T0399832

Children and Adolescent's Experiences of Violence and Abuse at Home

Children and Adolescent's Experiences of Violence and Abuse at Home is a unique book that explores some of the main controversies and challenges within the field. The book is organised into three sections, the first covering work that has focused on the experiences of living in DV settings as a child or young person, the second offers overviews of the impact of child victimisation and the final section is about working with children in practice and service-based settings.

It includes extensive reviews of the literature, empirical research and practice observations, all of which provide compelling evidence of a need to change how we construct victims and design services. It provides evidence for the need to work sensitively, inclusively and responsively around issues of victim identification, support and prevention. Moreover, the evidence urges us to include children's and adult victim/survivor's experiences and contributions in the creation of services.

Concluding with a series of recommendations for both future research, and ways in which we can help use the research findings to inform practice, it is a must-read for researchers, practitioners and educators working with children and young people within the field of domestic violence and abuse. It will also be of interest and value to policy makers who are reviewing legislation and those involved in commissioning psychological services, and victim services that work with child and adolescent victims.

Dr Julie C. Taylor is Head of Learning, Teaching and Student Experience for the Institute of Health at the University of Cumbria, UK. A chartered psychologist by background, Julie's passion is research that is participatory and collaborative. In recent years the focus has been children's experience of domestic violence, an interest that burgeoned following a 3-year study of sentenced women in the criminal justice system, all of whom related accounts of their victimisation as children and the impact this had on their schooling, relationships and subsequent opportunities.

Dr Elizabeth A. Bates is Principal Lecturer in Psychology and Psychological Therapies at the University of Cumbria, UK. Her research focus is on working with male victims of domestic violence including their experiences of physical and psychological abuse, the impact on them and the ways the abuse can continue and change post separation.

Children and Adolescent's Experiences of Violence and Abuse at Home

Current Theory, Research and Practitioner Insights

Edited by Julie C. Taylor and Elizabeth A. Bates

Routledge
Taylor & Francis Group

LONDON AND NEW YORK

Designed cover image: © Getty Images

First published 2024
by Routledge
4 Park Square, Milton Park, Abingdon, Oxon OX14 4RN

and by Routledge
605 Third Avenue, New York, NY 10158

Routledge is an imprint of the Taylor & Francis Group, an informa business

British Library Cataloguing-in-Publication Data
A catalogue record for this book is available from the British Library

Library of Congress Cataloging-in-Publication Data
Names: Taylor, Julie C., editor. | Bates, Elizabeth A., editor.
Title: Children and adolescent's experiences of violence and abuse at
home : current theory, research and practitioner insights / edited by
Julie C. Taylor, Elizabeth A. Bates.
Description: Abingdon, Oxon ; New York, NY : Routledge, 2024. |
Includes bibliographical references and index. | .
Identifiers: LCCN 2023027684 (print) | LCCN 2023027685 (ebook) |
ISBN 9780367644659 (hardback) | ISBN 9780367644642 (paperback) |
ISBN 9781003124634 (ebook)
Subjects: LCSH: Family violence. | Intimate partner violence.
Classification: LCC HV6626 .C45 2024 (print) | LCC HV6626 (ebook) |
DDC 362.8292--dc23/eng/20230725
LC record available at https://lccn.loc.gov/2023027684
LC ebook record available at https://lccn.loc.gov/2023027685

ISBN: 978-0-367-64465-9 (hbk)
ISBN: 978-0-367-64464-2 (pbk)
ISBN: 978-1-003-12463-4 (ebk)

DOI: 10.4324/9781003124634

Typeset in Times New Roman
by MPS Limited, Dehradun

Contents

Contributor Biographies

Dr Elizabeth A. Bates is a Principal Lecturer in Psychology and Psychological Therapies at the University of Cumbria, UK. Her research focus is on working with male victims of domestic violence including their experiences of physical and psychological abuse, the impact on them, and the ways the abuse can continue and change post separation.

Angie Boyle is a Senior Lecturer in Social Work at the University of Cumbria. She has previously worked as a Trainer and Independent Domestic Violence Advisor (IDVA) for a charity based in Cumbria. Her doctoral research is concerned with exploring the retrospective experiences of adults who grew up experiencing domestic violence and abuse as children and young people in the UK.

Professor Jane E.M. Callaghan is the Director of the Centre for Child Wellbeing and Protection. She is a Psychologist and Interdisciplinary Researcher, with an established record of research in areas related to childhood, violence, family life, relationships, discrimination and exclusion, and mental health and identity. Two clear strands are in evidence in her research – research focused on violence, health, children's mental health, social vulnerability, and family life, and a related strand focused on gender, professional identities, and ethnicity. She has been the Principal Investigator on the four-nation European Commission funded project "Understanding Agency and Resistance Strategies – Children's Experiences of Domestic Violence", the largest qualitative study of children who live with domestic violence conducted to date.

Dr Bethan Carter is a Post-doctoral Researcher at the School of Psychology, Cardiff University. Her research interests include investigating the impact of domestic violence on the mental health of children and young people using cohort studies and routinely collected administrative data. Bethan's PhD explored the effects of family violence (domestic violence and direct child abuse) on child and adolescent internalising symptoms, and the causal pathways between child abuse and internalising symptoms within the Avon Longitudinal Study of Parents and Children (ALSPAC).

Dr Grace Carter is a Chartered Psychologist and Research Fellow at the Institute of Health and Wellbeing. Grace conducts research in the fields of domestic abuse, sexual violence, and health. Her research broadly focuses on the development and robust evaluation of interventions for young people and adults who have experienced domestic abuse and/or sexual violence, and ensuring that the voices of victims/survivors are central to intervention design and evaluation. Grace's PhD thesis examined the development of the evidence base of interventions for children and young people who have experienced domestic violence and abuse.

Dr Daniela Di Basilio is a Post-doctoral Research Associate in Digital Mental Health, an HCPC Registered Clinical Psychologist, and a CBT therapist with extensive clinical experience in both the public and private sector. Her clinical work encompasses a wide range of disorders and conditions, including trauma-related ones. She has worked with victims of domestic abuse and people who have experienced direct or indirect violence in the household. This sparked her interest in meaningful ways in which practitioners can support people whose development has been affected by violence to live a fuller life, producing in-depth changes in their psychological functioning. Her publications on the themes of trauma and abuse call for a combination of individual-level and systemic ways to address trauma and promote post-traumatic growth.

Dr Joshua Eldridge is a Clinical Psychologist and Service Lead for a CAMHS Education Wellbeing Service in Southwest London and St George's NHS trust. His background experiences including working in CAMHS getting help, getting more help and within specialist Children's Services settings. His specialist interests include attachment-based interventions and working systemically to strengthen networks around young people who have experienced adversity and developmental trauma.

Dr Tanya Frances is a Lecturer in Psychology and Counselling based at The Open University in the UK. Tanya has an interest in gender-based violence, domestic abuse, social inequalities, and broadly, critical approaches to exploring eating disorders/eating distress. Tanya is interested in feminist and narrative approaches to research that centres victim-survivor voices and that attends to personal-socio-political intersections. Tanya is also a Counsellor and Psychotherapist. She integrates an intersectional, relational, and power-sensitive approach to working in practice.

Professor Nicola Graham-Kevan conducts research on vulnerable populations particularly within the Criminal Justice System. She is interested in trauma-informed approaches and is an internationally recognised expert in domestic abuse. Nicola has published widely in intimate partner violence perpetration and victimisation, and the psychological impact of adversity and trauma. She was one of the first researchers to explore typologies of coercive control within intimate relationships. She has led research projects and evaluations for a range of clients including the European Union, the Home Office, Police and Crime Commissioners. Nicola is the Director of the Centre for Criminal Justice Research and Partnership and a Lead for research on violence and aggression.

Elizabeth Harper is a Lecturer in Psychology and Health and Social Care at the University of Cumbria. Liz is currently studying for a PhD in how gender normative views influence the experienced victimisation of intimate partner violence (IPV).

Professor Susan Heward-Belle is a Professor of Social Work at the University of Sydney and is a recognised leader in domestic and family violence research. Sue has almost 30 years' experience in the domestic violence and child protection fields and has conducted many studies in these areas. Her PhD research examined the fathering experiences and practices of domestically violent men. She has a particular interest in advancing gender equitable and socially just approaches to practice that counter mother blaming.

Dr Stephanie Holt background is in social work practice across a variety of settings including residential child care, child protection, and family support. Since 2000 Stephanie has been lecturing in social work at Trinity College, Dublin. Stephanie's teaching and research expertise is on Domestic, Sexual and Gender Based Violence, with a particular emphasis on the impact of Domestic Violence on children and young people. Stephanie's research in this field is internationally renowned. In addition, Stephanie is an Associate Editor for the *Journal of Family Violence* (*JoFV*).

Dr Niamh Ingram is a Senior Clinical Psychologist and CBT Lead within NHS Child and Adolescent Mental Health Services. Her specialist areas of interests are supporting young people and their carers to heal from traumatic experiences, parent-child attachment, introducing yoga and movement into therapy, and creating sustainable and compassionate work environments for heath staff.

Dr Nassra Khan is a Registered Counselling Therapist in the province of Alberta, Canada. She works with individuals struggling with different mental health issues and traumatic life events to improve their mental and emotional wellbeing. She also provides counselling to individuals and families affected by domestic violence. Nassra adopts a culturally responsive framework in her counselling practice. Nassra's research interests are in the areas of acculturation, refugee issues, and experiences of people fleeing war-torn countries. She would also like to further explore how these issues may contribute to incidents of domestic violence in the home.

Dr Samuel Larner is a Senior Lecturer in Forensic Linguistics at Manchester Metropolitan University. His research explores children's disclosures of serious crimes perpetrated against them – particularly sexual abuse – and the role that trusted adults play in facilitating and scaffolding such disclosures. Samuel is a Member of the Manchester Centre for Youth Studies: an interdisciplinary youth-informed and youth-led research centre (https://www.mmu.ac.uk/mcys/).

Kirsty Martin is a Lecturer in Psychology and Health and Social Care at the University of Cumbria. Kirsty's main research focus to date has been with offender/perpetrator populations.

Professor Katherine Maurer is an Assistant Professor in the School of Social Work at McGill University. Kathryn practiced in New York City as a Clinical Social Worker and a Trauma Therapist. Her interdisciplinary research focuses on adolescent mental and behavioural health during the transition to adulthood. Particularly, Dr Maurer studies the physiological impact of exposure to extreme stressors, such as interpersonal violence and poverty, on the development of self-regulation capacities in adolescence and adults. Dr Maurer is the recipient of a 2016 Social Sciences and Humanities Research Council of Canada (SSHRC) Insight Development Grant to conduct a phenomenological study of affect regulation with adolescents who have experienced violence in their family as part of her research agenda focusing on the intergenerational transmission of family violence.

Dr Lucy Maynard works with people and organisations with social purpose to have an even greater impact. Lucy's approach to research and impact consultancy is underpinned by the ACA framework for development: enabling Awareness–Choice–Action personally and collectively, in leadership and practice. Lucy's research and practice are founded in the area of children, young people and family wellbeing and social justice. She strives to influence from practice and has held research and leadership roles across the social sector and as a visiting Research Fellow at University of Cumbria.

Dr Mark McGlashan is a Senior Lecturer in English Language in the Birmingham Institute of Media and English at Birmingham City University. His research interests predominantly centre on Corpus-based (Critical) Discourse Studies and the analysis of a wide range of social issues typically relating to extremist ideologies and behaviours (e.g. nationalism, extremism, racism, sexism, homophobia).

Professor Carolina Øverlien has conducted research in the field of domestic violence and abuse (children and young people) for a number of years, and has published extensively on this topic. Her expertise includes children experiencing/exposed to domestic violence, Youth intimate partner violence, children's rights, and research ethics. Carolina is currently a Professor of Social Work at Stockholm University, and a Research Leader at the Norwegian Centre for Violence and Traumatic Stress Studies (NKVTS) in Oslo, Norway. Carolina is also an Associate Editor for the *Journal of Family Violence (JoFV)*.

Dr Alexandra Papamichail is a Clinical Psychologist. Prior to this role, she worked as a Post-doctoral Research Associate at the IoPPN, King's College, and at the University of Nottingham. Her research specialises in interpersonal, family violence, and mental health (e.g. IPV, child-to-parent violence, modern slavery and mental health, sexual violence, and mental health among others). She completed her PhD in developmental psychology and psychopathology at the University of Brighton investigating child to parent violence.

Dr Sabreen Selvik is an associate Professor at the Faculty of Teacher Education and International Studies at Oslo Metropolitan University (OsloMet), Norway. Her educational background is in the field of psychology and special needs education. She has several years prior work experience with children at refuges for abused women and at other institutions. She has written articles concerning children's experiences of living at refuges and their schooling. Her research interests are in the fields of educational psychology, domestic violence and children, refuges for abused women, teacher-pupils' interactions, and children with special needs.

Dr Ali Shnyien is a Clinical Psychologist and Professional Lead for Youth Justice and Pupil Referral Unit CAMH services at South West London and St George's NHS trust. His specialist interests lie in utilising AMBIT (Adaptive Mentalization Based Integrative Treatment), community psychology, systemic practice and neurosequential approaches to support adolescents and families who have experienced traumatic developmental histories. Ali is also interested in the use of self and the application of somatic approaches in helping make meaning from our lived experiences.

Professor Kaz Stuart is the Director of Strategy and Learning at the YMCA George Williams College and Professor Emerita at the University of Cumbria. Kaz is passionate about enabling all people to have a voice in society so we can build a better world for everyone. Kaz achieves this by researching issues of inequality, researching in equitable ways and in supporting people's development through awareness, choice, and action at ACA Development.

Dr Julie C. Taylor is Head of Learning, Teaching and Student Experience for the Institute of Health at the University of Cumbria. A Chartered Psychologist by background Julie's passion is research that is participatory and collaborative. In recent years, the focus has been children's experience of domestic violence, an interest that burgeoned following a 3-year study of sentenced women in the criminal justice system, all of whom related accounts of their victimisation as children and the impact this had on their schooling, relationships, and subsequent opportunities.

David Wright is a Senior Lecturer in Psychology and Counselling, at the University of Cumbria. Dave is a chartered psychologist and an HCPC registered person-centred counsellor with more than 15 years' experience working with child and adult clients who self-harm.

Introduction

The importance of this volume

Julie C. Taylor and Elizabeth A. Bates

In the last 30 years researchers and practitioners have gathered a wealth of evidence relating to children's experiences of growing up in families with domestic violence and abuse. In the UK, children growing up in homes where there was domestic violence were, until recently, defined as witnesses or observers as opposed to victims of abuse. The use of this nomenclature to describe their status was challenged primarily because of its influence on the construction and treatment of children within services (Callaghan et al., 2018). Being considered a witness to the abuse as opposed to being a victim of it had the potential to minimise the perceived impact and therefore reduce the requirements for intervention (Callaghan et al., 2017). One of the consequences being the lack of priority given to children's trauma and the potential impact this may have on their lives (e.g., Øverlien, 2011; Øverlien & Holt, 2019). To collapse all children into a bystander position minimises their distress and privileges that of the adult victim. Many children living in homes where there is violence and abuse between parents are not only victims of these trauma inducing living conditions but also of direct abuse and violence within the home and other areas of their ecosystems (e.g., Bacchini & Esposito, 2020).

The UK Domestic Abuse Act (2021) now makes explicit reference to children as **victims** if *"they see, hear, or experience the effects of the abuse ...,"* and many researchers in the field see this change as long overdue (e.g., Callaghan et al., 2016). The move from the label witness or observer to victim in the context of a legal system enables the children to move from the periphery to centre stage. To identify children as key victims prioritises their experiences and directs attention to their needs. This new legal position is therefore to be applauded as a significant move in a positive direction. However, this change is UK-based and by no means universal, moreover, it is yet to be accompanied by a radical change in the way we identify needs and construct services.

This text explores some of the main controversies and challenges within the field. There are five main themes: 1. The importance of accessing the child victim/survivor's voices as opposed to relying on the voices and assumptions of others. 2. The methodological challenges of working with child/adult victim

DOI: 10.4324/9781003124634-1

populations. 3. The gendered assumptions around children's experiences of domestic abuse. 4. The adult sequelae of child victimisation, strengths and challenges. 5. What the evidence tells us about ways of working in practice with children and young people affected by child victimisation. It is hoped that this collection will serve as a useful tool for scholars and practitioners.

Outline of the chapters

This book consists of 16 chapters, each covering an important area of research or practice. These chapters include extensive reviews of the literature, empirical research and practice observations, all of which provide compelling evidence of a need to change how we construct victims and design services. It provides evidence for the need to work sensitively, inclusively and responsively around issues of victim identification, support and prevention. Morcover, the evidence urges us to include children's and adult victim/survivor's experiences and contributions in the creation of services. The book is organised into three parts, the first covering work that has focused on the experiences of living in DV settings as a child or young person, the second offers overviews of the impact of child victimisation and the final section is about working with children in practice and service-based settings.

Part I

Our first chapter is written by Professor Jane Callaghan who opens the volume with reference to her pioneering work, within this chapter Jane explains why working directly with the children and acknowledging their victim status is so important. In Chapter 2, Professor Nicola Graham-Kevan examines the literature to explore two key questions: 1. Is it only fathers/stepfathers who expose children to parental intimate violence, as you might assume based on many ACE (Adverse Childhood Experiences) survey questions? and 2. What does the evidence suggest the impact of exposure is? These questions are asked in response to the pervasive gendered narrative that infers that exposed boys become perpetrators and girls victims in the future.

In Chapters 3–5, children's experiences of growing up in homes where there has been domestic abuse and violence is explored, from a UK, European and a South Asian perspective. In Chapter 3, Dr Julie Taylor and colleagues draw upon data from adults in the United Kingdom who, as children, lived in homes where there was domestic abuse. Much of what we know about childhood experiences of domestic abuse comes from mothers or professionals working with children, often in refuge scenarios. Such studies provide invaluable insight and give the children a voice. However, many children who have grown up in a home where there is violence and abuse are never brought to the attention of services and so their voices remain unheard. The data drawn upon for this chapter comes from a retrospective study where adults were invited to reflect on their childhood experiences and their perception of how these experiences have influenced their adult lives. The experiences shared by participants show that growing up in homes where there is domestic abuse has had a long-lasting impact on their lives. In Chapter 4, Professors Holt and Øverlien offer a wider European perspective on children's experiences of domestic abuse. Positioned against the backdrop of the United Nations Convention on the Rights of the Child (UNCRC) and the Istanbul Convention, and grounded in a rights-based approach, their chapter celebrates the critical and burgeoning empirical knowledge base on children's experiences of living with domestic violence in Europe. Respecting and upholding children's right to participate in research and have a say in all matters affecting them, this chapter further positions children not only as victims in need but also as subjects and rights holders. In Chapter 5, Dr Nassra Khan provides a unique insight into the construction of domestic violence and abuse in rural Pakistan and the impact of this on the children. The chapter reports on Dr Khan's doctoral studies which sought to examine the cultural and structural factors that supported the perpetration of domestic violence in the home. The observations reported were made within the social environment that shaped the views and perceptions of the villagers towards domestic violence. Her detailed conversations with the villagers revealed that they did not recognise exposure to domestic violence at home as having a negative impact on children; nor did they consider these children as victims of domestic violence. Dr Khan's account concludes the first part of the book.

Part II

In Part II, the impact of childhood and adolescent domestic violence and abuse victimisation becomes the focus. In the first chapter of this section Dr Bethan Carter discusses the impact of domestic violence and abuse (DVA) on children and young people's (CYP) mental health. The focus being the development of internalising symptoms (e.g., anxiety and somatic complaints). The evidence base for the effect of DVA on internalising symptoms is discussed followed by presentation of recent research which aimed to overcome some of the previous limitations observed within the field. This chapter is followed by Professor Kathryn Maurer who discusses the effects of exposure to violence in the home on adolescents and emerging adults. Professor Maurer introduces a summary of current research on the psychophysiological consequences of high stress environments, such as the impact of exposure to family violence on the development of the capacity to self-regulate during adolescence and the transition to adulthood. Professor Maurer includes reference to findings from a recent study to illustrate her points using the lived experiences of family violence-exposed youths self-regulation capacities and reactions to situations of high stress. In Chapter 8, Dr Sabreen Selvik and Professor Carolina Øverlien discuss the role of school for children experiencing domestic violence (DV). School has repeatedly been recognised as important, yet despite the recognition of the importance of school for children experiencing DV, little research has been conducted in this field. Dr Selvik and Professor Øverlien begin by reviewing the existing research on the impact of DV on children's schooling and school experiences. They then share their participants perspectives on school attendance and absence, their experiences of 'coming and being' at school, and their experiences of teacher recognition and school strategies. In Chapter 9, Dr Elizabeth Bates and colleagues discuss some of the barriers and opportunities associated with help-seeking for children who live in homes where there is domestic abuse. The chapter begins by exploring the literature relating to barriers to help-seeking, drawing specifically on Overstreet and Quinn's (2013) theory of the Stigmatised Identity. The theory and evidence are then discussed in the context of data provided by adults who were victims of domestic abuse as children. The final chapter in this section comes from Angie Boyle whose doctoral research explores the concept of recovery in an adult population who were victims of domestic violence and abuse as children. Angie shares some of her findings and introduces her recovery framework. The framework has been designed in response to the contributions of her participants and offers potential insight into the process of victimisation recovery.

Part III

In Part III of the volume, the emphasis is placed on insights, experience and research from professionals working with child victims across a range of services. Drs Tanya Frances and Grace Carter introduce Part III by exploring how professionals can negotiate power, ethics and agency when working with children and young people to centralise their voice in the design and eva-luation of services. They draw upon recent qualitative research with children aged 7–12 years about their experiences of DVA interventions. The children's accounts reflect how they negotiate agency and power in adversity, in their recoveries and in research interviews. They also highlight that a reliance on limited outcome measures can constrain how children articulate their recovery. They conclude the chapter with a discussion of how academics, practitioners and intervention stakeholders can begin to prioritise centralising children's voices and inclusion in research, evaluation and service develop-ment. In the chapter that follows, Drs Samuel Larner and Mark McGlashan offer an alternative way to gain insight into children's experiences, they analysed data from support network forums for children and young people and made some discoveries that may assist practitioners working in the field and those designing forums for children and young people in the future. In Chapter 13, Dr Daniela Di Basilio explores ways to help children and young people make positive changes to their sense of self and attachment styles. Di Basilio explains that one of the challenges faced by practitioners is that they tend to work at a cognitive or behavioural level with victims of domestic abuse which may yield some superficial positive development but may fail to access the individual's emotional core. According to Di Basilio, this deeper level work is required for longer term sustainable change. This focus on deeper emotional level needs is expanded on in the next chapter where Dr

Alexandra Papamichail and colleagues, offer guidance to practitioners on ways of responding to the mental health needs of children who have experienced intimate partner violence (IPV). They use the principles of trauma-informed practice as a guiding framework, informing potential mental health responses for young people, their families and the professional networks around them. They discuss ways to engage therapeutically with children and their parents/caregivers to build collaborative understandings of their current mental health needs. They also explore the ways in which mental health interventions can be sequenced to respond to children's most pressing needs within their wider contexts. In the penultimate chapter of this section Professor Susan Heward-Belle critically considers the way practitioners view the role of fathering when working with children from domestically violent homes. Professor Heward-Belle examines what she refers to as inherently sexist institutional practices which adopt an exonerated father/responsible mother paradigm. Heward-Belle presents research in this area and then shares findings from a research study conducted in Australia with men who were involved in a men's behaviour change programme regarding their accounts of exposing children to domestic violence. Heward-Belle findings provide important insights into how fathers' behaviours and attitudes may contribute to childhood development and the ecology of the family. She closes the chapter with recommendations for the professional assessment of domestically violent men's fathering. The final chapter of the volume is a contribution by Professor Kaz Stuart and Dr Lucy Maynard, whereby they present a model of wellbeing development for young people who have experienced violence and abuse. The model presented seeks to respond to the challenge for practitioners, the creation of an environment for young people to develop power and feel able to take some control over their sense of wellbeing and future.

The volume concludes with the editors looking across the insights and evidence provided by contributors and uses these to offer a series of recommendations for both future research, and ways in which we can help use the research findings to inform practice. We hope that it will prove to be a useful resource for scholars and practitioners working in the sector. This volume contributes to the wider body of literature by bringing together a detailed, rigorous critique of current research and practice, and by presenting both research and practice around child victimisation within the same text.

References

Bacchini, D., & Esposito, C. (2020). Growing up in violent contexts: Differential effects of community, family, and school violence on child adjustment. *Children and Peace: From Research to Action*, 157–171.

Callaghan, J. E., Alexander, J. H., & Fellin, L. C. (2016). Children's embodied experience of living with domestic violence: "I'd go into my panic, and shake, really bad". *Subjectivity*, 9, 399–419.

Callaghan, J. E., Alexander, J. H., Sixsmith, J., & Fellin, L. C. (2018). Beyond "witnessing": Children's experiences of coercive control in domestic violence and abuse. *Journal of Interpersonal Violence, 33*(10), 1551–1581.

Callaghan, J. E. M., Fellin, L. C., Alexander, J. H., Mavrou, S., & Papathanasiou, M. (2017). Children and domestic violence: Emotional competencies in embodied and relational contexts. *Psychology of Violence, 7*(3), 333.

Øverlien, C. (2011). Women's refuges as intervention arenas for children who experience domestic violence. *Child Care in Practice, 17*(4), 375–391.

Øverlien, C., & Holt, S. (2019). Research on children experiencing domestic violence. *Journal of Family Violence, 34*, 65–67.

Part I

Children and young people's experiences of DVA

1 Children's experiences of domestic violence and abuse

Resistances and paradoxical resiliencies

Jane E. M. Callaghan
University of Stirling

The impact of domestic violence and abuse

Most research on children and domestic violence and abuse has focused on the impact "exposure to" domestic violence and abuse has on children. This literature is largely quantitative in nature, and is predominantly concerned with the harms children experience as a consequence of domestic violence and abuse. This negative impact on children's mental health, wellbeing, social and educational outcomes both in childhood and across the lifespan is not surprising. Growing up in a hostile environment where one parent attacks, undermines and controls the other can disrupt early attachments (Noonan & Pilkington, 2020) and unsettle development (Carlson et al., 2019).

Children who experience domestic violence and abuse are more at risk of a range of mental health difficulties, like depression and anxiety (Gondek et al., 2023; Silva et al., 2021), eating difficulties (Kimber et al., 2017) and behavioural difficulties (Chander et al., 2017; Chung et al., 2021; Holmes, 2015). Children also face an increased risk of sleep disturbance (Berg et al., 2021; Insana et al., 2014) and they are more prone to low levels of social-emotional competence, and higher levels of emotional dysregulation (Bender et al., 2022). Challenges in education have also been well documented, including lower achievement and attainment, higher rates of expulsion and suspension and greater risk of absenteeism (Cage et al., 2022). Research has also highlighted increased risks of physical health challenges like asthma and breathing problems, obesity and more use of emergency health care (Holmes et al., 2022) and heightened stress activation responses and dysregulation of the sympathetic and parasympathetic nervous systems (Berg et al., 2022). This group of children and young people are also at greater risk of a range of social challenges, like increased risk of involvement in abusive dating relationships as teens (Evans, Lee, et al., 2022) and bullying and being bullied (Lee et al., 2022; Nicholson et al., 2018). They are also more likely to hold attitudes that are accepting of parental violence and abuse as normal (Evans, Schmidt-Sane, et al., 2022).

There are some notable features in this literature. What stands out most is how little of it involves direct interaction with children and young people

DOI: 10.4324/9781003124634-3

themselves. Instead, it generally relies on clinical observation, clinician scored assessment and parent and teacher rating scales. This literature, focused on children, is glaringly lacking in child voice. At the same time, children are described as "exposed to" or "witness to" violence. This language has the effect of rendering children relatively passive in relation to the violence and abuse in their home – they are "mere witnesses," contaminated by this "exposure." This may seem merely a matter of language choice, but it does a particular job in the literature on domestic violence and abuse. By positioning children as witnesses, they are rendered as beings with limited agency, who are *external to* the abuse going on in their families. Domestic violence and abuse are therefore seen as something limited to the intimate adult dyad, that impacts children. This construction limits the potential to recognise both children's experiences as direct victims of domestic abuse (Callaghan et al., 2018) and their capacity to resist and manage its impact in the everyday (Callaghan, Alexander, & Fellin, 2016; Callaghan, Alexander, Sixsmith, et al., 2016; Callaghan et al., 2017, 2019; Callaghan et al., 2018; Fellin et al., 2019).

Further, in a literature that overwhelmingly assumes a male perpetrator and a female adult victim, it has remarkably little to say on the impact of abusive men on children's outcomes. Instead, mothers come under considerable scrutiny. Their mothering is typically presented as the key determinant of their children's mental health outcomes, whilst their (ex) partner's behaviour and its effects remain largely unexamined. For example, in one study, parent reported questionnaires were used to track the mental health trajectories of children impacted by domestic violence and abuse (Meijer et al., 2019). The study only gathered data from "one parent" and they rated their children's emotional security, mental health symptoms and their own rates of post-traumatic symptomatology (PTS). The study then reported that *maternal post-traumatic symptomatology* predicted children's mental health trajectories. Of course, given that it only assessed the mental health functioning of the non-violent parent, it is not possible to ascertain what role the other parent or other systemic factors might have played in children's outcomes.

This is a common oversight in outcomes research in this area. What is further problematic is the focus only on the role of the adult victim in children's outcomes, and in so doing produces a literature that "pathologises" and "responsibilises" adult victims of domestic violence and abuse, whilst making the perpetrators relatively invisible. It also potentially further silences children's experiences of domestic abuse, including their resistant and resilient strategies.

Resilience

This pattern of largely overlooking the role of the perpetrator of domestic violence and abuse, and focusing on the adult victim-survivor and their impact on their children, is also a feature of much of the literature on resilience. Children's capacity for resilience has been attributed primarily to maternal mental health (Fogarty, Wood, et al., 2019). In the Fogarty,

Woolhouse, et al. (2019) systematic review on resilience, of the 15 studies included, two focused on individual child factors that have been found to support resilience – "ease of temperament" (Martinez-Torteya et al., 2009), emotionality and shyness, socialbility (just for boys) and social development (just for girls; Bowen, 2017). In contrast, nine studies measured maternal mental health, and twelve assessed aspects of maternal parenting and attachment. Only two of the included studies appeared to assess qualities or behaviour of the abusive partner or their parenting. Interestingly, only one study identified in the Fogarty et al., systematic review looked at other contextual factors in the fostering of resilience. This study found that children whose parents were not involved in prolonged court disputes were more likely to be resilient (Georgsson et al., 2011). This perhaps most keenly demonstrates that perpetrators and their behaviour (before and after separation) play a significant role in children's outcomes, and yet are largely overlooked in domestic abuse research. A similar pattern is evident in more recent reviews (e.g., see Cameranesi et al., 2020, scoping review), and in subsequent research in the field.

It is therefore clear that most resilience research in domestic violence and abuse has focused overwhelmingly *on mothers* as victims with abusive parents or step-parents being almost entirely invisible. This reiterates a pattern identified by feminist authors who highlight that the research in this field both overwhelmingly focused on, and overwhelmingly "responsibilised," adult victim-survivors for the impact of domestic violence and abuse on their children. In focusing on maternal qualities and behaviours, this research also largely overlooks children's own resilient capacity and the agentic role children might play in managing domestic violence and abuse and its impacts. As a consequence, we actually know relatively little about *children's resilience*, compared to what we know about how adult victims' parenting impacts it.

By interviewing female victim-survivors of domestic abuse about how they supported their children's resilience, Fogarty, Woolhouse, et al. (2019) were able to move beyond mere focus on maternal mental health, to explore the complex and nuanced strategies women use. Women described a range of parenting strategies, like role modelling, consistent parenting and providing stability. They described the importance of talking about healthy relationships with their children and of protecting and shielding them from exposure to violence and abuse. These clearly protective strategies might be lost in research that simply focused on overall maternal symptomatology. The women in this study also commented on how difficult it can be to maintain a focus on their child's emotional wellbeing when they themselves were distressed and experiencing ongoing disruption through, for instance, contact disputes and post-separation abuse.

In their subsequent population-based study Cameranesi et al. (2022) explored risk and protective factors and the adjustment of children who had experienced domestic violence and abuse. They found that children who had no adjustment problems despite these experiences were distinguished by

having positive maternal physical and mental health. However, their conclusion pushes researchers to consider how maternal health is predicted by
biopsychosocial factors. They suggested the need for a multisystemic biopsychosocial resilience paradigm to make sense of maternal wellbeing and
children's outcomes. More recently, developmental resilience researchers
have turned to systems theory for a more nuanced account of resilience. For
example, the mental health impact of domestic violence and abuse is mediated by a range of positive experiences, like growing up in a safe neighbourhood, enjoying school and having a positive relationship with peers
(Gondek et al., 2023).

This emphasis on social and cultural factors in understanding resilience
gained traction with the work of Michael Ungar (Ungar, 2012, 2021; Ungar
& Theron, 2020). Ungar's social-ecological theory of resilience explains how
individuals and communities overcome adversity and can negotiate their way
to positive outcomes. According to Ungar (2011), resilience is "the capacity
of individuals, families, communities and systems to adapt and thrive in the
face of significant adversity or stress" (p.2). Ungar conceptualises resilience as
a dynamic process that involves interactions between individuals, their environments and the systems that support them. In his framework, Ungar
identifies seven key factors that contribute to resilience (see Figure 1.1). These
are seen as interconnected and interactive. Children and young people are
more likely to be resilient when they can enjoy and sustain relationships, have
a sense of identity, feel empowered in their social, political or personal lives,
feel like they "fit" and belong and have access to the material resources that
they need. The emphasis on context suggests that resilient young people live
in places where they feel there is social justice and fairness, and where they
feel culturally connected.

Figure 1.1 Ungar's multisystemic model of resilience.

Ungar's theory of resilience emphasises the importance of a holistic approach to promoting resilience, which involves addressing all these factors in a coordinated and integrated manner (Ungar & Theron, 2020). This approach requires collaboration across multiple sectors, including health, education, social services and community development (Lester et al., 2019). These findings were confirmed in our research on coping with domestic abuse, which emphasised the importance of sibling relationships (Callaghan et al., 2017), creativity (Fellin et al., 2019), belonging and a feeling of empowerment and identity (Callaghan & Alexander, 2015) and safe spaces and places (Callaghan et al., Callaghan 2017) in supporting children's recovery from domestic abuse.

In the context of domestic abuse, this theory underpins the importance of an approach to resilience that recognises not just the characteristics of caregivers and their children, but that also acknowledges that mother-child dyads cannot be "resilient" in isolation. The capacity of children to flourish after domestic abuse relies on access to safe and stable environments in a social context that is just and promotes a sense of belonging and value. For example, housing stability in itself has adverse effects on children and unstable housing produces a sense of "ontological insecurity" that parenting practice alone surely could not remediate. Interventions for parents and children to support resilience must move beyond purely parenting and emotional regulation, to look comprehensively at a more socially just context in which key material needs are addressed, the existing protective efforts of the non-abusive parent are recognised and supported and children and young people are supported to find their place in their community and the world around them.

What is resistance?

One aspect that is insufficiently addressed in Ungar's model is the issue of power and the way that this plays out in children's experiences of home, family and community. Domestic abuse does not just impact the intimate dyad, it pervades family life (Callaghan et al., 2018, 2019). Power is exerted through the control of space, of embodied subjects and of relationships. Family relationships are shaped as relationships of power, particularly in situations of coercive control and violence. Children manage the way they speak, play, interact with friends and family, use the space of their home and express their emotions, to manage the impact of coercive control and the risk of violence and harm for themselves and others in their family (Callaghan, Alexander, & Fellin, 2016; Callaghan, Alexander, Sixsmith, et al., 2016; Callaghan, Fellin, Alexander, et al., 2017; Callaghan, Fellin, Mavrou, et al., 2017; Fellin et al., 2019).

Ungar stressed the importance of an empowered sense of identity for children who experience adversity, arguing that this is a foundation for resilience. One consequence of coercive control is the steady erosion of a victim's sense of identity (Neale, 2023). Holding onto to some sense of "me" in the context of domestic abuse is therefore a powerful act of resistance to the oppressive action of the abuser. Consider this example from interviews with children impacted by domestic abuse completed as part of the UNARS project (see Callaghan & Alexander, 2015). Mark is talking about his father's financial control over his mother and his father's attempts to extract information about her finances from Mark:

Mark: *[…] when my mum gets money he takes it off her, so I say, I don't say anything, she don't get no money … . I mean like when she gets money out of the bank my dad takes it off her. So I have to lie to him.*

Here, Mark, who is 10 years old, explains the dynamics of financial control and the strategy he has developed to manage that control. He understands the moral dilemma of *lying* to his father, but recognises that in this case, it is a strategic and appropriate act of resistance to the control imposed by his father on him and on his mother.

Similarly, Dylan (10) commented on his father's offer to give him gifts in exchange for information about his mother:

Dylan: *I don't know ((erm)) I can't really explain it, I didn't really have a feeling ((.)) like I knew he wanted like information for exchange, but ((.)) at the end of the day, I have the information, he doesn't so I could technically control it so ((.)) it's easier for me to just ((.)) get gifts ((laughs)) and it's harder for him to get the information, so it was, ((.)) yeah*

In this extract he makes it clear that he fully understands that his father is attempting to manipulate him into providing information, to enable him to further control Dylan's mother. He recognises the power he holds in this situation (knowledge) and uses it to his own advantage. He giggles as he tells this story, seemingly half in joy and half in shame. He knows that in doing this, he is upending the traditional power dynamic of abuser and abused, and of father and son.

Talking about her experiences of living with domestic abuse, Emma (17) talks about how she would use the "cover" of visiting friends to resist the control her stepfather exerted over the physical spaces of the home.

Emma: *When I had friends around, nothing would happen, he wouldn't dare try anything, so then, when I did realise that, I used to get friends round all the time.*
Interviewer: *And how did you feel when they were there?*
Emma: *Safe. I could just go wherever I wanted. I'd go downstairs, sit in the living room, be a bit of a daredevil, in my head.*

Emma makes it explicit in her statement "be a bit of a daredevil, in my head" that she knows she is playing with power here. Having gained insight into her stepfather's patterns of behaviour, she was able to temporarily take control of space, exerting a sense of resistance to his control. Her little joke about being a daredevil makes it quite clear that she is aware of the power inversion and is taking pleasure in the temporary shift in power relations.

Each of these examples make it clear that children and young people directly experience the power and control that underpins the perpetrator's abuse. They also reveal the importance to the child of offering even a token of resistance to that control. Even where the disruption of power is short lived, nonetheless their ability to seize it is empowering to them. It is notable too that these power inversions are only possible when children step outside the traditional normative conceptualisation of being a "good child." Resistance involves rational and safe choices to beat the perpetrator at their own game. As such, each requires some taking on of characteristics that in other contexts might be seen as a problem – lying, manipulating, withholding information. To see their true meaning to the child however requires that we understand the function of each behaviour in the context of domestic abuse within the family.

Paradoxical resilience

The harms of domestic abuse for children and young people are as complex and nuanced as they are for adults. Abuse permeates familial relationships, the spaces of home, outdoors, emotions, identities, embodied selves. It is resisted in a similarly complex and multidimensional way. It is often the case that our resistances necessarily reflect the form of the thing we are resisting. This is clear in the extracts in the previous section, where children and young people used deception and manipulation – the tools of the oppressor – to resist. This matters because, when looking for traces of children's capacity to be resilient, we surely similarly need to understand the way that such resilience might also bear the marks of that which they are resisting. Elsewhere, we have explored, for instance, how *caring* for siblings and non-abusive parents is a key aspect of resilience for children (Callaghan, Alexander, Sixsmith, et al., 2016). Their identity as carer was a source of pride for some children and young people, an area in which they felt empowered and knew they excelled. However, "parentification" is often pathologized and problematised in clinical and social care responses to domestic abuse, and professionals often focus on restoring "normal" power dynamics between adult and child. This, we argued, is a misunderstanding of the complex and located nature of children's coping after domestic abuse. Domestic abuse typically involves direct attacks on adult and child victims' relationships, through practices of isolation and alienation. Caring therefore is a direct resistance to abuse, that carries within it the mark of the very thing it is resisting.

This is evident throughout children's narratives of domestic abuse. They cope through resistance, and resistance often bears the mark of that which it resists. Consider this extract from an interview with George (8) talking about his relationship with his brother (age 6):

George: *Yeah, I sent a letter to ((my social worker)) saying I don't want to*
           see my dad, and my dad found out and he got really angry and we
           never spoke to each other for a long time. And then ((my support
           worker)) got some people in, and I didn't speak a lot, my brother
           did because I got my brother to speak, I told him what to say.
           Because I like, if I tell him and he says it, then if he's doing all the
           speaking and it doesn't get back to dad, then he'll get hmm hmm,
           and I wouldn't
Int: *you'll hide behind your brother.*
George: *Yeah. Sometimes*

This extract might be read as quite chilling – as an example of a brother's willingness to "throw his brother under a bus" to get out of trouble. But it seems there's something more to be grappled with here. Whilst "caring" as an example of a *paradoxical* kind of resilience may seem palatable, George's admission that he would "hide behind" his younger brother is less palatable. It is not what a "nice child" would do. However, often young people's expressions of resilience are not "prosocial" or particularly "nice." In our drive for happy endings and closure, our need to restore a sense of "normal childhood" to children, we need to be careful that we are not also obscuring children's expressions of resilience and resistance. George was describing getting his brother to speak for him as part of his answer to our questions about how he coped living with domestic abuse. What he narrates here is a powerful strategy of resistance. However, it seems a relatively ambivalent strategy of resilience. Nonetheless, if you consider what he is doing here, it is creative and it is safe – both for him and for his brother. George is potentially at risk as a result of the social worker disclosing his position to his father. His brother, on the other hand, is younger and less likely to be judged harshly by his father. George knows this. He can read his family very effectively and understands its dynamics. Staying quiet, staying out of the way is a protective strategy. Finding safe ways to speak out is a resilient one. Whilst we may always want to see positive qualities like kindness and openness as resilient, these are not strategies that work in oppressive regimes. And families impacted by domestic abuse are, often, best understood as oppressive regimes. Resilient responses often contain seeds of the thing they are responding to, and consequently, resilience in the context of domestic abuse might be best understood as *paradoxical resilience.*

In our work with children who had experienced domestic abuse, we (the UNARS team, Callaghan & Alexander 2015, Callaghan, Alexander, & Fellin,

Figure 1.2 Photograph of a window with shattered glass.

2016; Callaghan, Alexander, Sixsmith, et al., 2016; Callaghan et al., 2017, 2019) asked children and young people to bring us photographs that captured their sense of how they coped with abuse. One of our participants brought this image of a broken window:

Electra:	*And this broken glass*
Interviewer:	*What does this represent?*
Electra:	*Broken heart?*

At first glance, this image might seem to be one that reflects the harms Electra has experienced as a consequence of domestic abuse. However, she brought it to express something about her capacity to cope. The image represents "her broken heart." But the window is not entirely smashed. It is damaged and marked, but it is still a whole pane. It has not fallen out or smashed to pieces. The window is still intact, arranged around the break. I would argue that in this image, Electra is communicating that her capacity for resilience, her ability to stay standing, is arranged around the harms she has experienced. Her capacity for resilience is entwined around her sense of woundedness. Resilience and woundedness are intertwined with each other, like a double helix. One strand cannot be understood without understanding the other.

When young people live in conflict laden environments, they have to find complex ways of coping and managing themselves and their relationships.

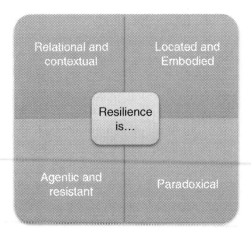

Figure 1.3 Illustration of the relationship between resilience and its elements.

When power imbalances are so stark, and when children's relational experiences are characterised by coercive, controlling and manipulative behaviours, their *resistances* to those behaviours are shaped by the context in which the violence and abuse takes place. What appears to be "dysfunctional" and difficult is often the way that children have found to cope. Resilience is inherently paradoxical and inherently reflects the oppressive practices that it is responding to. If power and control in domestic abuse are exerted in ways that are relational and contextual, embodied and located, then resistance to these must be similarly understood as relational, embodied and contextual. If domestic abuse is inherently about relationships of power and control, then there will necessarily be elements within the expression of resilience that expresses that sense of power and control.

References

Bender, A. E., McKinney, S. J., Schmidt-Sane, M. M., Cage, J., Holmes, M. R., Berg, K. A., Salley, J., Bodell, M., Miller, E. K., & Voith, L. A. (2022). Childhood exposure to intimate partner violence and effects on social-emotional competence: A systematic review. *Journal of Family Violence, 37*(8), 1263–1281. Springer. 10.1007/s10896-021-00315-z

Berg, K. A., Francis, M. W., Ross, K., & Spilsbury, J. C. (2021). Opportunities to improve sleep of children exposed to interpersonal violence: A social-ecological perspective. *Children and Youth Services Review, 127*. 10.1016/j.childyouth.2021.106082

Berg, K. A., Evans, K. E., Powers, G., Moore, S. E., Steigerwald, S., Bender, A. E., Holmes, M. R., Yaffe, A., & Connell, A. M. (2022). Exposure to intimate partner violence and children's physiological functioning: A systematic review of the literature. *Journal of Family Violence, 37*(8), 1321–1335. 10.1007/s10896-022-00370-0

Bowen, E. (2017). Conduct disorder symptoms in pre-school children exposed to intimate partner violence: Gender differences in risk and resilience. *Journal of Child and Adolescent Trauma, 10*(2), 97–107. 10.1007/s40653-017-0148-x

Cage, J., Kobulsky, J. M., McKinney, S. J., Holmes, M. R., Berg, K. A., Bender, A. E., & Kemmerer, A. (2022). The effect of exposure to intimate partner violence on children's academic functioning: A systematic review of the literature. *Journal of Family Violence, 37*(8), 1337–1352. 10.1007/s10896-021-00314-0

Callaghan, J. E. M., Alexander, J. H., & Fellin, L. C. (2016). Children's embodied experience of living with domestic violence: "I'd go into my panic, and shake, really bad." *Subjectivity, 9*(4). 10.1057/s41286-016-0011-9

Callaghan, J. E. M., Alexander, J. H., Sixsmith, J., & Fellin, L. C. (2016). Children's experiences of domestic violence and abuse: Siblings' accounts of relational coping. *Clinical Child Psychology and Psychiatry, 21*(4), 649–668. 10.1177/1359104515620250

Callaghan, J. E. M., Fellin, L. C., Alexander, J. H., Mavrou, S., & Papathanasiou, M. (2017). Children and domestic violence: Emotional competencies in embodied and relational contexts. *Psychology of Violence, 7*(3). 10.1037/vio0000108

Callaghan, J. E. M., Fellin, L. C., Mavrou, S., Alexander, J., & Sixsmith, J. (2017). The management of disclosure in children's accounts of domestic violence: Practices of telling and not telling. *Journal of Child and Family Studies, 26*(12). 10.1007/s10826-017-0832-3

Callaghan, J. E. M., Alexander, J. H., Sixsmith, J., & Fellin, L. C. (2018). Beyond "Witnessing": Children's experiences of coercive control in domestic violence and abuse. *Journal of Interpersonal Violence, 33*(10). 10.1177/0886260515618946

Callaghan, J. E. M., Fellin, L. C., & Alexander, J. H. (2019). Promoting resilience and agency in children and young people who have experienced domestic violence and abuse: the "MPOWER" intervention. *Journal of Family Violence, 34*(6). 10.1007/s1 0896-018-0025-x

Cameranesi, M., Piotrowski, C. C., & Brownridge, D. A. (2020). Profiles of adjustment in children and adolescents exposed to intimate partner violence: A scoping review investigating resilience processes. *Journal of Positive School Psychology, 4*(1), 1–20.

Cameranesi, M., Shooshtari, S., & Piotrowski, C. C. (2022). Investigating adjustment profiles in children exposed to intimate partner violence using a biopsychosocial resilience framework: A Canadian population-based study. *Child Abuse and Neglect, 125*. 10.1016/j.chiabu.2021.105453

Carlson, J., Voith, L., Brown, J. C., & Holmes, M. (2019). Viewing children's exposure to intimate partner violence through a developmental, social-ecological, and survivor lens: The current state of the field, challenges, and future directions. *Violence Against Women, 25*(1), 6–28. 10.1177/1077801218816187

Chander, P., Kvalsvig, J., Mellins, C. A., Kauchali, S., Arpadi, S. M., Taylor, M., Knox, J. R., & Davidson, L. L. (2017). Intimate partner violence and child behavioral problems in South Africa. *Pediatrics, 139*(3). 10.1542/peds.2016-1059

Chung, G., Jensen, T. M., Parisi, A., Macy, R. J., & Lanier, P. (2021). Impact of intimate partner violence on parenting and children's externalizing behaviors: Transactional processes over time. *Violence Against Women, 27*(14), 2576–2599. 10.1177/1077801220985125

Evans, K. E., Lee, H., Russell, K. N., Holmes, M. R., Berg, K. A., Bender, A. E., & Prince, D. M. (2022). Adolescent dating violence among youth exposed to intimate partner violence: A systematic review. *Journal of Family Violence, 37*(8), 1245–1262. 10.1007/s10896-021-00289-y

Evans, K. E., Schmidt-Sane, M. M., Bender, A. E., Berg, K. A., & Holmes, M. R. (2022). Children's exposure to intimate partner violence and acceptance or appraisals of IPV: A systematic review. *Journal of Family Violence, 37*(8), 1301–1319. 10.1007/s10896-021-00318-w

Fellin, L. C., Callaghan, J. E. M., Alexander, J. H., Mavrou, S., & Harrison-Breed, C. (2019). Child's play? Children and young people's resistances to domestic violence and abuse. *Children and Society, 33*(2). 10.1111/chso.12302

Fogarty, A., Wood, C. E., Giallo, R., Kaufman, J., & Hansen, M. (2019). Factors promoting emotional-behavioural resilience and adjustment in children exposed to intimate partner violence: A systematic review. *Australian Journal of Psychology, 71*(4), 375–389. 10.1111/ajpy.12242

Fogarty, A., Woolhouse, H., Giallo, R., Wood, C., Kaufman, J., & Brown, S. (2019). Promoting resilience and wellbeing in children exposed to intimate partner violence: A qualitative study with mothers. *Child Abuse and Neglect, 95*. 10.1016/j.chiabu.2019. 104039

Georgsson, A., Almqvist, K., & Broberg, A. G. (2011). Dissimilarity in vulnerability: Self-reported symptoms among children with experiences of intimate partner violence. *Child Psychiatry and Human Development, 42*(5), 539–556. 10.1007/s10578-011-0231-8

Gondek, D., Feder, G., Howe, L. D., Gilbert, R., Howarth, E., Deighton, J., & Lacey, R. E. (2023). Factors mitigating the harmful effects of intimate partner violence on adolescents' depressive symptoms—A longitudinal birth cohort study. *JCPP Advances*. 10.1002/jcv2.12134

Holmes, M. R. (2015). Physical and sexual intimate partner violence negatively affects women's mental health and their children's behaviour. *Evidence-Based Nursing, 18*(3), 94. 10.1136/eb-2014-102026

Holmes, M. R., Berg, K. A., Bender, A. E., Evans, K. E., Kobulsky, J. M., Davis, A. P., & King, J. A. (2022). The effect of intimate partner violence on children's medical system engagement and physical health: A systematic review. *Journal of Family Violence, 37*(8), 1221–1244. 10.1007/s10896-021-00291-4

Insana, S. P., Foley, K. P., Montgomery-Downs, H. E., Kolko, D. J., & McNeil, C. B. (2014). Children exposed to intimate partner violence demonstrate disturbed sleep and impaired functional outcomes. *Psychological Trauma-Theory Research Practice and Policy, 6*(3), 290–298. 10.1037/a0033108

Kimber, M., McTavish, J. R., Couturier, J., Boven, A., Gill, S., Dimitropoulos, G., & MacMillan, H. L. (2017). Consequences of child emotional abuse, emotional neglect and exposure to intimate partner violence for eating disorders: A systematic critical review. *BMC Psychology, 5*(1), 33. 10.1186/s40359-017-0202-3

Lee, H., Russell, K. N., O'Donnell, K. A., Miller, E. K., Bender, A. E., Scaggs, A. L., Harris III, L. A., Holmes, M. R., & Berg, K. A. (2022). The Effect of Childhood Intimate Partner Violence (IPV) exposure on bullying: A systematic review. *Journal of Family Violence, 37*(8), 1283–1300. 10.1007/s10896-021-00299-w

Lester, S., Lorenc, T., Sutcliffe, K., Khatwa Claire Stansfield, M., Sowden, A., Thomas, J., Khatwa, M., Stansfield, C., & Thomas, J. (2019). *What helps to support people affected by Adverse Childhood Experiences? A review of evidence What helps to support people affected by Adverse Childhood Experiences? A review of evidence.* Institute of Education. http://eppi.ioe.ac.uk/

Martinez-Torteya, C., Anne Bogat, G., Von Eye, A., & Levendosky, A. A. (2009). Resilience among children exposed to domestic violence: The role of risk and protective factors. *Child Development, 80*(2), 562–577. 10.1111/j.1467-8624. 2009.01279.x

Masten, A. S. (2001). Ordinary magic: Resilience processes in development. *American Psychologist, 56*(3), 227–238. 10.1037/0003-066X.56.3.227

Meijer, L., Finkenauer, C., Tierolf, B., Lünnemann, M., & Steketee, M. (2019). Trajectories of traumatic stress reactions in children exposed to intimate partner violence. *Child Abuse and Neglect, 93*, 170–181. 10.1016/j.chiabu.2019.04.017

Neale, J. (2023). Identity erasure: Women's experiences of living with domestic violence and abuse. *Journal of Gender-Based Violence*, 1–17. 10.1332/239868021X1675 7857695474

Nicholson, J. V., Chen, Y., & Huang, C.-C. (2018). Children's exposure to intimate partner violence and peer bullying victimization. *Children and Youth Services Review, 91*, 439–446. 10.1016/j.childyouth.2018.06.034

Noonan, C. B., & Pilkington, P. D. (2020). Intimate partner violence and child attachment: A systematic review and meta-analysis. In *Child Abuse and Neglect* (Vol. 109). Elsevier Ltd. 10.1016/j.chiabu.2020.104765

Silva, E. P., Emond, A., & Ludermir, A. B. (2021). Depression in childhood: The role of children's exposure to intimate partner violence and maternal mental disorders. *Child Abuse and Neglect, 122*. 10.1016/j.chiabu.2021.105305

Ungar, M. (2011). The social ecology of resilience: Addressing contextual and cultural ambiguity of a nascent construct. *American Journal of Orthopsychiatry, 81*(1), 1–17.

Ungar, M. (2012). Social ecologies and their contribution to resilience. In S. Goldstein & R. Brooks (Eds.), *Handbook of Resilience in Children* (pp. 19–31). Springer.

Ungar, M. (2021). *Multisystemic Resilience: Adaptation and Transformation in Contexts of Change*. Oxford University Press.

Ungar, M., & Theron, L. (2020). Resilience and mental health: How multisystemic processes contribute to positive outcomes. *The Lancet Psychiatry, 7*(5), 441–448. 10.1016/S2215-0366(19)30434-1

2 The impact of exposure to domestic violence in childhood

What can reviews of the literature tell us about sex-differences?

Nicola Graham-Kevan
University of Central Lancashire

Introduction

Interest in adverse childhood experiences (ACEs) is growing (e.g., Bellis et al., 2014; Hughes et al., 2017; Bellis et al., 2019). ACEs include not only physical abuse, sexual abuse and neglect of children but also exposure to parental intimate partner violence (IPV), all of which are associated with poorer outcomes across the lifespan. You would be mistaken for thinking that only fathers expose their children to domestic abuse. Many ACE surveys only include questions on childhood exposure to IPV (EIPV) in relation to exposure to mothers'/stepmothers' victimisation, this is found both in the original ACE survey (Felitti et al., 1998) and currently for example, both the Scottish and the Welsh ACE surveys, asked only if participants had seen their mother or step-mother assaulted by her partner. Similarly, organisations which support children implicitly reinforce the notion that it is only fathers IPV to mothers that is aversive (e.g., "our programme allows children and *mothers* [italics added] to talk openly, learn to communicate about what's happened and rebuild their relationship," NSPCC, 2022). The current review will seek to explore whether there is empirical support for the assumption that children only witness the abuse of their mothers.

There is another assumption however regarding sex and exposure to IPV that interacts with the belief that fathers are responsible for EIPV, whereby explanations as to the impact of this type of ACE are framed around exposed boys becoming perpetrators and girls becoming victims. These two examples illustrate this clearly:

> Boys who witness their mothers' abuse are more likely to batter their female partners as adults than boys raised in nonviolent homes. For girls, this may result in the belief that threats and violence are the norm in relationships. (Admin, Stop Violence Against Women, 2020)
>
> In these cases, male children might physically abuse their partners after watching their fathers do the same. Likewise, women from homes that witness domestic violence are more likely to be sexually assaulted by their partners in adulthood. (ONS, 2017)

DOI: 10.4324/9781003124634-4

A review by Spencer et al. (2020) found that dating violence by males and females was predicted by the same risk factors (i.e., age, alcohol and drug use, weapon carrying, depressive symptoms, risky sexual behaviours, suicidality and violence towards peers), suggesting more similarity than differences in the psychology of IPV. This is consistent with a 2018 review that also found that gender was not predictive of dating IPV (Grest et al., 2017).

Research reviews therefore suggest there is little justification for adopting a gendered interpretation when attempting to understand the aetiology of men's and women's IPV perpetration; instead, what needs to be acknowledged is the overwhelming evidence for the role of ACEs in the lives of IPV perpetrators (Cascardi & Jouriles, 2018; Clare et al., 2021; Costa et al., 2015; Godbout et al., 2019: Karakurt et al., 2019; Mackay et al., 2018; Stith, et al., 2000). Consistent with this argument is that other known correlates of ACEs such as psychiatric disorders (e.g., anxiety and depression) (Yapp et al., 2021; Spencer et al., 2020) and alcohol and illicit drug use are also associated with IPV perpetration (Choenni, et al., 2016; Dowling, 2016).

Therefore, the second aim of this chapter is to explore the research on the impact EIPV on development and subsequent perpetration of IPV.

EIPV is a common ACE with approximately a quarter of boys and girls experiencing it (Martin et al., 2006). EIPV includes witnessing IPV, awareness of IPV and also living in a home where IPV occurs (Kimber et al., 2018). EIPV is associated with an elevated risk of also experiencing child maltreatment (Hamby et al., 2010). EIPV is also likely to be associated with poorer parenting experiences (i.e., less parental warmth (e.g., Lapierre, 2008; Levendosky, & Graham-Bermann, 2000: 2001), although whether that is solely due to the impact of one or both parents experiences IPV or indicative of parents with a constellation of complex needs such as their own ACEs exposure, mental health and substance use is not clear from the current literature (Fogarty et al., 2019). Findings from Christie et al. (2019) found that that parental PTSD was associated with impaired parenting which is consistent with longitudinal research that found mothering to be predicted by the mother's own childhood experiences and not the relationship quality of her adult intimate relationship (Belsky et al., 2005); unfortunately data on fathering is largely lacking.

EIPV is distressing for children and this distress is felt similarly for boys and girls, both of whom are significantly more likely to have diagnoses of anxiety and depression by the age of 21 years compared to non-exposed peers (Martin et al., 2006). From a trauma-informed perspective, witnessing or hearing about a parent's suffering is sufficiently distressing to precipitate post traumatic stress disorder (PTSD) or due to the potential chronic nature of such exposure Complex PTSD. Complex PTSD is more severe when: (a) the traumatic events happen early in life; (b) the trauma is caused by a parent or carer; (c) the person was experiencing the trauma for a long time; all features of EIPV. Unlike PTSD, in complex trauma it may take years for the symptoms to be recognised, and even then, it may be labelled externalising (e.g., aggression to others) or internalising (e.g., depression) behaviour and/or lead to diagnosis of personality disorder. The reason that ACEs are related to a host of problematic behaviour is due to the impact that exposure has on children's brain development, undermining the efficacy of the regulatory systems that govern emotion reactivity and problem-solving, altering the very architecture of the brain (Shonkoff et al., 2012).

Also, consistent with a trauma-informed understanding of the impact of EIPV is the finding from Yule, Houston & Grych's (2019) review that cross-sectional studies report that self-regulation was most closely associated with adaptive functioning in exposed children and was the only protective factor that remained significant in the eight studies they included that utilised longitudinal designs (Yule et al., 2019). Emotion regulation is likely to be key to predicting whether an exposed child experiences post traumatic growth or develops mental health challenges in adult life (Carter et al., 2021).

In summary, the research on EIPV finds that it is associated with the development of serious and persistent problems across the social, emotional and behavioural areas. It negatively impacts an individual's ability to establish and maintain healthy relationships and is associated with elevated risk of adult use of IPV (Levendosky et al., 2013; Osofsky, 2003; Renner & Slack, 2006).

The purpose of this section is to explore whether there is empirical support for the assumptions that: 1. children only witness the abuse of their mothers, and 2. that the impact EIPV has on development and subsequent perpetration and victimisation of IPV differs for boys and girls. To do this research examining the prevalence of EIPV across nations and the factors relating to this exposure was explored. It was found that there is a tendency in the literature to only discuss violence from Fathers to Mothers (e.g., Mabanglo, 2002). Similarly in the WHO report by Sethi et al. (2013) only one nation, Turkey, asked respondents about their exposure to IPV from fathers and mothers. Indeed, in the reports included in Table 2.1 only researchers in Turkey enquired specifically about EIPV that was enacted by mothers.

This section therefore reviews the evidence of both men's and women's parental use of IPV. In it I explore the impact on both boys/men and girls/women. Where the data was available, I also investigated whether there was evidence for differences in outcomes in families with same-sex or opposite-sex perpetrator/child dyads. The sheer volume of research on this topic led to the decision to take a two-pronged approach. The first approach was to explore the prevalence of male and female EIPV from a variety of nations. The second approach was to summarise the findings of review articles on EIPV over the past decade.

Table 2.1 Prevalence of EIPV by nation and exposed victim sex

Nation	Boys %	Girls %	Study
South Africa	47%	45.4%	Swart, L. A., Seedat, M., Stevens, G., & Ricardo, I. (2002).
Taiwan	22%	24%	Feng, J. Y., Chang, Y. T., Chang, H. Y., Fetzer, S., & Wang, J. D. (2015).
Hong Kong	By father 22.4% By mother 18.5% By either 25.9%	By father 21.4% By mother 20.1% By either 26.0%	Chan, K. L. (2011).
Austria	30.9%	41.2%	Völkl-Kernstock et al. (2015).
Russia	8.4%	12.9%	World Health Organisation. (2014).
Serbia	19.8%	18.1%	World Health Organisation. (2012).
Romania	15.0%	18.7%	World Health Organisation (2013).
USA	Before 15 years 1.2 Father - Mother Before 15 years 897,000 Father – Mother Mother – Father 380,000	Before 15 years 1.2 Father - Mother Before 15 years 1.2 million Mother – Father 0.5 million	Sandison, B. (2018) (Australian Institute of Health and Welfare).
Canada	20%	25%	Chartier, M.J., et al., 2010
Brazil	7.8%	12.7%	Soares, A.L.G., et al., 2016

Exploring rates of EIPV from different nations

Prior to exploring review articles on EIPV exposure, a range of data from different nations where information was available by sex of the child EIPV was available were collated (see Table 2.1).

The prevalence rates for EIPV are based on estimates from different measures, for example WHO reports ask only of fathers' violence to mothers, whereas AIHW (Australian Institute of Health and Welfare) include violence by both parents. Where data is presented separately (e.g., Chan, 2011) there appears to be a small increase in prevalence compared to mother victimised only data. This suggests that the exposure to parental IPV is frequently bidirectional between parents, which is consistent with a 2012 systematic review that found that in over half of relationships where IPV is a factor, aggression is used by both partners towards each other (Langhinrichsen-Rohling et al., 2012). I use the term bidirectional abuse in this chapter because it acknowledges that both partners use aggression, without implying that in all these relationships this aggression is mutual in terms of aggressor/victim retaliation or self-defence. Research across nations shows variability which is likely to represent both population (e.g., Archer, 2006) and measurement differences as much if not more than actual prevalence rate disparity. There is also some variability across genders, although this is not particularly striking in magnitude. What is apparent is that EIPV is a common ACE and that both boys and girls are victims of this, from both female and male caregivers.

Review articles exploring EIPV between 2009 to 2022

Review articles were identified using a rapid evidence assessment PsychInfo. The search terms were "*Children* OR *adolescents* OR *youth or child* OR *teenager*" AND "*domestic violence* OR *domestic abuse* OR *intimate partner violence*" AND "*review of literature* OR *literature review* OR *meta-analysis*"
   And the data parameters were the following:

- published between from 2009 to 2022
- peer-reviewed journal article
- present data disaggregated by EIPV child gender

From this search 15 review articles that included data disaggregated by gender of the child exposed were identified and included (see tables that follow). These review papers included papers found collectively from searching numerous databases (e.g., PsychInfo, Medline, PubMed, ERIC, Social Work abstracts). There is overlap amongst the reviews, with the most recent (presented order of publication date with the most recent appearing first in the table) being most likely to contain most of the current data for the specific topic under review. Where nationality of participants was identified (four review articles), there is evidence of data from across the globe. Although later reviews are likely to contain the best estimates, the specific focus of the 15 reviews differed and so additional information regarding impact of EIPV is also available and therefore included.

The overview of papers (Table 2.2) presents a pattern of methodology where EIPV is measured using only father to mother data (14 articles) or an aggregated variable where participants were either asked about EIPV from fathers and mothers individually with these subsequently being aggregated into one variable or participants were asked about "violence" between parents/caregivers. Therefore, the predominance of information is for either or both parents using IPV. Where data for the sex of the parent using IPV was available there was no significant differences between exposure to men's or women's IPV. This suggests that there is no justification for limiting research to fathers' use of IPV, nor is there any justification in failing to target women's use of IPV to reduce ACEs exposure.

When looking at the impact of EIPV across the reviews, it is clear that EIPV is problematic across all age groups (Table 2.3). It impacts infants' threat sensitivity and increases the prevalence of childhood externalising (e.g., aggression) and internalising (e.g., depression and anxiety) behaviours and disorders. EIPV increases the probability that a child will be a perpetrator and/or victim of cyberbullying and will engage in risky sexual behaviour, including perpetrating sexual violence, in childhood. It is also a significant risk factor for perpetrating, and being a victim of, IPV in their own subsequent adult relationships.

Where there were sex-differences these were inconsistent. For example, Debowska et al. (2017) found females were more likely to experience sexual abuse if EIPV was present, while van Rosmalen-Nooijens et al. (2017) found inconclusive results. van Rosmalen-Nooijens et al. (2017) reviewed 45 studies on EIPV whereas Debowska et al's., (2017) work included only three papers on EIPV. The sex-difference with the most support was the difference in externalising and internalising behaviour in children, with the former being more common in boys and the latter being more common in girls.

In addition, the literature suggests that EIPV can come via father's, mother's or both parents' perpetration and there is no empirically supported reason to conclude that men are more likely to expose their children to IPV than are women. Additionally, there is no support for sex-differences in adult outcomes of EIPV in terms of the likelihood that any exposed child would become an adult victim or perpetrator of IPV themselves. Indeed, boys and girls appear similarly exposed and similarly harmed by EIPV.

Table 2.2 Overview of peer-reviewed review papers from the last 10 years

Study	Number papers DV exposure	Countries	Interest variable	Males	Females	Father IPV only	Mother IPV only	Parental IPV	Both
Kimber, M., Adham, S., Gill, S., McTavish, J., & MacMillan, H. L. (2018).	19	Canada India New Zealand Sri Lanka South Africa USA	Adult use of IPV	√	√	9		6	6
McGeough, B.L., & Sterzing, P. R. (2018).	5		Sexual minority youth (SMY)	√	√			1	
Nocentini et al. (2018).	2		Ethnicity	√	√			2	
	46		Cyberbullying	√	√			46	
Debowska, A., Willmott, D., Boduszek, D., & Jones, A. D. (2017).	3		Non-suicidal injury group & clinical disorders	√	√			3	
van Rosmalen-Noojens, K. A., Lahaije, F. A., Lo Fo Wong, S. H., Prins, J. B., & Lagro-Janssen, A. L. (2017).	45	Africa Asia Europe North-America South-America Oceania	Sexual risk-taking behaviour	√	√				
Vu, N. L., Jouriles, E. N., McDonald, R., & Rosenfield, D. (2016).	74		Child externalising and externalising problems	√	√				

Reference		Country	Topic				
Benavides, L. E. (2014).	9	UK	Protective factors	✓	✓		
Costa, B. M., Kaestle, C. E., Walker, A., Curtis, A., Day, A., Toumbourou, J. W., & Miller, P. (2015).	8	New Zealand	Longitudinal predictors of DV	✓	✓		8
Mandelli, L., Petrelli, C., & Serretti, A. (2015).	2	USA	ACEs as predictors of adult depression	✓	✓	1	1
Miller, L. E. (2015).	4		Threat sensitivity of children exposed to DV	✓	✓		4
Smith-Marek, E. N., Cafferky, B., Dharmidharka, P., Mallory, A. B., Dominguez, M., High, J.,...... & Mendez, M. (2015).	86		Exposure to DV & child abuse and adult DV	✓	✓	64	17
Tailor, K., & Letourneau, N. (2012).	4		Infants exposed to DV	✓	✓		
Wood, S. L., & Sommers, M. S. (2011).	24		Consequences of witnessing DV on children	✓	✓		
Chan, Y. C., & Yeung, J. W. K. (2009).	37		Children living with violence in the family	✓	✓		

Table 2.3 Impact of EIPV exposure

Study	Study focus	Males	Females	Combined	Father IPV only	Mother IPV only	Parental IPV	Both
Fogarty, A., Giallo, R., Wood, C., Kaufman, J., & Brown, S. (2019).	EIPV and Child resilience			Parental exposure – no sex-differences for pre-school or school aged children's resilience				
Kimber, M., Adham, S., Gill, S., McTavish, J., & MacMillan, H. L. (2018).	Parental exposure and adult use of DV			Parental exposure – adult use of those with adult exposure 84% used IPV; odds 4.35	9		6	6
McGeough, B. L., & Sterzing, P. R. (2018).	EIPV sexual minority youth			Compared heterosexual youth Sexual minority youth had significantly higher exposure				
Nocentini et al. (2018).	EIPV & child cyberbullying perpetration &victimisation			IPV exposure significantly related to cyberbullying perpetration in 95% of studies, and cyberbullying victimisation in 77%				
Debowska, A., Willmott, D., Boduszek, D., & Jones, A. D. (2017).	EIPV & clinical diagnosis		Of these, females with this exposure experienced high levels of sexual abuse	Those with the constellation of high abuse/neglect and EIPV had the highest rates of disorders.			3	
van Rosmalen-Nooijens, K. A., Lahaije, F. A., Lo	Witnessing DV increases some sexually risky	No consistent differences		EIPV increases sexual risk-taking and sexual violence perpetration			45	

(Continued)

Author	Variables	Findings	Notes
Fo Wong, S. H., Prins, J. B., & Lagro-Janssen, A. L. (2017).	behaviour in boys & girls.		but results on sexual victimisation and adolescent pregnancy were inconclusive. Pubertal timing appears not to be influenced by witnessing DV.	No difference whether it was exposure to fathers' or mothers' DV
Vu, N. L., Jouriles, E. N., McDonald, R., & Rosenfield, D. (2016).	DV exposure & child externalising/ externalising behaviour	Gender not associated with internalising/externalising	Results indicated that children's exposure to IPV is linked prospectively with child externalising, internalising and total adjustment problems. Child sex, sample type and whether only the male partner's violence or both partners' violence was measured did not predict the association between children's exposure to IPV and later adjustment problems.
Benavides, L. E. (2014).	Protective factors for children exposed to DV Ethnicity	Review stated 4/7 studies which analysed sex-differences found significant effects. It only details one study's finding (O'Keefe, 1998) which found for Males self-	Protective factors included: Proactive orientation (e.g., sense of control, hope, self-esteem), self-regulation, intelligence, positive

Table 2.3 (Continued)

Study	Study focus	Males	Females	Combined	Father IPV only	Mother IPV only	Parental IPV	Both
			esteem was protective and for females' educational attainment protective. Family support/cohesion is protective for African Americans	interpersonal relationships				
Costa, B. M., Kaestle, C. E., Walker, A., Curtis, A., Day, A., Toumbourou, J. W., & Miller, P. (2015).	Parental exposure and adult use of DV		No clear sex-differences	Data from cohorts from New Zealand and the USA found that exposure to DV predicted DV perpetration and victimisation				
Mandelli, L., Petrelli, C., & Serretti, A. (2015).	ACEs as predictors of adult depression			Comparing Exposure to DV, those participants had childhood exposure had prevalence of adult depression				
Miller, L. E. (2015).	Children's threat appraisal			Infants are sensitive to threatening stimuli. 3–7-year-olds exposed to DV show heighted threat detection & threat responses. 8–12-year-olds threat sensitivity may be				

Smith-Marek, E. N., Cafferky, B., Dharnidharka, P., Mallory, A. B., Dominguez, M., High, J.,...... & Mendez, M. (2015).	Exposure to DV & child abuse and adult DV	No significant sex-difference for the relationship between exposure to DV and perpetrating or being a victim of DV in adulthood. mediated by cognitive appraisal.	No significant sex-differences for the relationship between exposure to mother's or father's DV and perpetrating DV in adulthood. No significant sex-differences for the relationship between exposure DV and being the victim of DV in adulthood.
Tailor, K., & Letourneau, N. (2012).	Infants exposed to DV	One (7 mths to 16 years) study found no sex-differences. One study (2years to 12 years) found males significantly higher in aggression. Two studies (birth to 24 years) found boys showed significantly more externalising behaviour and girls more internalising behaviour	

(Continued)

Table 2.3 (Continued)

Study	Study focus	Males	Females	Combined	Father IPV only	Mother IPV only	Parental IPV	Both
Wood, S. L., & Sommers, M. S. (2011).		Boys show more externalising behaviour than girls, but aggression is directed primarily at boys. Girls demonstrated more internalising behaviour such as depression but also had higher rates of dating aggression than boys.		Differences were found in the behaviours of children who witness and do not witness IPV that have short- and long-term consequences and affect relationships with same-sex peers, dating partners and future partners with a clear pattern of dose-response				
Chan, Y. C., & Yeung, J. W. K. (2009).	Children living with family violence	Child sex did not moderate effect sizes, suggesting that the relationship between exposure to DV & child adjustment outcomes may be less affected by these factors than by other more consequential factors, such as children's individual resilience and their support network.						

References

Admin. (2020, March 17). *More Effects of Abuse on Child*. Stop Violence against Women. https://www.domesticviolenceinfo.ca/more-effects-of-abuse-on-child/

Archer, J. (2006). Cross-cultural differences in physical aggression between partners: A social-role analysis. *Personality and Social Psychology Review, 10*(2), 133–153. 10.1207/s15327957pspr1002_3

Bellis, M. A., Hughes, K., Leckenby, N., Hardcastle, K. A., Perkins, C., & Lowey, H. (2014). Measuring mortality and the burden of adult disease associated with adverse childhood experiences in England: A national survey. *Journal of Public Health, 37*(3), 445–454. 10.1093/pubmed/fdu065

Bellis, M. A., Hughes, K., Ford, K., Ramos Rodriguez, G., Sethi, D., & Passmore, J. (2019). Life course health consequences and associated annual costs of adverse childhood experiences across Europe and North America: A systematic review and meta-analysis. *The Lancet Public Health, 4*(10), e517–e528. 10.1016/s2468-2667(19)30145-8

Belsky, J., Jaffee, S. R., Sligo, J., Woodward, L., & Silva, P. A. (2005). Intergenerational transmission of warm-sensitive-stimulating parenting: A prospective study of mothers and fathers of 3-year-olds. *Child Development, 76*(2), 384–396. 10.1111/j.1467-8624.2005.00852.x

Benavides, L. E. (2014). Protective factors in children and adolescents exposed to intimate partner violence: An empirical research review. *Child and Adolescent Social Work Journal, 32*(2), 93–107. 10.1007/s10560-014-0339-3

Carter, L., Brooks, M., & Graham-Kevan, N. (2021). Emotion regulation mediates posttraumatic growth and cluster B personality traits after childhood trauma. *Violence and Victims, 36*(6), 706–722. 10.1891/vv-d-20-00022

Cascardi, M., & Jouriles, E. N. (2018). Mechanisms underlying the association of exposure to family of origin violence and adolescent dating violence [Review of *Mechanisms underlying the association of exposure to family of origin violence and adolescent dating violence*]. In *Adolescent dating violence* (pp. 159–188). Academic Press.

Chan, K. L. (2011). Children exposed to child maltreatment and intimate partner violence: A study of co-occurrence among Hong Kong Chinese families. *Child Abuse & Neglect, 35*(7), 532–542. 10.1016/j.chiabu.2011.03.008

Chan, Y.-C., & Yeung, J. W.-K. (2009). Children living with violence within the family and its sequel: A meta-analysis from 1995–2006. *Aggression and Violent Behavior, 14*(5), 313–322. 10.1016/j.avb.2009.04.001

Chartier, M. J., Walker, J. R., & Naimark, B. (2010). Separate and cumulative effects of adverse childhood experiences in predicting adult health and health care utilization. *Child Abuse & Neglect, 34*(6), 454–464. 10.1016/j.chiabu.2009.09.020

Choenni, V., Hammink, A., & van de Mheen, D. (2016). Association between substance use and the perpetration of family violence in industrialized countries. *Trauma, Violence, & Abuse, 18*(1), 37–50. 10.1177/1524838015589253

Christie, H., Hamilton-Giachritsis, C., Alves-Costa, F., Tomlinson, M., & Halligan, S. L. (2019). The impact of parental posttraumatic stress disorder on parenting: A systematic review. *European Journal of Psychotraumatology, 10*(1), 1550345. 10.1080/20008198.2018.1550345

Clare, C. A., Velasquez, G., Mujica Martorell, G. M., Fernandez, D., Dinh, J., & Montague, A. (2021). Risk factors for male perpetration of intimate partner violence: A review. *Aggression and Violent Behavior, 56*, 101532. 10.1016/j.avb.2020.101532

Costa, B. M., Kaestle, C. E., Walker, A., Curtis, A., Day, A., Toumbourou, J. W., & Miller, P. (2015). Longitudinal predictors of domestic violence perpetration and victimization: A systematic review. *Aggression and Violent Behavior*, *24*, 261–272. 10.1016/j.avb.2015.06.001

Debowska, A., Willmott, D., Boduszek, D., & Jones, A. D. (2017). What do we know about child abuse and neglect patterns of co-occurrence? A systematic review of profiling studies and recommendations for future research. *Child Abuse & Neglect*, *70*, 100–111. 10.1016/j.chiabu.2017.06.014

Dowling, E. (2016). Exploring the link between early adversity and behavioural health. *Public Health Theses*. http://elischolar.library.yale.edu/ysphtdl/1069

Felitti, V. J., Anda, R. F., Nordenberg, D., Williamson, D. F., Spitz, A. M., Edwards, V., Koss, M. P., & Marks, J. S. (1998). Relationship of childhood abuse and household dysfunction to many of the leading causes of death in adults. *American Journal of Preventive Medicine*, *14*(4), 245–258. 10.1016/s0749-3797(98)00017-8

Feng, J. Y., Chang, Y. T., Chang, H. Y., Fetzer, S., & Wang, J. D. (2015). Prevalence of different forms of child maltreatment among Taiwanese adolescents: A population-based study. *Child Abuse & Neglect*, *42*, 10–19. 10.1016/j.chiabu.2014.11.010

Fogarty, A., Giallo, R., Wood, C., Kaufman, J., & Brown, S. (2019). Emotional-behavioral resilience and competence in preschool children exposed and not exposed to intimate partner violence in early life. *International Journal of Behavioral Development*, 016502541983024. 10.1177/0165025419830241

Fogarty, A., Wood, C. E., Giallo, R., Kaufman, J., & Hansen, M. (2019). Factors promoting emotional-behavioural resilience and adjustment in children exposed to intimate partner violence: A systematic review. *Australian Journal of Psychology*, *71*(4). 10.1111/ajpy.12242

Godbout, N., Daspe, M.-È., Runtz, M., Cyr, G., & Briere, J. (2019). Childhood maltreatment, attachment, and borderline personality–related symptoms: Gender-specific structural equation models. *Psychological Trauma: Theory, Research, Practice, and Policy*, *11*(1), 90–98. 10.1037/tra0000403

Grest, C. V., Amaro, H., & Unger, J. (2017). Longitudinal predictors of intimate partner violence perpetration and victimization in Latino Emerging Adults. *Journal of Youth and Adolescence*, *47*(3), 560–574. 10.1007/s10964-017-0663-y

Hamby, S., Finkelhor, D., Turner, H., & Ormrod, R. (2010). The overlap of witnessing partner violence with child maltreatment and other victimizations in a nationally representative survey of youth. *Child Abuse & Neglect*, *34*(10), 734–741. 10.1016/j.chiabu.2010.03.001

Hughes, K., Bellis, M. A., Hardcastle, K. A., Sethi, D., Butchart, A., Mikton, C., Jones, L., & Dunne, M. P. (2017). The effect of multiple adverse childhood experiences on health: a systematic review and meta-analysis. *The Lancet Public Health*, *2*(8), e356–e366. 10.1016/s2468-2667(17)30118-4

Karakurt, G., Koç, E., Çetinsaya, E. E., Ayluçtarhan, Z., & Bolen, S. (2019). Meta-analysis and systematic review for the treatment of perpetrators of intimate partner violence. *Neuroscience & Biobehavioral Reviews*, *105*, 220–230. 10.1016/j.neubiorev.2019.08.006

Kimber, M., Adham, S., Gill, S., McTavish, J., & MacMillan, H. L. (2018). The association between child exposure to intimate partner violence (IPV) and perpetration of IPV in adulthood—A systematic review. *Child Abuse & Neglect*, *76*, 273–286. 10.1016/j.chiabu.2017.11.007

Langhinrichsen-Rohling, J., Misra, T. A., Selwyn, C., & Rohling, M. L. (2012). Rates of Bidirectional versus unidirectional intimate partner violence across samples, sexual orientations, and race/ethnicities: A comprehensive review. *Partner Abuse*, *3*(2), 199–230. 10.1891/1946-6560.3.2.199

Lapierre, S. (2008). Mothering in the context of domestic violence: the pervasiveness of a deficit model of mothering. *Child & Family Social Work*, *13*(4), 454–463. 10.1111/j.1365-2206.2008.00563.x

Levendosky, A. A., Bogat, G. A., & Martinez-Torteya, C. (2013). PTSD symptoms in young children exposed to intimate partner violence. *Violence Against Women*, *19*(2), 187–201. 10.1177/1077801213476458

Levendosky, A. A., & Graham-Bermann, S. A. (2000). Behavioral observations of parenting in battered women. *Journal of Family Psychology*, *14*(1), 80–94. 10.1037/0893-3200.14.1.80

Levendosky, A. A., & Graham-Bermann, S. A. (2001). Parenting in battered women: The effects of domestic violence on women and their children. *Journal of Family Violence*, *16*(2), 171–192. 10.1023/a:1011111003373

Mabanglo, M. A. G. (2002). Trauma and the effects of violence exposure and abuse on children: A review of the literature. *Smith College Studies in Social Work*, *72*(2), 231–251. 10.1080/00377310209517657

Mackay, J., Bowen, E., Walker, K., & O'Doherty, L. (2018). Risk factors for female perpetrators of intimate partner violence within criminal justice settings: A systematic review. *Aggression and Violent Behavior*, *41*, 128–146. 10.1016/j.avb.2018.06.004

Mandelli, L., Petrelli, C., & Serretti, A. (2015). The role of specific early trauma in adult depression: A meta-analysis of published literature. Childhood trauma and adult depression. *European Psychiatry*, *30*(6), 665–680. 10.1016/j.eurpsy.2015.04.007

Martin, J., Langley, J., & Millichamp, J. (2006). Domestic violence as witnessed by new zealand children. *The New Zealand Medical Journal (Online)*, *119*(1228), U1817. Retrieved from https://www.proquest.com/scholarly-journals/domestic-violence-as-witnessed-new-zealand/docview/1034194535/se-2

McGeough, B. L., & Sterzing, P. R. (2018). A systematic review of family victimization experiences among sexual minority youth. *The Journal of Primary Prevention*, *39*(5), 491–528. 10.1007/s10935-018-0523-x

Miller, L. E. (2015). Perceived threat in childhood: A review of research and implications for children living in violent households. *Trauma, Violence, & Abuse*, *16*(2), 153–168. 10.1177/1524838013517563

Nocentini, A., Fiorentini, G., Di Paola, L., & Menesini, E. (2018). Parents, family characteristics and bullying behavior: A systematic review. *Aggression and Violent Behavior*, *45*. 10.1016/j.avb.2018.07.010

NSPCC. (2022). How DART helps. https://www.nspcc.org.uk/what-is-child-abuse/types-of-abuse/domestic-abuse/

Office for National Statistics. (2017, September 27). *People who were abused as children are more likely to be abused as an adult - Office for National Statistics*. Ons.gov.uk. https://www.ons.gov.uk/peoplepopulationandcommunity/crimeandjustice/articles/peoplewhowereabusedaschildrenaremorelikelytobeabusedasanadult/2017-09-27

Osofsky, J. D. (2003). Prevalence of children's exposure to domestic violence and child maltreatment: Implications for prevention and intervention. *Clinical Child and Family Psychology Review*, *6*(3), 161–170. 10.1023/a:1024958332093

Renner, L. M., & Slack, K. S. (2006). Intimate partner violence and child maltreatment: Understanding intra- and intergenerational connections. *Child Abuse & Neglect*, *30*(6), 599–617. 10.1016/j.chiabu.2005.12.005

Sandison, B. (2018). Australian institute of health and welfare. *Impact*, *2018*(2), 80–81. 10.21820/23987073.2018.2.80

Sethi, D., Bellis, M., Hughes, K., Gilbert, R., Mitis, F., & Galea, G. (2013). *European report on preventing child maltreatment*. World Health Organization. Regional Office for Europe. May 6, 2021, from https://apps.who.int/iris/bitstream/handle/10665/326375/9789289000284-eng.pdf

Shonkoff, J. P., Garner, A. S., Siegel, B. S., Dobbins, M. I., Earls, M. F., Garner, A. S., McGuinn, L., Pascoe, J., & Wood, D. L. (2012). The lifelong effects of early childhood adversity and toxic stress. *Pediatrics*, *129*(1), e232–e246. 10.1542/peds.2011-2663

Smith-Marek, E. N., Cafferky, B., Dharnidharka, P., Mallory, A. B., Dominguez, M., High, J., Stith, S. M., & Mendez, M. (2015). Effects of Childhood Experienceschildhood experiences of Family Violencefamily violence on Adult Partner Violence:adult partner violence: A Meta-Analytic Reviewmeta-analytic review. *Journal of Family Theory & Review*, *7*(4), 498–519. 10.1111/jftr.12113

Soares, A. L. G., Howe, L. D., Matijasevich, A., Wehrmeister, F. C., Menezes, A. M. B., & Gonçalves, H. (2016). Adverse childhood experiences: Prevalence and related factors in adolescents of a Brazilian birth cohort. *Child Abuse & Neglect*, *51*, 21–30. 10.1016/j.chiabu.2015.11.017

Spencer, C. M., Anders, K. M., Toews, M. L., & Emanuels, S. K. (2020). Risk markers for physical teen dating violence victimization in the United States: A meta-analysis. *Journal of Youth and Adolescence*, *49*(3), 575–589. 10.1007/s10964-020-01194-1

Stith, S. M., Rosen, K. H., Middleton, K. A., Busch, A. L., Lundeberg, K., & Carlton, R. P. (2000). The intergenerational transmission of spouse abuse: A meta-analysis. *Journal of Marriage and Family*, *62*(3), 640–654. 10.1111/j.1741-3737.2000.00640.x

Swart, L.-A., Seedat, M., Stevens, G., & Ricardo, I. (2002). Violence in adolescents' romantic relationships: Findings from a survey amongst school-going youth in a South African community. *Journal of Adolescence*, *25*(4), 385–395. 10.1006/jado.2002.0483

Tailor, K., & Letourneau, N. (2012). Infants exposed to intimate partner violence: Issues of gender and sex. *Journal of Family Violence*, *27*(5), 477–488. 10.1007/s10896-012-9441-5

van Rosmalen-Nooijens, K. A. W. L., Lahaije, F. A. H., Lo Fo Wong, S. H., Prins, J. B., & Lagro-Janssen, A. L. M. (2017). Does witnessing family violence influence sexual and reproductive health of adolescents and young adults? A systematic review. *Psychology of Violence*, *7*(3), 343–374. 10.1037/vio0000113

Völkl-Kernstock, S., Huemer, J., Jandl-Jager, E., Abensberg-Traun, M., Marecek, S., Pellegrini, E., Plattner, B., & Skala, K. (2015). Experiences of Domesticdomestic and School Violence Among Childschool violence among child and Adolescent Psychiatric Outpatientsadolescent psychiatric outpatients. *Child Psychiatry & Human Development*, *47*(5), 691–695. 10.1007/s10578-015-0602-7

Vu, N. L., Jouriles, E. N., McDonald, R., & Rosenfield, D. (2016). Children's exposure to intimate partner violence: A meta-analysis of longitudinal associations with child adjustment problems. *Clinical Psychology Review*, *46*, 25–33. 10.1016/j.cpr.2016.04.003

Wood, S. L., & Sommers, M. S. (2011). Consequences of intimate partner violence on child witnesses: A systematic review of the literature. *Journal of Child and Adolescent Psychiatric Nursing, 24*(4), 223–236. 10.1111/j.1744-6171.2011.00302.x

World Health Organization. (2012). *Understanding and addressing violence against women: Intimate partner violence* (No. WHO/RHR/12.36). World Health Organization. https://apps.who.int/iris/bitstream/handle/10665/77432/?sequence=1

World Health Organization. (2013). *Global and regional estimates of violence against women: prevalence and health effects of intimate partner violence and non-partner sexual violence.* World Health Organization. https://apps.who.int/iris/bitstream/handle/10665/85239/?sequence=1

World Health Organization. (2014). WHO Country Cooperation Strategy for the World Health Organization and the Ministry of Health of the Russian Federation: 2014–2020. https://apps.who.int/iris/bitstream/handle/10665/179823/ccs_rus_en.PDF

Yapp, E., Booth, T., Davis, K., Coleman, J., Howard, L. M., Breen, G., Hatch, S. L., Hotopf, M., & Oram, S. (2021). Sex differences in experiences of multiple traumas and mental health problems in the UK Biobank cohort. *Social Psychiatry and Psychiatric Epidemiology.* 10.1007/s00127-021-02092-y

Yule, K., Houston, J., & Grych, J. (2019). Resilience in children exposed to violence: A meta-analysis of protective factors across ecological contexts. *Clinical Child and Family Psychology Review, 22*(3), 406–431. 10.1007/s10567-019-00293-1

3 Growing up with domestic abuse

Retrospective accounts

Julie Taylor, Elizabeth Bates, David Wright, and Kirsty Martin

University of Cumbria

Introduction

The impetus for this chapter came from a series of studies the main author carried out between 2010 and 2013, studies exploring the lived experiences of females who had been convicted of criminal acts. A key finding from this participatory research was that all the women involved described childhoods where IPV between the adults in their lives was commonplace. Moreover, whilst the violence and abuse experienced was not articulated by the women as a direct cause of their subsequent criminal behaviour, what they did describe suggested that their life choices were constrained as a result. For example, whilst school was occasionally characterised as a haven, in most cases the women described the pain of being at school, watching other children and feeling different, being victimised, or feeling compelled to use aggression to feel in control. With the cumulative effect of their experiences at school leading to high levels of truancy at formative stages in their educational career (often before 11 years of age). The truancy was explained in the context of avoiding bullying, social awkwardness and a fear of revealing what was happening at home if they forged friendships at school (Taylor et al., 2013; Taylor, 2019). The disengagement from school, often at such early stages, was reported as having many unintended consequences. The impact of these early experiences prompted a series of studies (2017–2021) that asked adults to reflect on their childhood experiences of domestic abuse, any barriers or opportunities for help seeking and the adult sequelae. This chapter draws on data from these studies to exemplify the heterogeneous nature of the children's lived experiences.

In the UK, children growing up in homes where there was domestic violence were, until recently, defined as witnesses or observers as opposed to victims of abuse. The use of this terminology to describe their status was challenged because of its influence on the construction and treatment of children within services (Callaghan et al., 2018). Witnessing the abuse as opposed to being a victim of it had the potential to minimise the perceived impact and therefore reduce the requirements for intervention (Callaghan et al., 2018). One of the consequences is the lack of priority given to children's

DOI: 10.4324/9781003124634-5

trauma and the potential impact this may have on their lives (e.g., Øverlien, 2010). To position children as peripheral and therefore not directly impacted is a socially convenient position that also enables homogeneous thinking. Homogeneity assumptions artificially simplify issues which whilst convenient for research design can lead to a perpetuation of injustice. To collapse all children into an onlooker position minimises their distress and privileges that of the adult victim. Whilst simple distinctions offer opportunities to artificially impose order on a complex multifaceted phenomenon, they simultaneously have the potential to obscure heterogeneity in pursuit of a one-size fits all approach. For example, the theory of intergenerational patterns of abuse has been a popular claim however one that makes a series of assumptions that fails to fully appreciate the diverse experiences of those involved. The desire for simplicity stands in opposition to the wealth of evidence contesting reductionist causal relationships. Many children living in homes where there is violence and abuse between parents are not only victims of these trauma inducing living conditions but also of direct abuse and violence within the home and in other areas of their ecosystems (e.g., Bacchini & Esposito, 2020). The search for homogeneity whilst appealing from a research design perspective, belies the lived reality of individuals.

It is precisely the complexity of lived experience that helps us understand why even similar looking experiences can lead to radically different outcomes. There exists a wealth of evidence (academic, anecdotal and observational) to show that children develop within complex ecosystems of which the home is only one of the socio-emotional contexts in which they participate (Margolin et al., 2010). The assumption that a child in a home where there is parental abuse who has positive relationships at school and who lives in a community where violence is unusual, is affected in the same way as a child who experiences violence within the home, school and the wider community seems somewhat naïve (Mrug & Windle, 2010).

Clearly, moving from the label witness or observer to victim retains the problem of making essentialist style statements. However, in the context of a legal system it enables the children to move from the periphery to centre stage. To identify children as key victims prioritises their experiences and directs attention to their needs. Fortunately, the Domestic Abuse Act (2021) now makes explicit reference to children as **victims** if "they see, hear, or experience the effects of the abuse … " many researchers in the field see this change as long overdue (e.g., Callaghan & Alexander, 2015). Several scholars in the field have for some years balked at the assumption that children could ever have been viewed as passive witnesses to the abusive behaviour patterns (e.g., Callaghan & Alexander, 2015; Eliffee & Holt, 2019). Asserting that such a position stood in contrast to what is known about stress, distress and trauma (e.g., Rossman & Ho, 2018). This new legal position is therefore to be applauded as a significant move in a positive direction, assuming it is accompanied by a radical change to the way we construct services for children and young people in the future.

The aim of this brief chapter is to share the accounts of child victims (birth to 18 years) and consider the impact of IPV on their lived experience. The accounts referred to here are from a self-selecting sample of adults (18 years and over) who were asked to look back on their experiences of growing up in a home where there was IPV between their adult caregivers. The study garnered responses from 110 male, female and non-Binary participants. In the chapter that follows we offer a summary of what is a growing body of literature examining the impact of living in an abusive home on children. We then introduce the experiences of the adults in our sample who were child victims, using their own words from their retrospective accounts. Whilst retrospective accounts are open to criticism on several grounds, for example, the accuracy of the memories recalled, to understand the lived experience and impact of childhood experiences on adult lives they are necessary. Moreover, whilst memory is fallible, it is not the veracity of recall that is of interest, it is how the persons perception and interpretation of their childhood experiences influenced their understanding and behaviour. Descriptive first-person accounts have the advantage of enabling the heterogeneity of experience to be shared and contextualised in the participants own words (Haselschwerdt et al., 2019).

Children and IPV

A growing body of evidence suggests that living in a home where there is domestic abuse can seriously impact a child's development (e.g., Wagner et al., 2019). These impacts can take several forms including: physical health issues (e.g., Bair-Merritt et al., 2006), poor mental health (e.g., Carpenter & Stacks, 2009; Gilbert, et al., 2009; Knefel et al., 2018), difficulty in managing emotions / emotional regulation (e.g., Peltonen et al., 2010). In particular, low self-esteem and social withdrawal have been associated with growing up in homes where there is domestic abuse (e.g., Wolfe et al., 2003). Additionally, studies have identified, problems in the maintenance of social and intimate relationships (e.g., Siegel, 2013), challenges with education including engagement, truancy and attainment (e.g., Carrell & Hoekstra, 2010) an increased probability of being convicted of an offence in adolescence or adulthood (e.g., Fox et al., 2015) and a greater likelihood of both internalising and externalising difficulties. An internalising behaviour may be anxiety, depression or self-harm and externalising difficulties may manifest in higher levels of aggression, substance misuse or anti-social behaviour (e.g., Vu et al., 2016). More recently, studies have shown attentional biases in preschool aged children who have been living in homes with domestic abuse. The biases observed were indicative of emotional difficulties with respect to sad or threatening targets (Mastorakos & Scott, 2019). The work relating to very young children has been gathering momentum in recent years for several reasons, in part because the younger the child the greater the likelihood of direct exposure to abusive behaviours, i.e., very young children are unable to remove themselves from danger in the way that older children might and in addition, neurological research shows just how critical the early years are for neurological development. Despite the plethora of evidence identifying negative outcomes, it is also important to note that through the management of complex relationships in the home children may also develop a level of competence that has the potential to be utilised positively in the future (e.g., Katz, 2016) and some studies have found that those who experience victimisation as children are less likely to be perpetrators in the future (e.g., Payne et al., 2011). Identifying strengths from adversity is important, however, efforts to prevent, intervene and treat remain the priority.

Whilst the last 30 years has seen significant developments in our understanding of the impact of domestic violence on children, developing a fuller first-hand understanding of the heterogeneity of children's experiences remains critical. This is particularly true in the UK with the recent legislative changes relating to how children living in homes with domestic abuse are defined. This change offers opportunities to reprioritise identification, intervention and treatment needs but to do so effectively the range of needs must be better understood. Moreover, a significant body of the extant literature comes from the US with less focus on the UK. Whilst all insights have value, with the recent legislative change in the UK, it is important to understand the experiences of those living in the UK to identify what resources may be needed to support children and adults who have experienced domestic abuse as children. Additionally, one of the biggest criticisms of the literature to date is methodological in nature, most of what we know about children's experiences comes from third parties, typically mothers or professionals working in refuges with children who are no longer residing within the abusive home. That is not to denigrate the importance of this evidence simply to acknowledge that other sources may be equally valuable and enable wider experiences to be included, for example, the voices of the children themselves, the voices of children whose mothers were the main perpetrators, the voices of those who were not able to leave the abusive home until they reached adulthood.

Childhood experiences of living in a home where there is domestic abuse?

The adults who participated in our study of retrospective experiences of growing up in homes with domestic abuse, identified as male, female and non-Binary and were aged between 18 and 61 years. It was a volunteer sample of UK residents who responded to one of a series of social media posts on Facebook, Instagram and Twitter. The data was collected using an ethically approved anonymous online survey which included a combination of open and closed questions. The first open question posed was: *How would you describe the nature of the domestic violence and abuse that occurred in your home when you were a child/young person?* The extracts that follow show that the abuse described included references to financial, physical, verbal, emotional, coercive and controlling behaviour, stalking, harassment, threats and manipulation.

> My father beat my mother and me … .He would lock me in a dark room all night as a punishment. I believe this was to give him free-reign to abuse my mother. His abuse of my mother and me blighted my life. (Participant 88, 47 years, Male)
>
> Most of the time it was my mum who had started the fights with her boyfriends. Just the boyfriend always took it to an unnecessary level. It would be a regular thing, happening most nights. My mum would use me as a defence. Putting me in-between her and her boyfriend while they were fighting. I was never hit from what I remember but for me it affected me more psychologically. (Participant 90, 18 years, Male)
>
> My step-father, physically abused my mother, usually after drinking. She came to antagonize him in the end, almost inviting the violence. As a teenage boy, I used to go to bed fully clothed in case I needed to get up quickly to intervene. This happened regularly, and twice led to me getting into a fight with him. He was also very controlling of my mother's comings and goings. (Participant 95, 51 years, Male)
>
> My parents separated, and we went to live with our father and step - mother. We had not experienced any physical chastisement or any type of abuse before then. I do not recall at what point it started but I do recall regular beatings, being physically hit, not a smack or an open-handed strike but with her fists and my brother too. My brother was beaten worse than me before he left at which point, I got his beatings as well as my own. We watched my father bullied, disrespected, controlled, coerced, exploited and abused for 40 more years, he couldn't get out of it, I don't think he recognised it as abuse, I did, my brother did. (Participant 103, 54 years, Male)
>
> On several occasions as a child, while in bed I heard my father in the next room shout at my mother in what I can only describe as a threatening outburst. I was only 8 at the time but I can still hear it now. I remember seeing my mum with a black eye. I also witnessed his shouting bad tempered outbursts many times. (Participant 8, 53 years, Female)
>
> My father and mother were separated when I was born but he continued to abuse my mother by stalking her, breaking in, or manipulating her into letting him stay the night and then refusing to leave. My mother was physically, emotionally and sexually abused by my father and I witnessed this. (Participant 57, 21 years, non-Binary)

In all cases the adult relationships were described as opposite sex. Of the relationships described by participants, 48% involved a male only perpetrator (father or stepfather), 16% female only (mother or stepmother), in 17% of cases the adults were involved in bi-directional violence, 12% of participants did not answer this question and 8% of participants identified grandparents.

My father was also extremely abusive towards my mum; she has depression and anxiety due to her childhood experiences and my father used this as a way of controlling her. For example, saying she couldn't leave him because she has mental health problems and will therefore never see her children again. He would be physically abusive, broken bones, thrown objects at her, pushed her down the stairs while pregnant, made her take sleeping pills to abuse her during the night. He was also psychologically abusive, controlling everything she done, took away any fun out of her life, putting her down and encouraging her to kill herself. (Participant 26, 25 years, Female)

Mostly verbal. My mother was very controlling and would scream and blow up at the slightest thing - towards us the kids and towards Dad. She has hit the boys but not me. With me it was emotional, threatening to withdraw emotionally and not meet my needs. Dad could never do anything right and was yelled at often in public. As I grew older and tried to gain independence, she stopped me from seeing friends. (Participant 5, 34 years, Female)

My mum went through domestic abuse for just over ten years. My father was an incredibly violent man who did not hide his abuse from me and my brother. We lived in a dangerous home environment. (Participant 7, 30 years, Female)

Grandparents were primarily mentally and verbally abusive with threats of violence. (Participant 14, 35 years, Female)

The responses also provided insight into how the participants experienced living in such complex abusive relationships and reported feeling that these formative relationships had contributed to later vulnerabilities

I was just miserable because I was bullied by other kids & by teachers too. But it was safer than home. The police came and put me into care. Then after a few years they put me back home again. I will never forgive them. I had a baby because they put me back home. (Participant 33, 43 years, Female)

I was a truant. Attendance around 30%. I was always the outsider. Never fitted in at all... ... lower class ... in council housing with damp walls and no heating. The bullies weren't always just the children. (Participant 10, 47 years, Female)

I was isolated because of my violent outburst because I was constantly stressed and fearful. Because of this I was picked on by those older and would often get in to fights with them. This isolated me even more and increased the bullying to the point where teachers would join in and always blame me. (Participant 52, 18 years, Male)

These extracts serve to exemplify the types of abuse that children were experiencing in the home and the diverse range of perpetrators involved, biological parents and grandparents as well as stepparents and partners. The proportion of males identified as main perpetrator was three times that of female only perpetrators and this is important to note, however, it is equally important that this size differential does not lead to myopia when it comes to individual domestic abuse reports. Men, women and children can all be victims and to assume all perpetrators are male has the potential to leave children whose perpetrators are female invisible.

How did "Home" feel?

Until the Domestic Abuse Act (2021), the marginal placement of children as external to the victim-perpetrator or perpetrator-perpetrator dyads in family relationships may have inferred that except when the abuse was occurring, their experiences at home were "typical." This perspective has been rejected by several scholars including Stark (2009) who argued that *"For children as well as their mothers, abuse is ongoing rather than episodic and its effects cumulative"* (p. 295). The newly ascribed victim status means that the abuse is no longer constructed as some distinct disruption to an otherwise "normally" functioning home rather it is acknowledged as being a manifestation of what is a dysfunctional home.

The accounts of the participants reinforce the argument that a home where there is domestic abuse is dysfunctional even in the absence of specific acts of abuse. Interestingly, many participants explicitly referred to "normal" or "calm" periods whilst at the same time acknowledging the underlying threat or undercurrent of tension and fear.

> Terrifying when he was out, as never knew what mood he'd be in when he got home. Worse when he was at home, as anything could trigger him. (Participant 5, 29 years, Male)
>
> Unstable. There would be calm and happy periods, but I always felt like there was a danger of the violence starting again if we weren't careful. (Participant 7, 32 years, Male)
>
> It was extremely frightening most of the time. Occasional bouts of normal kind behaviours, but very short lived. (Participant 16, 52 years, Male)
>
> My mother was volatile, easily upset and violent. Living at home was like constantly walking on glass, but this was 'normal' for me until I moved away. (Participant 24, 41 years, Female)

These extracts are a powerful indicator that the emotional tone of home was not perceived as typical by the many of the participants, suggesting instead a tone of emotional lability accompanied by fear. The heightened arousal and vigilance reported by participants has been identified as a classic symptom of trauma (e.g., Adams, 2006) and a state that can be transmitted intergenerationally (e.g., Fredland et al., 2015). Recent studies that build on these earlier findings focus on the mother as child victim and acknowledge that more attention is needed to understand how fathers who experienced victimisation in childhood are impacted (e.g., Lünnemann et al., 2019). Research has gathered momentum in terms of the adult sequelae of childhood victimisation, however, much ambiguity remains. The range of methods and measures employed, the sample composition and the extent to which the child's exposure/experience has been contextualised makes it difficult to draw clear conclusions. Compounded further by the range of outcomes explored e.g., from examining future parenting styles, a range of mental health conditions, educational outcomes, violence and aggression or future victimisation in intimate relationships. Clearly each of these outcomes warrants research attention but at the same time it means we have a large evidence base indicating lots of areas of need/concern but little in the way of consistency.

How do the participants themselves describe the longer-term impact of their childhood experiences?

We asked our participants whether they believed that their early experiences had impacted their adult relationships, six of the 110 participants identified positive outcomes, 104 negative impacts and one participant noted both positive and negative outcomes.

The positive responses included:

"In positive ways surprisingly. I recognised as I got older that there was abuse. I am estranged from my family and wanted to ensure that I nor my children were exposed to behaviours like that" (Participants 12, 45 years, Female)

"Made me a better parent through experiences I don't want my kids to experience the same" (Participant 67, 53 years, Male)

"They have allowed me to be mentally strong. I have been with my husband for 25 years. We have four children, three of whom are now adults. I have strong relationships with my children and husband and I make sure that I tell them that I love them everyday" (Participant 76, 41 years, Female)

"Positive effect I would never want a child to feel how I did or any partner I was with" (Participant 82, 35 years, Male)

"Yes, but only in the way that I would never tolerate any signs of domestic abuse. If anything, I am hyper aware of the behaviours and red flags, so I know what to look out for. And as such I have never suffered any abuse myself in my adult life" (Participant, years, Participant 16, 35 years, Female).

The mixed impact was described as

"Yes and no. I've enjoyed relationships and living with other people because its been more relaxed, I have been able to be me and constant threat was removed. I have probably stayed with people longer than I should just to stay away from my parents. I probably got more hurt by one and got together with others because of low self-esteem that results from walking on eggshells. My

drinking and need to talk about it was not compatible with another relationship. And a further person inspired me to get better. It's been a journey. Mostly they have helped me see things can be different" (Participant 35, 41 years, Female).

There were many negative outcomes identified that referred to mental health difficulties and relationship formation and maintenance.

"Yes. I have ongoing mental health input. My relationships are unstable" (Participant 2, 18 years, Male)

Yes. I find it very hard to trust people. I have depression and anxiety and very low self-esteem. I have tried to get treatment for this, but I think it's beyond repair (Participant 1, 37 years, Female)

"When I was at school I would regularly lash out at others and then isolate myself due to the bullying from those much older after each outburst" (Participant 22, 67 years, Male).

I suffered with depression, anorexia (6mths), bulimia (12 years), alcoholism, poor self-esteem, lack of confidence etc for years and although I've sought help, and made progress, I'm still aware of the effects lingering" (Participant 24, 41 years, Female).

"Yes. I have ongoing mental health input. My relationships are unstable" (Participant 26, 32 years, Male).

Overall, the negative outcomes were striking by their consistency, the following words/phrases were commonplace, *"fear, I don't trust people, I am needy people cannot give me what I need, isolated, terrified, fear of abandonment, cautious."*

"I don't trust anyone. I have control issues. I find emotional and physical intimacy challenging" (Participant 14, 35 Years, Female).

"Yes. Constant abandonment fears" (Participant 51, 20 years, Female).

Yes. I often self-isolate and become withdrawn. I struggle to form loving relationships because I fear that I will be hurt, harmed or let down (Participant 87, 30 years, Male).

"I trust no one. I believe that everyone is out for what they can get from me. I've got a wall built up and won't let anyone in. I don't speak well about my thoughts and feelings" (Participant 102, 35 years, Female).

"I find it difficult to trust, to be close to someone because of the anxiety I feel about losing them. I have never been married, nor do I have children. I feel jealous and insecure as soon as I enter a relationship and feel the anxiety around this outweighs any happiness" (Participant 107, 39 years, Female).

In addition, there was a theme of abusive relationships (real or feared).

"Yes- In so many ways. My first relationship was domestically violent. I then went on to be violent in a relationship because of that. I have struggled with violence as an adult because of my experience as a child and young person.

However, I vowed never to raise a hand to my own children, and I never have. I see the difference this has made to them" (Participant 74, 37 years, Female).

"Yes, I married an abusive woman who I accepted the emotional abuse as it was normal and a comfortable familiar way to be treated" (Participant 86, 42 years, Male)

"Yes, I have co-dependency issues, trust issues and have been in abusive relationships on two occasions" (Participant 90, 28 years, Female).

"Yes, I always thought I would never end up like my mum, I would say it all the time, but as it often happens you have that cycle and I fell into another statistic of growing up with domestic violence and ending up in a violent relationship, I was with a girl for 2 years who had hit me and beat me up a lot of times due to jealousy, I'd be emotionally manipulated and towards the end of the relationship ended up being attacked with a knife and stabbed … I am very self-conscious, I think witnessing abuse as a child has had a massive effect on my adult relationships because of trust issues" (Participant 110, 26 years, Female).

Finally, one of the key issues identified in the early research introduced at the beginning of this chapter was how child victims of adult IPV experienced school. In the main authors early work with female's who had been convicted of criminal offences school had largely been experienced as something to avoid which the women saw as a key turning point in their lives. Their truancy led to low educational attainment, low literacy and limited basic academic skills. They also reported few long-term friendships and acknowledged that they had not forged or maintained friendships in the same way they had seen their peers doing. Several of the participants reported feeling that this was because of their home circumstances and their general social awkwardness around others. The consequences of missing out academically and socially at school were reported to impact on their own personal development, ability to find employment and support their own children's educational journey. Whilst most of this cohort found school too difficult to cope with, a couple experienced it as a haven. Understanding the school experience is potentially key in terms of supporting children from complex abusive homes to find a safe space and become equipped to compete in a society that places considerable emphasis on qualifications and social competence.

Of the 110 respondents, 10 elected not to comment on their school experiences, 7 expressed mixed views, 45 reported positively on school and 48 negatively. It is worth noting that of those who reported positively almost 50% were positive because it felt safer than home even if they did not have any friends and felt isolated or bullied at school.

The positive experiences associated with school took a variety of forms, for some it was associated primarily with the emotional tone of the school, i.e., an escape from home.

I enjoyed school and looked forward to the normality and calmness of the school. I was an average student, tried hard and generally likeable (I hope),

I suffered from missing homework as sometimes the situation at home was not conducive - nor did it feel a place that I could focus on study. (Participant 31, 53 years, Male)

My behaviour at school was reserved. My relationship with my peers was positive. I found teachers to be authoritarian and issuing out rules which I thought was unreasonable. I was argumentative and was suspended on a few occasions. (Participant 3, 27 years, Male)

School was very much an escape. (Participant 62, 40 years, Female)

I really, really loved school, it was a break and I loved going to my grandparents who gave me shelter from the storm so to speak. (Participant 87, 30 years, Male)

School was a break from home life for me but I was still bullied for being 'weird'/'gay'. But it never phased me because I was going through worse verbal abuse at home. (Participant 44, 18 years, Male)

From an academic and social perspective some participants reported positive experiences including reference to strong peer groups and academic success.

School was fine. I was academically able so it wasn't hard. I had a really strong friendship group. (Participant 23, 41 years, Female)

I was lucky because school was very easy for me academically. As a result I received a lot of praise and special treatment at school which gave me some much needed validation and sense of achievement. (Participant 27, 43 years, Female)

I loved school. I had quite a few friends and overall school life was fine. (Participant 53, 22 years, Female)

Very positive, I really enjoyed school, learning and friendships with peers. (Participant 73, 33 years, Female)

However, for almost 50% of the participants who responded to this question, school was a negative experience that further compounded their feelings of isolation, fear and social awkwardness. In some cases, these feelings were reported as leading to disruptive, violent, or aggressive behaviours at school. In others leading to high levels of truancy.

I was isolated because of my violent outburst because I was constantly stressed and fearful. Because of this I was picked on by those older and would often get in to fights with them. This isolated me even more and increased the bullying to the point where teachers would join and always blame in when it comes to problems I was involved in. (Participant 52, 18 years, Male)

My behaviour in school was often unpredictable, depending on what had happened at home. Sometimes I was calm and engaged and happy to learn, but other times I would be violent, talk back to the teacher, and start fights. (Participant 54, 21 years, Non-Binary)

I was inattentive. I was polite but naughty- not a bully. I used to pretend everything was okay at home or make up stories. So, my parents were like other people's. (Participant 88, 33 years, Female)

I was a truant. Attendance around 30% I remember a middle-class colleague interpreting me as being home schooled. The bullies weren't always just the children. Just a total outsider. (Participant 10, 47 years, Female)

I barely went to school and didn't have any hobbies. I also didn't have any friends. (Participant 66, 23 years, Female)

I didn't want to be at school. I was distracted because I was thinking about mum. I was assumed to be a child/young person who was not bright. I became isolated at school and faced problems with bullying. (Participant 7, 30 years, Female)

Highly anxiety provoking. For many reasons. Clearly growing up in an emotionally intense environment impacted my own development. I was scared every time a person changed their tone of voice, until slowly realising that massive explosions were not normal reactions to someone not finishing their lunch, or hanging a coat up immediately after taking it off. (Participant 21, 35 years, Female)

Awful. I was bullied in the sense that for two years none of the children at school spoke/interacted with me. If they did, it was an insult. (Participant 64, 49 years, Female)

Introverted. We were very poor. Lack of social contact, poor school performance. (Participant 40, 46 years, Male)

These exemplars demonstrate that the respondents had very mixed experiences of school. Where school was seen as a haven, respondents have often gone on to higher level study and employment. These findings are consistent with recent work by Lloyd (2018), Lloyd concluded that whilst schools had the potential to make a positive difference to the children's experience, many teachers and educational professionals reported lacking the knowledge, understanding and confidence required to affect change. This is consistent with Selvik (2018) see also Chapter 8 of this volume for a discussion of the role of school in the lives of child victims of DVA. Further research is required in this area because it is evident that school has the potential to offer a safe environment where children can meet their academic potential and flourish socially. Whilst there are hints at how this could be achieved from the respondents' perspectives e.g., not engaging in triggering behaviours like shouting or appearing to join in with bullies, the data here does not enable any explicit recommendations to be made.

Conclusion

The experiences shared by our participants, to whom we are extremely grateful, show that growing up in homes where there is domestic abuse has a long-lasting impact on their lives. The perpetrators of the abuse may be male, female, there may be single perpetrators or multiple. Consistent with the literature the participants themselves, regardless of gender identification, overwhelmingly reported long-lasting negative outcomes, with respect to their future relationships (intimate or otherwise) and their mental health and wellbeing (e.g., Øverlien, 2010). There were some participants, albeit a small minority, that recognised that their negative childhood experiences had shaped them positively, giving them a determination to be better parents or partners themselves (Payne et al., 2011; Katz, 2016). Perhaps the most encouraging finding relates to school and the potential that schools have to identify, support and provide a haven for children. The relationship between child victims and school and school support services would benefit from further research because to meet victims' needs a more sophisticated understanding of the aspects of the school culture that are sensitive to the needs of victims is required. This is consistent with previous research (e.g., Taylor et al., 2013; Taylor, 2019). Ultimately, making school accessible and supportive may enable more children to see school as positive for reasons beyond offering an escape from home.

References

Adams, C. M. (2006). The consequences of witnessing family violence on children and implications for family counselors. *The Family Journal, 14*(4), 334–341. 10.1177/1 066480706290342.

Bacchini, D., & Esposito, C. (2020). Growing up in violent contexts: Differential effects of community, family, and school violence on child adjustment. In *Children and peace* (pp. 157–171). Springer, Cham.

Bair-Merritt, M. H., Blackstone, M., & Feudtner, C. (2006). Physical health outcomes of childhood exposure to intimate partner violence: A systematic review. *Pediatrics, 117*, e278–e290.

Callaghan, J.E.M., & Alexander, J.H. (2015). Understanding agency and resistance strategies (UNARS): Children's experiences of domestic violence. *Report*, University of Northampton, UK.

Callaghan, J. E. M., Alexander, J. H., Sixsmith, J., & Fellin, L. C. (2018). Beyond "witnessing": Children's experiences of coercive control in domestic violence and abuse. *Journal of Interpersonal Violence, 33*(10), 1551–1581. 10.1177/0886260515618946

Carpenter, G. L., & Stacks, A. M. (2009). Developmental effects of exposure to Intimate Partner Violence in early childhood: A review of the literature. *Children and Youth Services Review, 31*(8), 831–839. 10.1016/j.childyouth.2009.03.005

Carrell, S. E., & Hoekstra, M. L. (2010). Externalities in the classroom: How children exposed to domestic violence affect everyone's kids. *American Economic Journal: Applied Economics, 2*(1), 211–228. 10.1257/app.2.1.211

Elliffe, R., & Holt, S. (2019). Reconceptualizing the child victim in the police response to domestic violence. *Journal of Family Violence.* 10.1007/s10896-019-00055-1

Fox, B. H., Perez, N., Cass, E., Baglivio, M. T., & Epps, N. (2015). Trauma changes everything: Examining the relationship between adverse childhood experiences and serious, violent and chronic juvenile offenders. *Child Abuse & Neglect, 46*(1), 163–173. 10.1016/j.chiabu.2015.01.011

Fredland, N., Symes, L., Gilroy, H., Paulson, R., Nava, A., McFarlane, J., & Pennings, J. (2015). Connecting partner violence to poor functioning for mothers and children: Modeling intergenerational outcomes. *Journal of Family Violence, 30*(5), 555–566. 10.1007/s10896-015-9702-1

Gilbert, R., Kemp, A., Thoburn, J., Sidebotham, P., Radford, L., Glaser, D., & MacMillan, H. L. (2009). Recognising and responding to child maltreatment. *The Lancet, 373*(9658), 167–180. 10.1016/s0140-6736(08)61707-9

Haselschwerdt, M. L., Hlavaty, K., Carlson, C., Schneider, M., Maddox, L., & Skipper, M. (2019). Heterogeneity Within Domestic Violence Exposure:within domestic violence exposure: Young Adults' Retrospective Experiencesadults' retrospective experiences. *Journal of Interpersonal Violence, 34*(7), 1512–1538. 10.1177/0886260516651625

Katz, E. (2016). Beyond the physical incident model: How children living with domestic violence are harmed by and resist regimes of coercive control. *Child Abuse Review, 25*(1), 46–59. 10.1002/car.2422

Knefel, M., Lueger-Schuster, B., Karatzias, T., Shevlin, M., & Hyland, P. (2018). From child maltreatment to ICD-11 complex post-traumatic stress symptoms: The role of emotion regulation and re-victimisation. *Journal of Clinical Psychology, 75*(3), 392–403. 10.1002/jclp.22655

Lloyd, M. (2018). Domestic violence and education: Examining the impact of domestic violence on young children, children, and young people and the potential role of schools. *Frontiers in Psychology, 9*(1). 10.3389/fpsyg.2018.02094

Lünnemann, M. K. M., Horst, F. C. P. V. der, Prinzie, P., Luijk, M. P. C. M., & Steketee, M. (2019). The intergenerational impact of trauma and family violence on parents and their children. *Child Abuse & Neglect, 96*, 104134. 10.1016/j.chiabu.2019.104134

Margolin, G., Vickerman, K. A., Oliver, P. H., & Gordis, E. B. (2010). Violence exposure in multiple interpersonal domains: Cumulative and differential effects. *Journal of Adolescent Health, 47*(2), 198–205. 10.1016/j.jadohealth.2010.01.020

Mastorakos, T., & Scott, K. L. (2019). Attention biases and social-emotional development in preschool-aged children who have been exposed to domestic violence. *Child Abuse & Neglect, 89*, 78–86. 10.1016/j.chiabu.2019.01.001

Mrug, S., & Windle, M. (2010). Prospective effects of violence exposure across multiple contexts on early adolescents' internalizing and externalizing problems. *Journal of Child Psychology and Psychiatry, 51*(8), 953–961. 10.1111/j.1469-7610.2010.02222.x

Øverlien, C. (2010). Abused women with children or children of abused women? A study of conflicting perspectives at women's refuges in Norway. *Child & Family Social Work, 16*(1), 71–80. 10.1111/j.1365-2206.2010.00715.x

Payne, B. K., Triplett, R. A., & Higgins, G. E. (2011). The relationship between self-control, witnessing domestic violence, and subsequent violence. *Deviant Behavior, 32*(9), 769–789. 10.1080/01639625.2010.538317

Peltonen, K., Ellonen, N., Larsen, H. B., & Helweg-Larsen, K. (2010). Parental violence and adolescent mental health. *European Child & Adolescent Psychiatry*, *19*(11), 813–822. 10.1007/s00787-010-0130-8

Rossman, B. R., & Ho, J. (2018). Posttraumatic response and children exposed to parental violence. In *Children exposed to domestic violence: Current issues in research, intervention, prevention, and policy development* (pp. 85–106). Routledge.

Selvik, S. (2018). School strategies of children with multiple relocations at refuges for abused women. *Scandinavian Journal of Educational Research*, *64*(2), 227–241. 10.1 080/00313831.2018.1539032

Siegel, J. P. (2013). Breaking the links in intergenerational violence: An emotional regulation perspective. *Family Process*, *52*(2), 163–178. 10.1111/famp.12023

Stark, E. (2009). *Coercive control: The entrapment of women in personal life.* Oxford University Press.

Taylor, J., Convery, I., & Barton, E. (2013). Social connectedness and female offending. *Forensic Update*, *1*(111), 10–16. 10.53841/bpsfu.2013.1.111.10

Taylor, J. C. (2019). Childhood experiences of domestic violence and adult outcomes: Where are we now: challenges, debates, and interventions? In *Intimate Partner Violence* (pp. 154–171). Routledge.

Vu, N. L., Jouriles, E. N., McDonald, R., & Rosenfield, D. (2016). Children's exposure to intimate partner violence: A meta-analysis of longitudinal associations with child adjustment problems. *Clinical Psychology Review*, *46*, 25–33. 10.1016/j.cpr.2016.04.003

Wagner, J., Jones, S., Tsaroucha, A., & Cumbers, H. (2019). Intergenerational transmission of domestic violence: Practitioners' perceptions and experiences of working with adult victims and perpetrators in the UK. *Child Abuse Review*, *28*(1), 39–51. 10.1002/car.2541

Wolfe, D. A., Crooks, C. V., Lee, V., McIntyre-Smith, A., & Jaffe, P. G. (2003). The Effects of children's exposure to domestic violence: A meta-analysis and critique. *Clinical Child and Family Psychology Review*, *6*(3), 171–187. 10.1023/a:1024910416164

4 A European perspective on children and adolescents who experience domestic violence and abuse

Stephanie Holt[1] *and Carolina Øverlien*[2]

[1]*Trinity College, Dublin*
[2]*Norwegian Centre for Violence and Traumatic Stress Studies*

Introduction

Increasing attention to and focus on individual children's voices in research as well as practice and policymaking, has been evident since the early 1990s, with many countries ratifying the United Nations Convention on the Rights of the Child (UNCRC). Specifically, Article 12 and 13 of the UNCRC clearly states that children should be informed, involved and consulted on all decisions with which they and their lives are concerned. This reflects a theoretical, ontological, methodological and empirically grounded awareness that children's involvement in research values the original contribution that they can make to our understanding of how children experience their individual lives. The philosophical rhetoric underpinning the UNCRC also reflects a construction of childhood that appreciates children as competent social actors whose thoughts and opinions are worthy of consideration (Bosisio, 2012).

While this journey of involving children in research has far from been a trouble free endeavour, this chapter exposes an increasing body of European research and researchers that engage directly with children as expert informants on their own lives and lived experiences of living with domestic violence and abuse (DVA). With a starting point that respects and upholds children's right to participate in research and have a say in all matters affecting them, this chapter celebrates the critical and burgeoning empirical knowledge base on children's experiences of living with DVA in Europe, positioning them not only as victims in need but also as subjects and rights holders.

To this end, the chapter will begin by reflecting on the rationale, principles and challenges underlying the practice of engaging children in research. Next, we present a select overview of research conducted across Europe both with and about children and young people who experience living with DVA. Compared to the North American research that dominates the field, European research often has an explicit child-centred approach. As research on complex social issues is always contextual, situated in a specific time and context, we assert the utmost importance that European countries conduct their own research grounded in their own legislation, policies and practical realities. Finally, we conclude by arguing that participating in research should

DOI: 10.4324/9781003124634-6

not only be seen as a right but also that participation can be experienced as empowering for children, as their lived experience can contribute to research and, ultimately, to improved practice and policy.

The rationale for and the challenges involved in engaging children and young people in research

In this chapter the key rationale driving and underpinning the practice of engaging children in research on DVA, is that this knowledge is critical for all practitioners who work with children and adolescents in their everyday life; for researchers who develop and evaluate interventions and treatment methods; and indeed for policymakers who make decisions that affect children and adolescents' lives. Across the three domains of research, policy and practise therefore, we argue that we critically *need* children's knowledge about their own lives, but we further assert that children also have a *right* to make their voices heard in matters that concern them. This reflects a commitment to honouring the principle of "listening to the voice of the child" as demanded by nation-states across Europe and by recognising and accepting children as active sentient social actors in the unfolding story of their ongoing development in family life. Specifically, Article 12 of the UNCRC outlines that "States Parties shall assure to the child who is capable of forming his or her own views the right to express those views freely in all matters affecting the child, the views of the child being given due weight in accordance with the age and maturity of the child" (UNCRC, 1989).

Therein lies one of the first challenges to participation however: a child has the right to express his or her views, for example through participating in research, *but* in accordance with his or her age and maturity. As such, children's competence to participate can be questioned, and their participation can be restricted on the grounds of age and maturity (Cossar et al., 2014). However we would argue that broad general indicators of age and stage capacity as provided by developmental psychology (Buss, 1999), do not give the complete guidance that professionals may require, only a general picture. Concurring with this concern about the authority of that "general picture," and reflecting on a related context – that of children's participation in family law - James, James & McNamee's (2004) UK research concluded that interviewing each child was deemed unnecessary because the professional already "knew" what was best for the child based on universal assumptions of children's best interests. Adhering steadfastly to a "single voice of childhood" (Roche, 1999, p. 33) may preclude a child ever being heard, whether in research or indeed family law, particularly if the child's views deviates from universally held assumptions. Van Bijleveld et al. (2013) further comment that while it is clearly argued that the child's views should be ascertained in line with age and maturity, it is considerably less clear who should assess the maturity of the child and, indeed, what criteria should determine that assessment. Caffrey (2013), similarly found that the concept of the ascertainable wishes of the child is so ambiguous that it is potentially vulnerable to subjective understanding.

A second challenge to participation is located within the welfare discourse or protectionist agenda, a conservative view which adheres reverently to a belief in children's right to remain as children, protected from involvement in adult affairs (Holt, 2018). This includes every form of potential harm, including harm from participating in research. Neale (2002) condemns this orientation for critically limiting children's participation, for positioning them as subordinate to adults and rendering their right to speak at the discretion of the adults" judgement. Øverlien's (2012) research with children about their experiences of domestic violence counters this orientation, rather is a clear testimony to their capacity to participate.

This balance between an obligation to include *and* to protect, is aptly described by Lansdown (1994, p. 36) below as an "inherent tension," and can, as the authors of this chapter have experienced, be the core of the ethically sensitive child researcher's dilemma:

> [The debate] exposes the inherent tension between a view of children on the one hand, as dependent on adult protection and incapable of taking responsibility for their decision-making, and on the other, as people with basic civil rights including the right to participate fully in decisions that affect their lives.

This tension can leave adults struggling to translate the rhetoric of participation into meaningful research practice reality (Skjorten, 2013). In particular, barriers to children's research participation include ethical concerns for children's capacity to consent and worries over re-traumatising of children who participate in research on sensitive topics, which in turn potentially jeopardising and minimising their right to research participation (Øverlien & Holt, 2018). Research Ethics Committees" concerns for children's capacity to consent and the potential for re-traumatisation have been a common and dominant concern across many European research projects involving children and DVA (Callaghan et al., 2015; Katz, 2016; Øverlien, 2010; Øverlien & Holt, 2018). We would argue however as researchers, that we cannot categorically eradicate this risk, and neither can we guarantee that the study we conduct will not in any way cause upset or even harm. Reflecting on research with bereaved young people, we concur with Buckle et al.'s (2010, p. 117) question whether our research on painful issues including loss and bereavement causes undue harm or rather "bears witness to the pain that is already there?"

Drawing on evidence of research conducted with and about children and young people living with DVA and indeed our own experience of conducting such research, we further concur with Mantle et al. (2006, p. 792) who caution against a "naïve positivism underlying any assumption" that the views of the child are simply "out there waiting to be collected." Rather, as Smart (2005) has argued, we advocate for ethical and skilful research practice that elicits children's views, involving the ability to hear what they are saying in addition to considering what they are not saying, via their silences and non-verbal messages (Houghton, 2018; Øverlien & Holt, 2021). It requires an adept understanding of the psychological complexity of children and an ability to understand their "internal world," particularly where abusive experiences have rendered them confused and vulnerable (Schofield, 1998, p. 430).

Our aim as thoughtful and expert researchers is to strive to ensure that the probable gains outweigh the potential risks in our research (Øverlien & Holt, 2018). It is our duty as adult researchers, to create an environment that is predictable, respectful, considerate and attentive to the child's needs, where the child is in control of, can chose what to answer, when to take breaks and when to finish. Concurring with the observations of other children's researchers (Butler et al., 2002), we assert that the reality of children's experience of living with DVA has been emphatically established and remains unquestioned. This experience, therefore, needs to be acknowledged and respected, with the manner in which participation is achieved representing a "finely balanced position between recognising and respecting the abilities of children whilst at the same time viewing them as inherently vulnerable" (Emond, 2008, p. 192).

Employing a range of varying research designs, the research selectively drawn on for the purpose of this chapter is primarily qualitative in focus, conducted with children and adolescents who have had difficult life experiences, including living with DVA. However, we argue that children growing up with domestic violence are children first and foremost, and our starting point positions them as right holders and as experts. Mindful of the ethical challenges of conducting research on sensitive subjects like DVA with children and young people, the next section draws on empirical research across Europe, all the while maintaining a strong reflective awareness of a growing ethos of respect for the child's position in a process that involves all family members (Buckley et al., 2007; Mullender et al., 2002).

European research with and about children and young people experiencing DVA

Over the last 20 years, significant foundations have been laid by European researchers in building the empirical knowledge base on children's and young people's experiences of living with DVA. Building on, and being inspired by, the early and instrumental work of Caroline McGee (2002) and Audrey Mullender and colleague's (2002) in the UK, and Helen Buckley and colleagues' (2006) Irish research, much of the subsequent work in this space has turned to children themselves to gather empirical data on different aspects of living with domestic violence. Mullender et al. (2002) were clearly hoping for change, as they called in the first chapter in their book for a "shift of approach'. The authors wrote that "very little research to date has been designed with the intention of hearing the voices of children and young people about domestic violence, either in general terms or concerning how those who have lived with it cope with and make sense of their experiences" (2002: 2). Instead across many jurisdictions in Europe and elsewhere, mothers were often asked in research studies to represent their children, reporting on their experiences of violence and abuse (Øverlien, 2010).

In the 20-year intervening period, there has been a steady increase in scientific studies that include children as informants. Today, for example, researchers investigating treatment and interventions, often turn to the participating children and adolescents themselves to gather data on how the intervention is received and experienced. Reporting on an intervention that was delivered in four European countries for example, Callaghan et al., (2018) highlight improvement in subjective wellbeing as children and young people moved through the programme "MPOWER." In order to capture the young participants' wellbeing and perception of the intervention, the participants completed two scales. In addition, qualitative interviews were conducted with 21 children and young people, exploring their experience of the group intervention and its impact. Also focusing on group programme interventions in Sweden for children living with DVA, Pernebo & Almqvist (2014) interviewed nine children, aged 4 to 6 years following their participation in the intervention. This study clearly highlights the capacity of very young children to make valuable contributions to research on their experience of DVA interventions. Echoing Øverlien & Holt's (2018) earlier assertion that a developmentally sensitive and conducive approach to research can support children's participation, Pernebo & Almqvist (2014) concluded that the quality of the interview process can facilitate children's expression of how treatment may, or may not, be fruitful and enjoyable for them.

In addition to capturing young voices in order to increase our knowledge about the effectiveness and feasibility of interventions and treatments, we also need to turn to children and adolescents themselves to understand more about the dynamics of domestic violence from the perspective of the child. Emma Katz (2022) investigates the impact of coercive control on children, a phenomenon we previously primarily had knowledge about in regards to adult women. Kaltrina et al.'s (2019) study explores the co-existence of IPV and child maltreatment among adolescents in Kosovo. Drawing on a sample of 208 adolescents in Kosovo, the authors illustrate how adolescents who experienced parental IPV had an increased risk of experiencing psychological aggression and corporal punishment, underlining the importance of poly-victimisation. While Kelmendi et al. (2019) increased our phenomenological understanding of co-existence of different forms of violence by asking young people themselves, Sabreen Selvik (2018) explored children's strategies to cope with everyday life in schools in Norway, despite a violent situation at home. Selvik interviewed 20 children (6–16 years old) about how they manage to learn and play at school, although deeply engaged in, and worried, about their chaotic home situation (see chapter 8). Taking an interactive and creative approach to the interviews which Selvik (2018, p. 230) describes as "co-produced," the participating children were encouraged to draw a map illustrating their refuge moves, which then became the basis for the subsequent interview.

Focusing on adolescents, Siv-Britt Björktomta (2019) investigated the nature of honour-related domestic violence in Sweden as experienced by young female victims with non-Swedish born parents. Using Bourdieu's concept of symbolic violence and Stark's theory of coercive control, Björktomta illustrates how the violence is embedded in the young women's whole childhoods, the importance of non-physical forms of violence in controlling and restraining them and the young women's limited possibilities for resistance. Staying with adolescents but focusing on IPV in their own romantic/intimate relationships, Nardi and colleagues' (2019) study in Spain conducted an analysis of survey responses on boys' perpetration of psychological abuse, and girls' acceptance of the same. The analysis of results from the participation of 479 heterosexual adolescent boys and girls highlights that both positive and negative behavioural beliefs coexist for both girls and boys, and that peers seem to be a possible risk factor for boys, while this is not the case for girls. Finally, drawing on a mixed methods approach to data collection with young women across Wales, Davies' (2019) study addresses young women's understandings of healthy romantic/intimate relationships. The analysis of responses to an attitudinal questionnaire and qualitative interviews with young women revealed a tension between what the young women reported in the questionnaire, and shared in the interviews, as well as a gap between the young women's expectations and lived experiences. The young women were able to articulate "healthy" attitudes on relationships, but in the interviews they naturalised and justified abusive behaviour.

The importance of engaging directly with children is the focus of two doctoral studies concerning police responses to domestic violence, both reported on in 2019. Although the first professionals with whom many child victims of domestic violence come into contact with often are members of the police force, little is still known however about how children and police officers experience these encounters. Both papers respond to this dearth of empirical knowledge in two jurisdictions: the Republic of Ireland and Northern Ireland. The first paper by Millar and Devaney (2019), conducts a narrative review of the existing literature on the police response to children at domestic violence call outs through the lens of Emotional Intelligence. Significant among the findings are reports by police officers feeling overwhelmed and uncertain at domestic violence incidents involving children and indeed children reporting significant differences in empathy of officers, which impacted their feelings of safety and visibility at these incidents. The second study draws on this concept of visibility, stating that a reconceptualising of the child victim as involved actor in the DV home is required if police are to involve children in the response and for the child's experience to be fully acknowledged. Elliffe & Holt's (2019) paper reports on qualitative research conducted in Ireland involving interviews with 10 children (most aged 7–9 years) and 14 police officers. Utilising a story-telling approach, the children were encouraged through the use of fictitious vignettes and a set of child friendly images to co-construct an interactive story about the police arriving to a home where DVA had been reported and where children were living. This research concluded that children continue to be unseen by police and are not engaged with in a way that recognises their victim status at a domestic violence incident.

While the studies referred to above have included children and young people themselves, and used their reports and voices as empirical data, other studies have turned to professionals in order to increase our knowledge about society's ability and preparedness to handle and address children who experience domestic violence. De Puy et al. (2019) address the assessment needs of children living with domestic violence, in a health setting in Switzerland. The authors describe the nature and circumstances of children's experiences, as reported to nurses by parents. The analysis illustrates how children's lives were marked by severe and repeated violence but also that the children's parents often experienced multiple vulnerabilities. Münger & Markström's (2019) study focuses on two other professional arenas important for children living with violence, child protection services (CPS) and schools. In this study two professional groups were interviewed in order to shed light on professional views of the school and CPS on the school's mission and responsibilities for children experiencing DV. The findings reveal a lack of a commonly understood and established terminology, as well as an absence of a shared understanding of children living with domestic violence as a form of "child abuse."

Perhaps in response to the "shift" that Mullender et al. called for in 2002, participatory research or engaging children as peer researchers has become increasingly common in recent years (Bradbury-Jones & Taylor, 2013). The adult researcher conducting interviews with children can decide to engage (or employ) a child as a researcher or co-researcher, both in terms of designing, implementing and interpreting the research findings. In her chapter "Voice, Agency, Power. A Framework for Young Person's Participation in National Domestic Abuse Policy Making," Houghton (2018) describes how a group of young survivors of domestic abuse greatly changed the research, policy and service landscape in Scotland. Houghton was the manager of the group of young experts, but did not speak for them and was their equal. During their two-and-a-half-year engagement, the group was given direct access to politicians and national representatives of the Scottish local authorities. Also, using creative methods to engage the children in research as a way to conduct research with them, has become increasingly popular. A UK research project reported on in Gabriel et al. (2017) involved developing in-depth research conversations with three mothers and their children who had experienced domestic violence. The project included the use of photographs, using video clips, using a secret box, drawing activities and mind-mapping. The mothers and children chose themselves the setting for the conversations. Although the methods were described as successful in developing rich data, the study also highlights the complexities and challenges of developing a participatory approach with vulnerable populations. One of the challenges include the emotional impact on the researchers. Finally and also engaging both mothers and children in research, Emma Katz's (2019) project based in the midlands region of England engaged with 15 mothers and 15 children (aged 10–14 years) to elicit their views on mother-child relationships in the context of DVA. The findings highlight a number of factors impacted mother-child relationships which the author asserts has global significance for service delivery and practice.

Conclusion

To conclude this chapter we return to Mullender et al.'s (2002) call for a "shift of approach" in how we capture and understand children's experiences of living with domestic violence and abuse. Reflecting on the evidence selectively represented above, we assert that this research capacity has gained sophistication of both depth and breadth in the intervening 20 years, significantly informing our knowledge about the extent of children's experiences of domestic abuse, the short- and long-term consequences and what it means to be a child and live with violence. This clear theoretical and conceptual "shift" from viewing children as "mere objects of enquiry," to dynamic and key participants, recognises not only children's capacity to operate within "adult-centred socially constructed meanings of citizenship" but also their capacity to influence them as well (Bacon & Frankel, 2014, p. 22). Located firmly within a children's rights position which accepts children's capacity to participate in research which is after all about them, we concur with Birnbaum et al. (2011, p. 415) who argue that to "build an ethic for children's participation," adults need to "listen respectfully and engage in a dialogue" with children that respects their capacity rather than focusing on their perceived limitations. The evidence of conducting research with children and young people as presented in this chapter is testament to Birnbaum and colleagues claim. It also underscores the importance of Houghton's (2018) call for those in policy, research and practice to "listen louder" to the views and experiences of children and young people and recognise them as experts in their own lives.

References

Bacon, K., & Frankel, S. (2014). Rethinking children's citizenship. *The International Journal of Children's Rights, 22*(1), 21–42. 10.1163/15718182-55680003

Björktomta, S.-B. (2019). Honor-based violence in Sweden – Norms of honor and chastity. *Journal of Family Violence.* 10.1007/s10896-019-00039-1

Bosisio, R. (2012). Children's right to be heard: What children think. *The International Journal of Children's Rights, 20*(1), 141–154. 10.1163/157181811x573462

Bradbury-Jones, C., & Taylor, J. (2013). Engaging with children as co-researchers: Challenges, counter-challenges and solutions. *International Journal of Social Research Methodology*, *18*(2), 161–173. 10.1080/13645579.2013.864589

Birnbaum, R., Bala, N., & Cyr, F. (2011). Children's experiences with family justice professionals in Ontario and Ohio. *International Journal of Law, Policy and the Family*, *25*(3), 398–422. 10.1093/lawfam/ebr014

Buckle, J. L., Dwyer, S. C., & Jackson, M. (2010). Qualitative bereavement research: Incongruity between the perspectives of participants and research ethics boards. *International Journal of Social Research Methodology*, *13*(2), 111–125. 10.1080/13 645570902767918

Buckley, H., Holt, S., & Whelan, S. (2007). Listen to me! Children's experiences of domestic violence. *Child Abuse Review*, *16*(5), 296–310. 10.1002/car.995

Buss, E. (1999). Confronting developmental barriers to the empowerment of child clients. *Cornell Law Review*, *84*, 895–966.

Butler, I., Scanlan, L., Robinson, M., Douglas, G., & Murch, M. (2002). Children's involvement in their divorce: Implications for practice. *Children & Society*, *16*(2), 89–102. 10.1002/chi.702

Caffrey, L. (2013). Hearing the 'voice of the child'? The role of child contact centres in the family justice system. *Child and Family Law Quarterly*, 25, 357–3179. https://heinonline.org/HOL/LandingPage?handle=hein.journals/chilflq25&div=33&id=&page=

Callaghan, J. E. M., Fellin, L. C., & Alexander, J. H. (2018). Promoting resilience and agency in children and young people who have experienced domestic violence and abuse: The "MPOWER" intervention. *Journal of Family Violence*, *34*(6), 521–537. 10.1007/s10896-018-0025-x

Callaghan, J. E. M., Alexander, J. H., Sixsmith, J., & Fellin, L. C. (2015). Beyond "witnessing": Children's experiences of coercive control in domestic violence and abuse. *Journal of Interpersonal Violence*, *33*(10), 088626051561894. 10.1177/08862 60515618946

Cossar, J., Brandon, M., & Jordan, P. (2014). "You've got to trust her and she's got to trust you": Children's views on participation in the child protection system. *Child & Family Social Work*, *21*(1), 103–112. 10.1111/cfs.12115

De Puy, J., Radford, L., Le Fort, V., & Romain-Glassey, N. (2019). Developing assessments for child exposure to intimate partner violence in Switzerland – A study of medico-legal reports in clinical settings. *Journal of Family Violence*, *34*(5), 371–383. 10.1007/s10896-019-00047-1

Elliffe, R., & Holt, S. (2019). Reconceptualizing the child victim in the police response to domestic violence. *Journal of Family Violence*. 10.1007/s10896-019-00055-1

Emond, R. (2008). Children's voices, children's rights. In A. Kendrick (Ed.), *Residential child care: Prospects and challenges* (pp. 183–195). London: Jessica Kingsley.

Gabriel, L., James, H., Cronin-Davis, J., Tizro, Z., Beetham, T., Hullock, A., & Raynar, A. (2017). Reflexive research with mothers and children victims of domestic violence. *Counselling and Psychotherapy Research*, *17*(2), 157–165. 10.1002/capr.12117

Holt, S. (2018). A voice or a choice? Children's views on participating in decisions about post-separation contact with domestically abusive fathers. *Journal of Social Welfare and Family Law*, *40*(4), 459–476. 10.1080/09649069.2018.1519653

Houghton, C. (2018). Voice, agency, power: A framework for young survivors' participation in national domestic abuse policy-making. In S. Holt, C. Overlien, & J. Devaney (Eds.), *Responding to Domestic Violence: Emerging Challenges for Policy, Practice and Research in Europe* (pp. 77–96). London: Jessica Kingsley.

James, A. L., James, A., & McNamee, S. (2004). Turn down the volume-not hearing children in family proceedings. *Child & Fam. LQ, 16*, 189.

Katz, E. (2016). Beyond the physical incident model: How children living with domestic violence are harmed by and resist regimes of coercive control. *Child Abuse Review, 25*(1), 46–59. 10.1002/car.2422

Katz, E. (2022). *Coercive Control in Children's and Mothers' Lives.* Oxford University Press.

Kelmendi, K., Duraku, Z. H., & Jemini-Gashi, L. (2019). Coexistence of intimate partner violence and child maltreatment among adolescents in Kosovo. *Journal of Family Violence, 34*(5), 411–421. 10.1007/s10896-018-00034-y

Lansdown, G. (1994). Children's rights. In B. Mayall (Ed.), *Children's Childhoods Observed and Experienced,* London: The Falmer Press, pp. 33–45.

Mantle, G., Moules, T., Johnson, K., Leslie, J., Parsons, S., & Shaffer, R. (2006). Whose wishes and feelings? Children's autonomy and parental influence in family court enquiries. *British Journal of Social Work, 37*(5), 785–805. 10.1093/bjsw/bcl035

McGee, C., & Kingsley, J. (2000). *Childhood Experience of Domestic Violence by Caroline McGee, Jessica Kingsley.* 235. ISBN 1-85302-827-4

Millar, A., Devaney, J., & Butler, M. (2018). Emotional intelligence: Challenging the perceptions and efficacy of 'Soft Skills' in policing incidents of domestic abuse involving children. *Journal of Family Violence, 34*, 577–588.

Mullender, A., Hague, G., Imam, U. F., Kelly, L., Malos, E., & Regan, L. (2002). *Children's Perspectives on Domestic Violence.* London: Sage.

Münger, A.-C., & Markström, A.-M. (2019). School and child protection services professionals' views on the school's mission and responsibilities for children living with domestic violence – tensions and gaps. *Journal of Family Violence, 34*(5), 385–398. 10.1007/s10896-019-00035-5

Neale, B. (2002). Dialogues with children. *Childhood, 9*(4), 455–475. 10.1177/09075682 02009004006

Overlien, C. (2012) *Våld i hemmet, barns strategier [Domestic Violence, Children's Strategies].* Oslo, Norway: Universitetsforlaget.

Øverlien, C. (2010). Children exposed to domestic violence. *Journal of Social Work, 10*(1), 80–97. 10.1177/1468017309350663

Øverlien, C., & Holt, S. (2018). Including children and adolescents in domestic violence research: When myths and misconceptions compromise participation. In S. Holt, C. Øverlien & J. Devaney (Eds.) *Responding to Domestic Violence – Emerging Challenges for Policy, Practice and Research in Europe.* Jessica Kingsley Publishers.

Øverlien, C., & Holt, S. (2021). Qualitative interviews with children and adolescents who have experienced domestic violence and abuse. In J. Devaney, C. Bradbury-Jones, R. J. Macy, C. Øverlien & S. Holt (Eds.) *The Routledge International Handbook of Domestic Violence and Abuse.* Routledge.

Pernebo, K., & Almqvist, K. (2014). Young children's experiences of participating in group treatment for children exposed to intimate partner violence: A qualitative study. *Clinical Child Psychology and Psychiatry, 21*(1), 119–132. 10.1177/13591 04514558432

Roche, J. (1999). Children and divorce: A private affair?, in Slater, S. & Piper, C. (eds) *Undercurrents of Divorce* (pp. 35–75). Aldershot: Darthmouth.

Schofield, G. (1998). Making sense of the ascertainable wishes and feelings of insecurely attached children. *Child and Family Law Quarterly*, *10*(4), 429–443.

Selvik, S. (2018). School strategies of children with multiple relocations at refuges for abused women. *Scandinavian Journal of Educational Research*, *64*(2), 227–241. 10.1080/00313831.2018.1539032

Skjorten, K. (2013). Children's voices in norwegian custody cases. *International Journal of Law, Policy and the Family*, *27*(3), 289–309. 10.1093/lawfam/ebt011

Smart, C. (2005). From children's shoes to children's voices. *Family Court Review*, *40*(3), 307–319. 10.1111/j.174-1617.2002.tb00842.x

UNCRC (United Nations Convention on the Rights of the Child) (1989) Accessed on 4/7/2017 at www.ohchr.org/EN/ProfessionalInterest/Pages/CRC.aspx

van Bijleveld, G. G., Dedding, C. W. M., & Bunders-Aelen, J. F. G. (2013). Children's and young people's participation within child welfare and child protection services: A state-of-the-art review. *Child & Family Social Work*, *20*(2), 129–138. 10.1111/cfs.12082

5 Children's exposure to domestic violence in rural Pakistani societies

Nassra Khan

Registered Counselling Therapist, Alberta, Canada

Children's exposure to domestic violence in rural Pakistani societies

It had only been two weeks since the 17-year-old got married to his mother's best friend's daughter when rumours began to circulate that the marriage was in serious trouble. The mother-in-law was dissatisfied with the new daughter-in-law, while the young man constantly threatened to leave the new bride if she did not get her act together. The neighbours reported hearing loud bangs and shouting coming from the young couple's home. Some said that the bride appeared emaciated after just two weeks of marriage, others reported that the bride had threatened to take her own life if the abuse did not stop. Some of the villagers sided with the young man and his mother suggesting that the new bride should learn to keep her mouth shut and get used to her new role as a wife and daughter-in-law. Nonetheless, no one in the neighbourhood showed much concern. When asked why this was so, the response was that it is not a big deal, a little bit of hitting and yelling is a common practice in every other household in the village.

Introduction to the research study

The situation described above may not be atypical in patriarchal rural communities in Pakistan. Accounts such as this were frequently described in a research study that became the basis of my PhD thesis. The data collection for which took place between December 2012 and February 2015 in a rural Pakistani village. The purpose of the study was to investigate how *battered* women in Pakistani rural societies experience domestic violence in their marriages. At the time this study was carried out there was little published research on domestic violence in Pakistan and much less on the marginalised and underrepresented rural women in the area. As the first qualitative study conducted in a patriarchal rural Pakistani village, the findings contributed to the limited body of knowledge that sought to understand domestic violence in this area.

The goals of the research were to examine the cultural and structural factors that supported the perpetration of domestic violence in the home. The

DOI: 10.4324/9781003124634-7

factors that shaped women's attitudes towards domestic violence were also explored. The study identified risk factors for domestic violence and investigated barriers that prevented women from leaving their abusive marriages. Although the study's primary focus was women's perceptions of their experiences of domestic violence, it also explored the process of childhood socialisation and gender roles within the home. This offered insight into how exposure to violence in the home may have the potential to impact children in a rural Pakistani society.

This chapter adds a unique perspective because little is known about rural Pakistani children's experiences of domestic violence. Although the limited literature on domestic violence in South Asian communities recognises that exposure to domestic violence affects children of all ethnic and cultural backgrounds (Dalal et al., 2012; Ragavan, Fikre, Millner & Bair-Merritt, 2018; Zhu & Dalal, 2009), it has failed to adequately address how cultural norms and other environmental factors can affect children differently. This chapter argues that to gain a more accurate understanding of children's exposure to domestic violence in rural Pakistani societies it is important to be culturally aware.

Exposure to violence in the home and community

Rural Pakistani communities are characterised as being highly patriarchal adhering to traditional family values (Zakar, Zakar & Abbas, 2015). A common feature of a typical household observed in the village was its extended family system, in which children, parents, aunts, uncles, cousins and paternal grandparents all lived under the same roof. The villagers recounted experiences of poverty and deprivation, which were further compounded by the large extended family size as everyone competed for the same limited resources.

Moreover, the data collected during the research study in the Pakistani village indicated that the villagers adopted an authoritarian or discipline-oriented style of parenting in the home. As the women recounted their childhood experiences, they explained that parents were expected to discipline their children. Disciplinary tactics might include aggression, force and punishment. The women went on to explain that a parent who used punishment to reprimand their child could anticipate praise for their good parenting skills. The rural Pakistani children may therefore gradually internalise these disciplinary child-raising practices and acquire similar behavioural patterns, as suggested by the women (Jabeen, 2021).

The field observations made as part of this research study showed that the villagers generally lived in an extended family setup in which parents, paternal grandparents, uncles and aunts become the first "socialising agents" for children living in the household. Morgan (2013) described the process of socialisation as "learning by example." He argued that through the socialisation process which mainly takes place in the home, children acquire skills, norms, values and beliefs that they then carry over into adulthood. Correspondingly, through gender role socialisation the rural Pakistani children internalise the cultural attitudes and expectations that regard men as the guardians and providers, legitimising their use of aggression to keep the family in control (Fernandez, 2006; Hussain, Naz, Khan, Daraz & Khan, 2015; Sugarman & Frankel, 1996). In contrast, different messages and gender stereotypes are conveyed to girls in the village through their mothers and senior women in the family. They are taught to be shy, submissive and grateful for what they have. The girls are often reminded of the *hadith* indicating that displeasing the husband invites the wrath of God, compelling them to accept abuse in their marriages later in life (Hoel, 2013).

The research findings of the current study demonstrated that a certain amount of violence in the home was not only normal but also necessary to keep the wife or the daughters-in-law in line. In fact, abuse occurred in intergenerational and hierarchical relationships in the home. For example, children in the village often experienced physical and emotional violence at the hands of their parents, uncles, aunts and older siblings. The children were routinely exposed to extreme emotional outbursts, including beatings, shaming and name-calling by family members. They grew up witnessing their father assaulting their mother and their grandfather abusing their grandmother. They also observe the abuse inflicted on their mother by their paternal grandmother. The children in the village essentially see their grandparents as perpetrators and instigators of violence in the home, which is in stark contrast to Sandberg's (2013) and Hampton's (2006) findings that grandparents play a protective role in the lives of children exposed to domestic violence. However, concurs with Åkerlund (2019) who sought children's perspectives on grandparenting in homes with domestic abuse and they reported feeling unprotected. The children in the village watch their mother go from being a victim to becoming a perpetrator as she takes on the role of a mother-in-law. This means that the Pakistani village children are routinely exposed to intergenerational cycles of familial abuse and violence.

It has been suggested that children with high exposure to domestic violence may experience some desensitisation to violence (Fleckman, Drury, Taylor & Theall, 2016). The women's accounts revealed that the children in the village were exposed to violence not only in their home but also in the community. The village children become witnesses to long-standing bitter family feuds and altercations between neighbours. The events reported by the women suggested that disputes over land, resources and rejected marriage proposals were commonplace in rural Pakistani communities. A typical dispute resolution process in the village was described as maintaining feelings of revenge and animosity because this reflects "standing one's ground." In addition, the conversations with the villagers suggested that school teachers, who are generally viewed as "substitute parents," often rely upon corporal punishment to reprimand students, which is an accepted mode of punishment in Pakistani schools (Ahmad, Said & Khan, 2013; Holden & Ashraf, 2016). It may be inferred from the data that there is a cultural desensitisation process that might normalise aggression in the village to a certain degree.

It seems that the casual acceptance of violence in the village sends a strong message to the children that some degree of physical aggression is in the best interest of children and those in a subordinate position in the family. Domestic violence is therefore seen in the village as having reformatory value. Much of the violence reported by the villagers was considered normative. The findings from the study supported the view that accepting domestic violence as a normal part of family life, as opposed to recognising it as an inappropriate behaviour, leads to the tolerance of domestic violence. Consequently, the children come to see violence as an appropriate way of resolving conflicts in the home, a view which is consistent with Markowitz (2001), who found that witnessing and experiencing violence as a child can result in internalising abusive behaviour as an acceptable form of conflict resolution later in their own marriages.

Effects of early exposure to domestic violence on rural children

Gender differences

Despite immense interest in understanding gender differences, the published research has fallen short of explaining how domestic violence exposure may affect girls and boys differently (Jung et al., 2018; Sousa et al., 2011). This is an important consideration in understanding children's exposure to domestic violence in rural Pakistani communities because the observations made in the village suggested that patriarchal societies maintain distinctive gender role expectations. According to the rural cultural discourse a man who is ascribed an authoritative position is entitled to act aggressively in the face of marital conflict (Riddell et al., 2009). For example, the scenarios described in the study indicated that in the village a man who does not beat up his wife is ridiculed and labelled a "wimp," who is not in control of his wife. In other words, a man in the rural Pakistani society is under a great deal of pressure to uphold his position of power in a marriage by any means necessary (Zakar et al., 2013). Those who fail to live up to their masculine role are subjected to societal scrutiny. The boys in the village may internalise these cultural practices and recognise the consequences of nonconformity. This apparent normative use of violence makes direct comparisons with other researcher's conclusions complex e.g., Davis and Carlson (1987), Kalmuss (1984) and Kwong, Bartholomew, Henderson and Trinke (2003) because whilst they largely attribute the likelihood of becoming a battering husband or a male aggressor to the theory of intergenerational transmission (Hou, Yu, Fang & Epstein, 2015; Widom & Wilson, 2014), they are not working on the basis that domestic violence is the cultural norm. So whilst my findings partially support the intergenerational theory, they go beyond this suggesting that cultural norms and practices play a profound role in shaping male behaviour in a patriarchal rural Pakistani society.

Conversely, the reports of childhood experiences shared by women in the village indicated that they were taught by their own mothers and other senior women in the family to display self-constraint and show unquestionable obedience to the male members of their family. The women reported that they were reprimanded in early childhood for raising their voice at their brothers and male cousins. Correspondingly, the women's accounts of their marriages revealed that they were praised for remaining steadfast in the face of their husband's atrocities. This means that women in the village were taught to view submissive traits in a favourable light. While on the surface these findings appear to agree with the suggestion that girls exposed to domestic violence between their parents have a higher probability of becoming victims of domestic violence in their own intimate relationships (e.g., Levendosky, Huth-Bocks & Semel, 2002; Artz et al., 2014) to adopt this as an explanation may obfuscate the wider cultural patriarchal norms that indoctrinate women from an early age to accept their husband's abuse.

These findings demonstrate that the existing domestic violence literature generally assumes that all children have common domestic violence experiences, while failing to address cultural beliefs and values that may distinguish them. There is widespread agreement in the literature that in response to children's exposure to domestic violence boys exhibit externalising problems including aggressiveness and defiance, while girls develop internalising issues including depression, withdrawal and low self-esteem (Edleson, Shin & Armendariz, 2008; Evans, Davies & DiLillo, 2008; Graham-Bermann & Perkins, 2010; Herrenkohl et al., 2008). Although there is much agreement that exposure to domestic violence leaves children traumatised, the internalising and externalising outcomes set forth by these researchers does not consider the cultural norms that promote distinct gender behaviours, namely male dominance and female submissiveness. Further research is necessary to determine the extent to which these behavioural outcomes are a product of cultural conditioning as opposed to childhood exposure to domestic violence in the home.

Whilst my study raised some interesting questions relating to the universal applicability of popular European and US research evidence, it was a relatively small-scale study of one rural location in Pakistan. In addition, it is difficult to understand the impact of exposure to domestic violence on rural Pakistani children because abusive events at home are kept a secret from the outside world. As a researcher therefore, whilst accepted to a degree within the village, I remained part of that outside world. It was evident from my work, however, that domestic violence in patriarchal rural Pakistan was regarded as a "private family matter" and outside intervention was very much frowned upon.

Conclusion

The detailed conversations with the villagers revealed that they did not recognise exposure to domestic violence at home as having a negative impact on children; nor did they consider these children as victims of domestic violence.

The data indicated that the children in the village were expected to learn their gender roles and display culturally desirable behaviours. This rural Pakistani society sought to transform young children into "obedient" community members who learned to remain within the parameters of their assigned gender roles, a pattern of behaviour that extends into their adulthood. This type of "cultural conditioning" runs the risk of undermining and masking the devastating psychological and emotional repercussions of early exposure to domestic violence. It is worth noting that while the children in the village may appear to be coping well with the incidents of domestic violence at home, at school and in the community, they may internally be dealing with feelings of deep sadness, fear and distress, which are not exhibited and therefore remain unobserved. Further research is needed to explore the issues raised here further, with cultural awareness and sensitivity underpinning all aspects of the research process, including design, implementation, analysis and interpretation.

References

Ahmad, I., Said, H., & Khan, F. (2013). Effect of corporal punishment on students' motivation and classroom learning. *Review of European Studies*, 5(4). 10.5539/res.v5n4p130

Åkerlund, N. (2019). "They could have defended my mum and me": Children's perspectives on grandparent responses to intimate partner violence. *Families, Relationships and Societies*, 8(2), 179–195. 10.1332/204674318x15199991640641

Artz, S., Jackson, M. A., Rossiter, K. R., Nijdam-Jones, A., Géczy, I., & Porteous, S. (2014). A comprehensive review of the literature on the impact of exposure to intimate partner violence for children and youth. *International Journal of Child, Youth and Family Studies*, 5(4), 493. 10.18357/ijcyfs54201413274

Dalal, K., Lee, M. S., & Gifford, M. (2012). Male adolescents' attitudes towards wife beating: A multi-country study in South Asia. *Journal of Adolescent Health*, 50(5), 437–442. 10.1016/j.jadohealth.2011.09.012

Davis, L. V., & Carlson, B. E. (1987). Observation of spouse abuse. *Journal of Interpersonal Violence*, 2(3), 278–291. 10.1177/088626087002003004

Edleson, J. L., Shin, N., & Johnson Armendariz, K. K. (2008). Measuring children's exposure to domestic violence: The development and testing of the Child Exposure to Domestic Violence (CEDV) Scale. *Children and Youth Services Review*, 30(5), 502–521. 10.1016/j.childyouth.2007.11.006

Evans, S. E., Davies, C., & DiLillo, D. (2008). Exposure to domestic violence: A meta-analysis of child and adolescent outcomes. *Aggression and Violent Behavior*, 13(2), 131–140. 10.1016/j.avb.2008.02.005

Fernandez, M. (2006). Cultural beliefs and domestic violence. *Annals of the New York Academy of Sciences*, 1087(1), 250–260. 10.1196/annals.1385.005

Fleckman, J. M., Drury, S. S., Taylor, C. A., & Theall, K. P. (2016). Role of direct and indirect violence exposure on externalizing behavior in children. *Journal of Urban Health*, 93(3), 479–492. 10.1007/s11524-016-0052-y

Graham-Bermann, S. A., & Perkins, S. (2010). Effects of early exposure and lifetime exposure to Intimate Partner Violence (IPV) on child adjustment. *Violence and Victims*, 25(4), 427–439. 10.1891/0886-6708.25.4.427

Herrenkohl, T. I., Sousa, C., Tajima, E. A., Herrenkohl, R. C., & Moylan, C. A. (2008). Intersection of child abuse and children's exposure to domestic violence. *Trauma, Violence, & Abuse, 9*(2), 84–99. 10.1177/1524838008314797

Hoel, & Shaikh. (2013). Sex as Ibadah: Religion, gender, and subjectivity among South African Muslim Women. *Journal of Feminist Studies in Religion, 29*(1), 69. 10.2979/jfemistudreli.29.1.69

Holden, G. W., & Ashraf, R. (2016). Children's right to safety: The problem of corporal punishment in Pakistan. In *Child safety, welfare and well-being* (pp. 59–74): Springer.

Hou, J., Yu, L., Fang, X., & Epstein, N. B. (2015). The intergenerational transmission of domestic violence: The role that gender plays in attribution and consequent intimate partner violence. *Journal of Family Studies, 22*(2), 121–139. 10.1080/132294 00.2015.1045923

Hussain, M., Naz, A., Khan, W., Daraz, U., & Khan, Q. (2015). Gender stereotyping in family. *SAGE Open, 5*(3), 215824401559525. 10.1177/2158244015595258

Jabeen, T. (2021). Challenges in the prevention of child maltreatment in Pakistan: An interplay of the culture and the context. *International Journal on Child Maltreatment: Research, Policy and Practice.* 10.1007/s42448-021-00095-5

Jung, H., Herrenkohl, T. I., Skinner, M. L., Lee, J. O., Klika, J. B., & Rousson, A. N. (2018). Gender differences in intimate partner violence: A predictive analysis of IPV by child abuse and domestic violence exposure during early childhood. *Violence against Women, 25*(8), 903–924. 10.1177/1077801218796329

Kalmuss, D. (1984). The intergenerational transmission of marital aggression. *Journal of Marriage and the Family, 46*(1), 11. 10.2307/351858

Kwong, M. J., Bartholomew, K., Henderson, A. J. Z., & Trinke, S. J. (2003). The intergenerational transmission of relationship violence. *Journal of Family Psychology, 17*(3), 288–301. 10.1037/0893-3200.17.3.288

Levendosky, A. A., Huth-Bocks, A., & Semel, M. A. (2002). Adolescent peer relationships and mental health functioning in families with domestic violence. *Journal of Clinical Child & Adolescent Psychology, 31*(2), 206–218. 10.1207/s153 74424jccp3102_06

Markowitz, F. E. (2001). Attitudes and family violence: Linking intergenerational and cultural theories. *Journal of Family Violence, 16*(2), 205–218. 10.1023/a:1011115104282

Morgan, D. (2013). Socialization and the family. *Families, Education and Social Differences, 4.*

Ragavan, M. I., Fikre, T., Millner, U., & Bair-Merritt, M. (2018). The impact of domestic violence exposure on South Asian children in the United States: Perspectives of domestic violence agency staff. *Child Abuse & Neglect, 76*, 250–260. 10.1016/j.chiabu.2017.11.006

Riddell, T., Ford-Gilboe, M., & Leipert, B. (2009). Strategies used by rural women to stop, avoid, or escape from intimate partner violence. *Health Care for Women International, 30*(1-2), 134–159. 10.1080/07399330802523774

Sandberg, L. (2013). Being there for my grandchild - grandparents' responses to their grandchildren's exposure to domestic violence. *Child & Family Social Work, 21*(2), 136–145. 10.1111/cfs.12123

Sousa, C., Herrenkohl, T. I., Moylan, C. A., Tajima, E. A., Klika, J. B., Herrenkohl, R. C., & Russo, M. J. (2011). Longitudinal study on the effects of child abuse and children's exposure to domestic violence, parent-child attachments, and antisocial behavior in adolescence. *Journal of Interpersonal Violence, 26*(1), 111–136. 10.1177/0886260510362883

Sugarman, D. B., & Frankel, S. L. (1996). Patriarchal ideology and wife-assault: A meta-analytic review. *Journal of Family Violence, 11*(1), 13–40. 10.1007/bf02333338

Widom, C. S., & Wilson, H. W. (2014). Intergenerational transmission of violence. *Violence and Mental Health,* 27–45. 10.1007/978-94-017-8999-8_2

Zakar, R., Zakar, M. Z., & Abbas, S. (2015). Domestic violence against rural women in Pakistan: An issue of health and human rights. *Journal of Family Violence, 31*(1), 15–25. 10.1007/s10896-015-9742-6

Zakar, R., Zakar, M. Z., & Kraemer, A. (2013). Men's beliefs and attitudes towards intimate partner violence against women in Pakistan *Violence Against Women, 19*(2), 246–268. 10.1177/1077801213478028

Zhu, Y., & Dalal, K. (2009). Childhood exposure to domestic violence and attitude towards wife beating in adult life: A study of men in India. *Journal of Biosocial Science, 42*(2), 255–269. 10.1017/s0021932009990423

Part II

The impact of DVA on children

6 The impact of domestic violence and abuse on children and young people
Internalising symptoms and mental health

Bethan Carter
Cardiff University

Background

Experience of DVA during childhood is a global public health concern. It is thought that in the UK one in four children have been exposed to DVA during their childhood (Radford et al., 2011). The costs of DVA during childhood and adolescence are significant and the support of these children has been estimated to cost UK taxpayers £1.4 billion in education, health care, residential and crime costs (Pro Bono Economics, 2018). Furthermore, the lifetime economic costs of childhood experience of DVA are estimated to be $70,000 per victim in the USA (Holmes, Richter, Votruba, Berg, & Bender, 2018).

Exposure to DVA in childhood has been linked to psychosocial difficulties, physical and mental health problems among children and young people (Holt, Buckley, & Whelan, 2008; Wolfe, Crooks, Lee, McIntyre-Smith, & Jaffe, 2003). Meta-analyses of early research within the field (Kitzmann, Gaylord, Holt, & Kenny, 2003; Wolfe et al., 2003) concluded that exposure to DVA was associated with increased internalising and externalising symptoms (conduct problems and hyperactivity). However, the studies included within these analyses had many methodological flaws such as failure to define the extent of the DVA children were exposed to, reliance on shelter or clinical populations and none of the studies were longitudinal, thus preventing causal inference. Furthermore, data collected on child outcomes were most frequently reported by mothers rather than the children themselves (Fantuzzo & Lindquist, 1989). It should also be highlighted that these early reviews, like all syntheses of evidence, may suffer from publication bias towards positive results, leading to an inflated estimated effect size of DVA on behavioural and emotional outcomes.

A more recent meta-analysis found evidence for significant direct associations between DVA and children's internalising, externalising and trauma symptoms (Evans, Davies, & DiLillo, 2008), yet methodological limitations remained. Many studies relied on mother's reports of children's emotional and behavioural symptoms and few utilised longitudinal methods. Furthermore, the review showed that previous studies have rarely accounted

DOI: 10.4324/9781003124634-9

for the necessary potential confounds, e.g., factors that are considered to cause both the exposure (DVA) and the outcome (children's emotional and behavioural symptoms) and thus introduce bias to the results. These confounding factors are likely to include direct child abuse, parental psychopathology, parental substance misuse, deprivation and community violence. Consequently, despite many studies measuring the association between DVA and negative child and adolescent developmental outcomes, causal inferences about the effect of DVA on child outcomes cannot not be drawn.

It is important to highlight that numerous studies have also shown that some children exposed to DVA do not appear to be adversely affected and develop healthily (Edelson, Edelson, Kerr, & Grandin, 1999; Graham-Bermann, Gruber, Howell, & Girz, 2009; Herman-Smith, 2013; Holt, Buckley, & Whelan, 2008; Kimball, 2016; Laing & Humphreys, 2013). For example, following an extensive review of the literature, Laing and colleagues (2013) reported that 26% to 50% of children exposed to violence between caregivers were functioning as well as those who were not exposed. Thus, researchers have started to explore potential protective factors, as well as risk factors, to better understand how DVA impacts on child health and well-being and what helps some children and young people to be resilient. This knowledge may then help inform the development of preventative interventions and enable practitioners to better help vulnerable children. However, the methodological limitations associated with DVA research remain and these studies have been based on statistically significant associations rather than causal inferences. Therefore, it is not yet clear whether DVA does in fact cause the negative outcomes among those exposed or whether other factor/s are responsible for the outcomes such as those described earlier.

Recognising the dearth of research within the field moving beyond simple associations between DVA and children's internalising symptoms to determining a "true" or causal effect of DVA on child and adolescent internalising symptoms, the author and her team conducted a recent, population-based cohort study (unpublished) utilising data from the Avon Longitudinal Study of Parents and Children (ALSPAC). The study aimed to investigate the effect of early and middle-childhood exposure to DVA on internalising symptoms at six and thirteen years controlling for a myriad of potential confounders (variables that cause both the exposure and the outcome and bias the results) including, but not limited to, direct child abuse, parent substance misuse, parental psychopathology and numerous socio-demographic variables such as financial difficulties and maternal education status. Given the in-depth, longitudinal nature of ALSPAC, there was a large amount of missing data within the dataset which was addressed using multiple imputation and inverse probability weighting to account for missed questions and participant attrition respectively. DVA was measured using binary (yes/no) variables when children were 0–3 years and 6–9 years and internalising symptoms were measured using mother-reports of the Strengths and Difficulties Questionnaire (SDQ; Goodman & Scott, 1999) when the children were six and 13 years old. It was found that although simple, crude regression models indicated significant effects of early exposure to DVA (0–3 years) on internalising symptoms at six years and DVA in middle-childhood exposure (6–9 years) on internalising symptoms at 13 years (controlling for previous DVA), once relevant confounders were included in the models, these effects were no longer significant. Thus, it may be concluded that it is not the exposure to DVA itself, but the factors within the broader picture of child's home environment that contribute to the development of internalising symptoms.

It is vital to highlight the limitations of the study described earlier, and extreme caution should be taken when interpreting the results. In no way do we advocate that somehow DVA has no effect on children's mental health. We know in practice that children exposed to DVA do often experience internalising symptoms, but how DVA exerts its effect remains unclear. It could be that DVA is manifesting through something else or other symptoms that were not measured. First, although the exposure was reported by both parties, the psychometric properties of the measure have not been assessed. It simply asked mothers and partners "Has your partner been physically/emotionally cruel to you (since the previous survey)?" which is highly subjective and given the socially undesirable nature of DVA coupled with the fear that reports may lead to social services intervention, the number of children exposed is likely to be underestimated. This measure also meant that parental reports were taken as evidence that the children were exposed and impacted in some way by the DVA, yet their involvement and both the severity and frequency of the abuse was unknown. Additionally, the child and adolescent internalising symptoms, although measured utilising the validated SDQ (Goodman, 1999), were only reported by the mothers, and evidence suggests that parent and child reports of their internalising symptoms may differ greatly (Achenbach, McConaughy, & Howell, 1987; Van Roy, Groholt, Heyerdahl, & Clench-Aas, 2010). More research is urgently needed to explore this finding further utilising longitudinal methods and child reports of both exposure to DVA (including a measure of severity and frequency of the abuse) and internalising symptoms in order to provide further evidence for or against these results. However, there are many methodological, legal and ethical issues with conducting such research (Carroll-Lind, Chapman, Gregory, & Maxwell, 2006; Knight et al., 2000; Morris, Hegarty, & Humphreys, 2012).

Domestic violence and direct child abuse

DVA has been regarded as a form of child maltreatment (Gilbert et al., 2009) as children growing up in violent and abusive households have been found to experience similar rates of internalising and externalising problems as those who have been directly abused (Moylan et al., 2010). However, it is not always easy to distinguish between the effects of DVA and direct child abuse given that that the two often co-occur (Appel & Holden, 1998; Jouriles &

LeCompte, 1991) and thus, children are often exposed to multiple types of family violence (Dodge, Pettit, & Bates, 1997; Margolin, 1998).

Despite often overlapping and sharing similar negative outcomes (Herrenkohl, Sousa, Tajima, Herrenkohl, & Moylan, 2008), DVA and direct child abuse have traditionally been addressed in isolation by researchers, policy makers and programmes. Interventions addressing one of these in isolation may be less effective if the other is experienced alongside and targeting both simultaneously may be beneficial. In fact, many forms of violence co-occur, and it has been persuasively argued that other forms of violence outside the family should be included in analyses such as child sexual abuse, bullying and witnessing community violence (Finkelhor, 2008; Hamby, Finkelhor, Turner, & Ormrod, 2010) as well as family factors such as poverty (Fahmy & Williamson, 2018), parental health (Herrenkohl et al., 2008), financial and parenting stress (Herrenkohl et al., 2008) and lower education (Herrenkohl et al., 2008). Interventions for children and young people which focus on one aspect of adversity may not be effective, therefore it is likely that a holistic approach is needed, addressing children's environment more broadly.

Understanding how child abuse, DVA exposure and other factors relate to one another, and the relative strength of each as a risk factor, particularly using longitudinal studies, is an important first step in setting the context for intervention and policy level change. Moylan et al. (2010) studied the effects of both domestic violence and child abuse and found that, when factors in the child's environment other than DVA and child abuse are accounted for, neither DVA nor direct abuse alone increased the risk of a child experiencing internalising symptoms, yet dual exposure did increase the risk compared to non-exposed adolescents.

My team and I also investigated the effect of direct child abuse, alongside DVA, in the study described earlier. Direct child abuse, like DVA was measured at 0–3 years and 6–9 years and both parents were asked whether they, or their partner had been physically or emotional cruel to their child/children since the previous wave of data collection. After controlling for relevant confounders including DVA, there was evidence that direct child abuse had an impact on child internalising symptoms at both six and 13 years. No evidence was found for DVA increasing the risk of internalising symptoms in combination with direct child abuse, nor was DVA found to be a significant confounder of the effect. However, reliance on the self-reports of cruelty by the potential abusers brings its own limitations.

Conclusion

Research exploring the impact of DVA on child and adolescent outcomes including internalising symptoms has been plagued by a host of significant limitations. Recent research aiming to overcome the limitations and take a causal approach, considering the many other factors that are likely to play a role in the effect of DVA and internalising symptoms, has found that DVA does not significantly affect internalising symptoms during childhood or adolescence. However, direct child abuse, which commonly occurs within violent homes, was found to significantly affect the development of internalising symptoms when children were six and 13 years old in the same population. Further research is needed, overcoming the remaining limitations, to assess the causal effect of DVA on internalising symptoms and other emotional and behaviour problems and better understand how best to support children and adolescents who have been exposed to DVA.

References

Achenbach, T. M., McConaughy, S. H., & Howell, C. T. (1987). Child/adolescent behavioral and emotional problems: Implications of cross-informant correlations for situational specificity. *Psychological Bulletin, 101*(2), 213–232. 10.1037/0033-2909.101.2.213

Appel, A. E., & Holden, G. W. (1998). The co-occurrence of spouse and physical child abuse: A review and appraisal. *Journal of Family Psychology, 12*(4), 578–599. 10.1037/0893-3200.12.4.578

Carroll-Lind, J., Chapman, J. W., Gregory, J., & Maxwell, G. (2006). The key to the gatekeepers: Passive consent and other ethical issues surrounding the rights of children to speak on issues that concern them. *Child Abuse & Neglect, 30*(9), 979–989. 10.1016/j.chiabu.2005.11.013

Dodge, K. A., Pettit, G. S., & Bates, J. E. (1997). How the experience of early physical abuse leads children to become chronically aggressive. In D. Cicchetti & S. L. Toth (Eds.), *Developmental perspectives on trauma: Theory, research, and intervention* (pp. 263–288). University of Rochester Press.

Edelson, S. M., Edelson, M. G., Kerr, D. C. R., & Grandin, T. (1999). Behavioral and physiological effects of deep pressure on children with Autism: A pilot study evaluating the efficacy of Grandin's hug machine. *American Journal of Occupational Therapy, 53*(2), 145–152. 10.5014/ajot.53.2.145

Evans, S. E., Davies, C., & DiLillo, D. (2008). Exposure to domestic violence: A meta-analysis of child and adolescent outcomes. *Aggression and Violent Behavior, 13*(2), 131–140. 10.1016/j.avb.2008.02.005

Fahmy, E., & Williamson, E. (2018). Poverty and domestic violence and abuse (DVA) in the UK. *Journal of Gender-Based Violence, 2*(3), 481–501. 10.1332/239868018x15263881184558

Fantuzzo, J. W., & Lindquist, C. U. (1989). The effects of observing conjugal violence on children: A review and analysis of research methodology. *Journal of Family Violence, 4*(1), 77–94. 10.1007/bf00985658

Finkelhor, D. (2008). *Childhood victimization: Violence, crime, and abuse in the lives of young people*: Oxford University Press.

Gilbert, R., Widom, C. S., Browne, K., Fergusson, D., Webb, E., & Janson, S. (2009). Burden and consequences of child maltreatment in high-income countries. *The Lancet, 373*(9657), 68–81. 10.1016/s0140-6736(08)61706-7

Goodman, R., & Scott, S. (1999). Comparing the strengths and difficulties questionnaire and the child behavior checklist: Is small beautiful? *Journal of Abnormal Child Psychology, 27*(1), 17–24. 10.1023/a:1022658222914

Graham-Bermann, S. A., Gruber, G., Howell, K. H., & Girz, L. (2009). Factors discriminating among profiles of resilience and psychopathology in children exposed to Intimate Partner Violence (IPV). *Child Abuse and Neglect, 33*(9), 648–660. 10.1016/j.chiabu.2009.01.002

Hamby, S., Finkelhor, D., Turner, H., & Ormrod, R. (2010). The overlap of witnessing partner violence with child maltreatment and other victimizations in a nationally representative survey of youth. *Child Abuse and Neglect, 34*(10), 734–741. 10.1016/j.chiabu.2010.03.001

Herman-Smith, R. (2013). Intimate partner violence exposure in early childhood: An ecobiodevelopmental perspective. *Health and Social Work, 38*(4), 231–239. 10.1093/hsw/hlt018

Herrenkohl, T. I., Sousa, C., Tajima, E. A., Herrenkohl, R. C., & Moylan, C. A. (2008). Intersection of child abuse and children's exposure to domestic violence. *Trauma Violence Abuse, 9*(2), 84–99. 10.1177/1524838008314797

Holmes, M. R., Richter, F. G. C., Votruba, M. E., Berg, K. A., & Bender, A. E. (2018). Economic burden of child exposure to intimate partner violence in the United States. *Journal of Family Violence, 33*(4), 239–249. 10.1007/s10896-018-9954-7

Holt, S., Buckley, H., & Whelan, S. (2008). The impact of exposure to domestic violence on children and young people: A review of the literature. *Child Abuse & Neglect, 32*(8), 797–810. 10.1016/j.chiabu.2008.02.004

Jouriles, E. N., & LeCompte, S. H. (1991). Husbands' aggression towards wives and mothers' and fathers' aggression towards children: Moderating effects of child gender. *Journal of Consulting and Clinical Psychology, 59*(1), 190–192. 10.1037/0022-006x.59.1.190

Kimball, E. (2016). Edleson revisited: Reviewing children's witnessing of domestic violence 15 years later. *Journal of Family Violence, 31*(5), 625–637. 10.1007/s10896-015-9786-7

Kitzmann, K. M., Gaylord, N. K., Holt, A. R., & Kenny, E. D. (2003). Child witnesses to domestic violence: A meta-analytic review. *Journal of Consulting and Clinical Psychology, 71*(2), 339–352. 10.1037/0022-006X.71.2.339

Knight, E. D., Runyan, D. K., Dubowitz, H., Brandford, C., Kotch, J., Litrownik, A., & Hunter, W. (2000). Methodological and Ethical Challenges Associated With Child Self-Report of Maltreatment. *Journal of Interpersonal Violence, 15*(7), 760–775. 10.1177/088626000015007006

Laing, L., & Humphreys, C. (2013). *Social work and domestic violence: Developing critical and reflective practice*. London:Sage.

Margolin, G. (1998). Effects of domestic violence on children. In P. K. Trickett & C. J. Schellenbach (Eds.), *Violence against children in the family and the community* (pp. 57–101). American Psychological Association. 10.1037/10292-003

Morris, A., Hegarty, K., & Humphreys, C. (2012). Ethical and safe: Research with children about domestic violence. *Research Ethics, 8*(2), 125–139. 10.1177/174701 6112445420

Moylan, C. A., Herrenkohl, T. I., Sousa, C., Tajima, E. A., Herrenkohl, R. C., & Russo, M. J. (2010). The effects of child abuse and exposure to domestic violence on adolescent internalizing and externalizing behaviour problems. *Journal of Family Violence, 25*(1), 53–63. 10.1007/s10896-009-9269-9

Pro Bono Economics. (2018). *The economic cost from childhood exposure to severe domestic violence*. Retrieved from https://www.probonoeconomics.com/the-economic-cost-from-childhood-exposure-to-severe-domestic-violence

Radford, L., Corral, S., Bradley, C., Fisher, H., Bassett, C., Howat, N., & Collishaw, S. (2011). Child abuse and neglect in the UK today. https://learning.nspcc.org.uk/ research-resources/pre-2013/child-abuse-neglect-uk-today

Van Roy, B., Groholt, B., Heyerdahl, S., & Clench-Aas, J. (2010). Understanding discrepancies in parent-child reporting of emotional and behavioural problems: Effects of relational and socio-demographic factors. *BMC Psychiatry, 10*(1), 56. 10.1186/1471-244X-10-56

Wolfe, D. A., Crooks, C. V., Lee, V., McIntyre-Smith, A., & Jaffe, P. G. (2003). The effects of children's exposure to domestic violence: A meta-analysis and critique. *Clinical Child and Family Psychology Review, 6*(3), 171–187. 10.1023/a:102491041 6164

7 The self-regulation capacities of young people exposed to violence

Kathryn Maurer
McGill University, Canada

Introduction

Our understanding of how exposure to violence in the home affects child and youth development has evolved rapidly over the past several decades. Exposure to the multiple forms of family violence (FV; child maltreatment, intimate partner violence [IPV], sibling abuse) and types (psychological, emotional, physical, neglect and sexual) is associated with short- and long-term changes in a complex array of biological, psychological and social functioning (Ungar et al., 2021). One process vulnerable to change or modification is the self-regulation of affect, defined as an effortful coordination of attention, cognitions, appraisal, internal emotional states and physiological processes to maintain affective homeostasis and inhibit behavioural reactivity in response to internal and external stimuli (e.g., FV; Taipale, 2016). An interdisciplinary knowledge base of the biological, psychological and social mechanisms by which violence exposure-related psychophysiological change occurs and manifests has emerged. Current transdisciplinary perspectives position the effects of FV exposure relative to developmental processes across childhood and within the complex biopsychosocial cultural and physical ecology in which children and families are situated (Ungar et al., 2021).

This chapter's focus is psychophysiological modification of the capacity to regulate affect when experiencing stress following caregiver enacted FV (child abuse/IPV) exposure for youth transitioning to adulthood. The capacity to self-regulate under stress is a primordial process that can be affected by FV exposure and differentially mediates the effects of exposure on individuals and their adaptive responses post-exposure (Ellis & Del Giudice, 2019). Exposure to FV is widely accepted as a psychobiological traumatogenic experience, the effects of which may, even with intervention, endure well into adulthood (Beauchaine, 2015). Significant rates of FV exposure occur during adolescence (Maurer, 2015), highlighting the need to study exposure effects on youth development as well as for younger children (Hambrick et al., 2019). Exposure is a general term that encompasses direct youth victimisation and witnessing of FV incidents, as well as living in a family in which violence occurs. When examined concurrently, research has shown that multiple forms

DOI: 10.4324/9781003124634-10

and types of violence frequently co-occur within families (see Hamby et al., 2010; Maurer, 2015) and effect the same biopsychosocial systems regardless of form/type of violence (Beauchaine, 2015; Perry, 2017). These same systems are also implicated in psychophysiological modifications, via self-regulation processes. Adolescence is a sensitive period for the development of self-regulation capacity, during which the neurobiological mechanisms of regulation have a heightened sensitivity to exposure to high stress/adversity, such as FV (Romeo, 2013). Thus, self-regulation processes are a salient focus in transdisciplinary study of the psychophysiological effects of FV exposure on adolescent functioning.

Western scholarship on the effects of adolescent FV exposure often focuses on behavioural outcomes, i.e., "anti-social" or "risky" behaviour and psychopathology (i.e., conduct disorder, anxiety, depression, etc.). Adolescent substance misuse, violence, precocious sexual activity, truancy, etc. In addition, distal behaviours of perpetrating FV and criminal justice involvement in adulthood are pathologised and stigmatised for their violation of Eurocentric norms of social behaviour (Beauchaine, 2015; Ellis & Del Giudice, 2019). Anti-social behaviours are often presumed to result from top-down cognitive regulation of conflict resolution and stress-reducing strategies learned in violent homes. Yet, despite the well-documented effectiveness of family-based social learning, only a small proportion of FV-exposed children and youth manifest substantial impulsive and aggressive behaviours (Smith-Marek et al., 2015). Even in the most chaotic family environments, most youth develop the capacity to regulate impulsive and aggressive reactivity under stress (Repetti et al., 2002; Tremblay, 2003). Transdisciplinary human development research (Cicchetti & Rogosch, 1996) understands engagement in "risky" behaviours as typical and fundamental to adolescent development of self-regulation capacity (Ellis, 2018). Thus, assessing and intervening in the effects of exposure to high adversity in general, and FV specifically, is predicated on understanding the differential effect of exposure.

Shifting perspectives in the social and neurosciences increasingly challenge discourses of pathologisation and stigmatisation of "non-typical" or disrupted development of "optimal" brain function, structure and behaviour, by conceptualising modifications as purposively adaptive to high adversity environments (Belsky & Pluess, 2013; Ellis, 2018). The shift from pathologizing individual behaviour to a focus on person-in-environment adaptive interactions critiques the imposition of a value hierarchy on the differential effects of FV exposure on adolescents (i.e., "good" vs. "bad" behaviours); this approach decentralises the individual and implicates the full sociocultural ecology in assessment and intervention. A critical approach to FV exposure effects is crucial given the many mezzo and macro systems which influence the behaviour of adolescents (i.e., school, child welfare and criminal justice) with potential profound and long-reaching effects on youths' life courses.

Indeed, many youth surveillance systems focus on behaviours. Yet, behaviours are but the tip of the iceberg of FV exposure's effects. What lies beneath behavioural outcomes are complex interactive interdependent processes of physical, emotional, cognitive and social functioning which precede and influence behavioural responses (Cicchetti & Rogosch, 1996; Ellis & Del Giudice, 2019). The study of the effects of adversity on child development has expanded rapidly over the past three decades with the explosion of information generated through neuroscience-related research. Given the daunting expanse of knowledge, a transdisciplinary integrated approach to human development is essential for a nuanced understanding of the differential impact of experiences, such as FV exposure, and to inform assessment and intervention. Transdisciplinary research demonstrates that markers of self-regulation such as attention, emotional lability, etc. result from many different psychophysiological adaptations (equifinality). Furthermore, changes in brain structure or function manifest heterogeneously, depending on contextual factors (multifinality; Perry, 2017). For example, changes in the amygdala can affect fear conditioning and emotional memory. Given the complex interactive nature of human development, the phenomenon of effects of FV exposure must be understood in context, including developmental, social, cultural and environmental contexts, the water in which the iceberg resides.

An ecological transactional developmental model of the effects of FV exposure

Linear acontextual risk and resilience modelling cannot encompass the entire micro to macro ecology and the considerable equifinality and multifinality of risk factors and differential effects on child and youth developmental outcomes post-FV exposure. Current theory, research, assessment and intervention on the effects of exposure to high stress/adversity has shifted to prioritise complex, interactional, developmental, process-informed modelling to understand the differential effects of adversity exposure on the individual and to responsibilise the exo- and mesosystem in the dynamics (Ungar et al., 2021). Three concepts are integral to this shift to a context-dependent psychophysiological developmental approach to adversity exposure: Developmental trauma ecological transactional model, person-in-environment adaptation and differential sensitivity to the environment.

Developmental ecological transactional model

The study of child development is inherently interdisciplinary given the "complex interactions across levels of analysis (i.e., genes, the epigenome, neural systems, physiological networks, organ systems, individuals, families, communities and cultures) and the developmental timing, patterns, intensity and nature of stress-activating experiences (i.e., sensitising vs. resilience-building) for any given individual" (Perry, 2017, p. 712). The ecological model facilitates mapping the most granular level interactions within the brain and body (e.g., synaptic connections) in relationship with social systems from micro (e.g., family) to macro sociocultural phenomena (e.g., racism) and the physical environment of our planet (Ungar, 2021). Although the person-in-environment model dates back to social work's foundations (see Richmond, 1917/1955), psychologist Bronfenbrenner's ecological systems theory is most commonly adopted by child and youth development theorists and researchers. Bronfenbrenner embeds all systems (micro to macro) within the Chronosystem which situates changes in the entire ecology in time, across the lifespan and specific developmental stages. Integrating Sameroff's (2009) conceptualisation of transactional interactions, i.e., the modifying, adaptive and dynamic nature of interactions between an individual and the many levels of their ecology, within the ecological framework is congruent with current neurobiological and sociocultural models of gene X environment and person X environment interactions (see Ungar et al., 2021; Ellis, 2018).

Thus, an ecological transactional framework facilitates the synthesis and integration of knowledge across and between disciplines to generate a holistic transactional developmental representation of the many biopsychosociocultural components, mechanism and processes that influence individuals interacting in their environment and across stages of human development. Furthermore, the transactional focus encourages integration of the adverse effects of sociocultural phenomena such as racism, colonialism, intergenerational systemic oppression, etc. on developmental adaptation at individual, community and structural levels. This framework is congruent with current psychobiological models of adaptation to environment post-adversity exposure, i.e., FV, which do not isolate or privilege the individual experience (Ungar, 2021).

Person-in-environment adaptation

Throughout history, humans have recognised a relationship between high stress/adversity exposure and changes or adaptations in a person's biological, psychological, behavioural and social functioning. The reigning western psychological paradigm conceptualises this relationship as trauma (Perry, 2017). By definition, trauma is a physical injury, the emotional, psychological, or behavioural responses (temporary or chronic) to injury, as well as an event/experience which causes injury (Merriam-Webster, n.d.). Based on the premise of mind-body duality, modern trauma theory initially focused on top-down cognitive and social processes (Beauchaine, 2015) to explain psychological states and behaviours deemed "non-normative," i.e., pathological. This dualism has largely been replaced by the understanding that trauma is fully embodied. Just as the individual cannot be separated from their environment, neuroscience-informed research has confirmed that what happens in the brain and mind cannot be understood disconnected from the physical body and the physical, social and cultural environment in which bodies reside.

Trauma-focused theory and research explore: 1) which experiences are traumatogenic, 2) which biological structures, systems and processes are vulnerable to modification following exposure to high stress events and experiences, 3) the mechanisms of stress-related modification and 4) the indicators or symptoms of modification. It is crucial to understand that events and experiences such as FV exposure are traumatogenic, meaning they have the potential to cause psychobiological modification, yet many individuals will not incur any long-term changes in functioning or behaviour post-exposure. For example, most FV-exposed youth do not become family-violent in adulthood (e.g., Smith-Marek et al., 2015; Maurer, 2015).

Advances in neuroscience technology (i.e., brain imaging, genetics, etc.) have revolutionised our understanding of trauma-related adaptation under conditions of high stress and adversity via the mechanisms of neuroplasticity (modifications to neural pathways) and epigenetics (modifications to gene expression). Neuroplasticity and epigenetics are experience- and context-dependent and occur across the lifespan (Ellis & Del Giudice, 2019).

The full biology of a person, especially the brain/nervous system, is in a continual dynamic responsive adaptive relationship between internal and external stimuli to maintain equilibrium. Enhancing experiences, as well as exposure to stress and adversity, change brain structure and function (Ellis & Del Giudice, 2019). Two counterbalancing processes, developmental plasticity (high sensitivity to the environment) and canalisation (environmental influence buffering; Del Giudice et al., 2018) result in differential susceptibility to environmental influence. Modifications may be minor or comprehensive, of short or long duration and equifinal or multifinal. Through repetition, changes in brain structure and function, including those in reaction to high stress (i.e., FV exposure), become physically entrenched to influence current and future functioning (e.g., Belsky & Pluess, 2013; Del Giudice et al., 2011; Karatsoreos & McEwen, 2013). Via this looping effect, reactions to past stress and adversity (and nurturing experiences) are reproduced in reaction to current stress and adversity (and nurturing experiences) to affect social functioning. Neuroplasticity is a self-reinforcing mechanism of substantive structural change, particularly in childhood and emergent adulthood, when the rapidly developing brain is highly susceptible to modification (Belsky & Pluess, 2013).

Acontextual, environmental adaptation and modification are value-neutral phenomena (Belsky & Pluess, 2013). The ecological transactional model demonstrates that environments are complex, dynamic and the valence of transactions is locally specific (see Cicchetti et al., 2000). Interactions are transactional in that they may act as vulnerabilities, buffers, potentiating and compensatory factors, which in combination mitigate or amplify the influence of environmental (internal and external) stimuli. Internal and external stimuli vary in intensity (severity of exposure), frequency (dose) and duration (chronic or episodic). Thus, just as event exposure is traumatogenic, the many risk factors associated with FV exposure are not deterministically causal of outcomes but probabilistic. Developmental biopsychosocial cultural adaptations following FV exposure are differential due to contextual, equifinal and multifinal variation (Perry, 2017).

Differential sensitivity to the environment

Variation in the effects of exposure to high adversity environments is also filtered through an individual's degree of sensitivity to environmental stimuli. Research on the diathesis stress model evolved into a theory of differential biological sensitivity to environment or context (BSC; see Del Giudice et al., 2011). Testing of the BSC theory demonstrates that in addition to the heterogeneity generated by the complex multilevel transactional nature of a person's ecology, individual sensitivity to the environment varies in general and in relation to the quality of the environment. Boyce (2019) popularised the metaphor of orchids and dandelions to describe those individuals who are more impervious to their environment - dandelions, which thrive under almost any conditions – in contrast to orchids who are highly impacted by unreliable high adversity environments (exposure to FV) as well as well-resourced responsive and predictable environments. Belsky et al. (2007) suggested an additional and independent sensitivity to enhancing environments, i.e., vantage sensitivity. More research is needed on phenotypes of BSC at the population level to understand patterns of sensitivity and buffering to environmental influence on adaptation processes (Del Giudice et al., 2011). Nonetheless, BSC is an essential concept for understanding the complexity of the differential effects of person-in-environment interactions of stress/adversity exposure such as FV on adolescent development.

Affect regulation

Affect regulation is centrally situated in adaptation to environment, BSC and the developmental transactional ecological model (see Maurer, 2020 Figure 1). The process of affect regulation includes appraisal of environmental stimuli, physiological response, emotion and cognitive processing, neurophysiological processes and subsequent behaviour of a person interacting with their internal and external environment (Ellis & Del Giudice, 2019; Karatsoreos & McEwen, 2013). Affect regulation is a person's effortful maintenance of, or return to, the internal state of affective equilibrium (homeostasis), which is in constant fluctuation. Under conditions of heightened stimulation, states of hyper- and hypo-arousal of affect may arise, leading to affect dysregulation and the loss of cognitive control of internal affect. These high arousal states are often described as the fight, flight, or freeze response and are associated with impulsivity, aggression, dissociation, limited attention and cognitive engagement. Intermittent or chronic FV-related hypo-/hyper-arousal can effectuate changes in the regulation process as well as affective homeostasis, particularly during the heightened sensitivity of adolescence. The greater an adolescent's BSC, the more impactful the environment is likely to be on their affect regulation capacity. Affect regulation is central to a continuous experience of the internal sense of self as well as patterns of interaction of the self with the external environment (Taipale, 2016). Adaptive modifications to high adversity environments often increase reactivity, including hypervigilance, dissociation and impulsive and aggressive behaviour. Such adaptations are ill-fitted to many environments outside of the family, such as school and workplaces, where they are construed as anti-social or pathological (Ellis & Del Giudice, 2019).

The centrality of affect regulation renders it an accessible and impactful process to target in interventions to modify adaptations to stress that may no longer meet the needs of an individual's environment. Data from a study we conducted on the affect regulation capacity of adolescents exposed to FV can help demonstrate the utility of the concepts of the transactional developmental ecological model, adaptation to environment and BSC in understanding the effects of high adversity exposure. Furthermore, these concepts are applicable to assessment and intervention when adaptations are ill-fitted to new or changing environments.

Researching the affect regulation experiences of FV-exposed adolescents

In a 2019 study conducted with adolescents FV-exposed to, we explored the relationship between biophysiological mechanism-focused and psychosocial experience-focused understandings of affect regulation when under stress through qualitative phenomenological research. Youth described their experiences of regulating affect when in an arousal state in two situations: one in which they took action and one in which they inhibited behavioural impulses. We asked participants to describe the physical, emotional and cognitive components of their stress responses. Stress physiology, complex trauma and resilience frameworks underpinned the study design (see Maurer, 2020 for a full description).

The sample included 16 participants, one gender non-binary, seven female and eight male youth, aged 15–25 years old. Youth reported witnessing caregiver IPV (81%) and child abuse victimisation (75%) in the previous 12 months. Six participants reported past youth protection services involvement.

Results: Examples of biopsychosocial model of the effects of FV exposure

Some participants described an association between high sensitivity to the environment and pervasive affect dysregulation: *"Sometimes I have a lot of tendencies to be hyper-sensitive and anxious, and I often get emotional ups and downs. I'm often out of control for a day, in fact, all the time, I'm out of control all the time"* (Participant 13).

Physiological arousal was described in detail; some associated it with behavioural reactivity: *"like when I get into that mode it feels like everything around me is shaking, as if it's almost like an earthquake. It's almost hard to balance, and I just quickly snapped at him for just being worried about me, and I started yelling at him. And then yelling at him quickly turned into me hitting myself"* (Participant 8).

Expressing aggression in a state of hyper-arousal can be adaptive in some environments, such as playing sports: *"Then in order to let off steam, I mean, when... ... when I was doing sports then I was in a bad mood like I didn't care you know, like I was just letting off steam on the ball then it's a way if you want to do things like everyone... ... . Like... ... not necessarily take it out on somebody, but at least take it out on something to get that energy out because in the end, the way I grew up it's like a poison"* (Participant 10).

Suppressing all emotions was a common adaptation to inhibit hyper-arousal: *"Like me, yes, I have no emotions. It's made me have these blocks. But at least I can stay rational and think logically, or get out of other situations where I have problems"* (Participant 11).

Reactivity, when repeated over time, becomes entrenched: *"No, I acted pretty fast. I've never had a really good relationship with mom, so when reacting to what she does, it takes about 30 seconds for me to just not be able to handle it and just explode ... Yeah, it's a reflex --because I've had so many bad situations with mom, that it's just a reflex to be angry towards her"* (Participant 5).

Participants were challenged to adapt to change, even positive change: *"Well, so much bad stuff has happened in my life that sometimes when good stuff happens, but I don't go through with it out of fear, because I tell myself it's not normal"* (Participant 7).

An ecological developmental trauma approach to intervention with FV-exposed adolescents

As one participant noted, it is the one time an adolescent fails to regulate their affect that draws attention and consequences, not the 100 times they are able to inhibit dysregulated behaviours of impulsivity and aggression (Maurer, 2020). Despite the expected variation in adolescent capacity to regulate affect during the maturation process, many behaviours and affective reactions are pathologised acontextually as dysfunctional (Belsky & Pluess, 2013; Ellis & Del Giudice, 2019; Maurer, 2020). Neurobiological-informed theory and research reconceptualises dysfunction as differential adaptation to high stress/adversity environments (FV exposure) resulting from complex, developmental, process-informed ecological interactions. This approach responsibilises the exo- and mesosystem in the dynamics as well as individuals, given the evidence of the impact of intergenerational transmission of traumatic stress, the collective stress of the global COVID-19 pandemic, climate change, racism, etc. Commensurate complex and dynamic ecological assessment and intervention strategies with engagement across the full social ecology are needed to increase flexibility and responsivity to environmental change and diversity in adaptations to high adversity environments (Ungar, 2021).

For example, precision medicine (a highly individualised approach to medical treatment; Fernandes et al., 2017) has been adapted by Perry & Hambrick (2008) in an individualised, neurobiological and development-informed assessment tool, the neurosequential model of therapeutics (NMT).

NMT mapping informs interventions for children and adolescents that engage family, peers and mezzo-level partners such as teachers in an iterative developmental-focused intervention process (see NMT website). A related trauma-informed model of intervention that brings together youth, parents, educators and clinicians is Blaustein and Kinniburgh's (2018) Attachment, Regulation and Competency (ARC) framework. Both adopt the adaptation conceptualisation of how high adversity exposure effectuates changes in function and behaviour and a complex, dynamic and transactional developmental approach engaged across multiple level of a youth's sociocultural ecology. Enhancing affect regulation capacity is central to each approach.

Bloom's (2013) trauma-informed Sanctuary Model is designed for organisation-level change in "structure, processes, and behaviours on the part of staff, clients, and the community" (Esaki et al., 2013, p. 119) to facilitate developmental ecological transactional interventions, like ARC (Blaustein & Kinniburgh, 2018). Kirmayer (2007) and colleagues have pioneered the field of transcultural psychiatry which insists on the contextualisation of clients in their full ecology to better meet their needs with culturally informed interventions. Similarly, Ungar's (2021) ecological transactional model of resilience responsibilises the mezzo and macro ecology to provide services and access to resources which are culturally meaningful to adaptation post-adversity exposure. Integrating these approaches to implicate all levels of a youth's ecology in mitigating the effects of exposure to FV is the foundation of a values and justice-based response to adversity exposure. A justice approach can be further enhanced by a global commitment to open access research and citizen researcher collaborators to revise the discourses of stigmatisation and pathologisation of adolescent behaviour associated with exposure to adversity including family violence.

References

Beauchaine, T. P. (2015) Future directions in emotion dysregulation and youth psychopathology. *Journal of Clinical Child & Adolescent Psychology*, *44*(5), 875–896. 10.1080/15374416.2015.1038827

Belsky, J., & Pluess, M. (2013). Beyond risk, resilience, and dysregulation: Phenotypic plasticity and human development. *Development and Psychopathology*, *25*(4pt2), 1243–1261. 10.1017/S095457941300059.x

Belsky, J., Bakermans-Kranenburg, M. J., & van IJzendoorn, M. H. (2007). For better and for worse. *Current Directions in Psychological Science*, *16*(6), 300–304. 10.1111/j.1467-8721.2007.00525.x

Blaustein, M. E., & Kinniburgh, K. M. (2018). *Treating traumatic stress in children and adolescents, second edition: How to foster resilience through attachment, self-regulation, and competency* (2nd ed.). Guilford Publications.

Bloom, S. L. (2013). *Creating sanctuary: Toward the evolution of sane societies* (2nd ed.). Routledge, Taylor & Francis Group.

Boyce, W. T. (2019). *The orchid and the dandelion: Why some children struggle and how all can thrive*. Alfred A. Knopf.

Cicchetti, D., & Rogosch, F. (1996). Equifinality and multifinality in developmental psychopathology. *Development and Psychopathology*, *8*(4), 597–600. 10.1017/S0954579400007318

Cicchetti, D., Toth, S.L., & Maughan, A. (2000). An ecological-transactional model of child maltreatment. In E.J. Sameroff, M. Lewis. & S.M. Miller (Eds.), *Handbook of Developmental Psychopathology?* (pp. 689–722). 2nd ed.). New York, NY: Springer.

Del Giudice, M., Ellis, B. J., & Shirtcliff, E. A. (2011). The Adaptive Calibration Model of stress responsivity. *Neuroscience & Biobehavioral Reviews*, *35*(7), 1562–1592. 10.1016/j.neubiorev.2010.11.007

Del Giudice, M., Barrett, E. S., Belsky, J., Hartman, S., Martel, M. M., Sangenstedt, S., & Kuzawa, C. W. (2018). Individual differences in developmental plasticity: A role for early androgens?. *Psychoneuroendocrinology*, *90*, 165–173. 10.1016/j.psyneuen.2018.02.025

Ellis, B.J. (2018). Toward an adaptation-based approach to resilience. In: J. Noll & I. Shalev (Eds), *The biology of early life stress*. Springer. 10.1007/978-3-319-72589-5_3

Ellis, B., & Del Giudice, M. (2019). Developmental adaptation to stress: An evolutionary perspective. *Annual Review of Psychology*, *70*(1), 111–139. 10.1146/annurev-psych-122216-011732

Esaki, N., Benamati, J., Yanosy, S., Middleton, J. S., Hopson, L. M., Hummer, V. L., & Bloom, S. L. (2013). The sanctuary model: Theoretical framework. *Families in Society*, *94*(2), 87–95. 10.1606/1044-3894.4287

Fernandes, B. S., Williams, L. M., Steiner, J., Leboyer, M., Carvalho, A. F., & Berk, M. (2017). The new field of 'precision psychiatry'. *BMC medicine*, *15*(1), 80. 10.1186/s12916-017-0849-x

Hamby, S., Finkelhor, D., Turner, H., & Ormrod, R. (2010). The overlap of witnessing partner violence with child maltreatment and other victimizations in a nationally representative survey of youth. *Child Abuse & Neglect*, *34*(10), 734–741. 10.1016/j.chiabu.2010.03.001

Hambrick, E. P., Brawner, T. W. & Perry, B. D. (2019) Timing of early-life stress and the development of brain-related capacities. *Frontiers Behavioural Neuroscience*, *13*(183). 10.3389/fnbeh.2019.00183

Karatsoreos, I. N., & McEwen, B. S. (2013). Annual research review: The neurobiology and physiology of resilience and adaptation across the life course. *Journal of Child Psychology and Psychiatry*, *54*, 337–347. 10.1111/jcpp.12054

Kirmayer, L. J. (2007). Psychotherapy and the cultural concept of the person. *Transcultural Psychiatry*, *44*(2), 232–257. 10.1177/1363461506070794

Maurer, K. (2015). *An examination of the dynamics of intergenerational transmission of family violence as mediated by affect regulation capacity* (unpublished doctoral dissertation). New York, NY: New York University.

Maurer, K. (2020). Exploring resilience in the affect regulation of family violence-exposed adolescents: « des fois ça marche, des fois, ça [ne] marche pas ». *International Journal of Child and Adolescent Resilience*, *7*(1), 195–210. https://ijcar-rirea.ca/index.php/ijcar-rirea/article/view/87/161

Merriam-Webster. (n.d.). Trauma. In *Meriam-Webster.com dictionary*. https://www.merriam-webster.com/dictionary/trauma

Perry, B., & Hambrick, E. (2008). The neurosequential model of therapeutics. *Reclaiming Children and Youth: Journal of Emotional and Behavioural Problems*, *17*(3), 38–43. https://www.complextrauma.ca/wp-content/uploads/C2-NMT-Therapy.pdf

Perry, B. D. (2017). Trauma- and stressor-related disorders in infants, children, and adolescents, in Hinshaw, S. P., & Beauchaine, T. P. (Eds.). (2017). *Child and adolescent psychopathology*, pp. 699–722.

Romeo, R. D. (2013). The teenage brain: The stress response and the adolescent brain. *Current Directions in Psychological Science*, *22*(2), 140–145. 10.1177/09637214134 75445

Repetti, R. L., Taylor, S. E., & Seeman, T. E. (2002). Risky families: Family social environments and the mental and physical health of offspring. *Psychological Bulletin*, *128*, 330–366. 10.1037/0033-2909.128.2.330

Richmond, M. E. (1917/1955). *Social diagnosis*. Russell Sage Foundation.

Sameroff, A. (2009). The transactional model. In A. Sameroff (Ed.), *The transactional model of development: How children and contexts shape each other* (pp. 3–21). American Psychological Association. 10.1037/11877-001

Smith-Marek, E. N., Cafferky, B., Dharnidharka, P., Mallory, A. B., Dominguez, M., High, J., …Mendez, M. (2015). Effects of childhood experiences of family violence on adult partner violence: A meta-analytic review. *Journal of Family Theory & Review*, *7*(4), 498–519. 10.1111/jftr.12113

Taipale, J. (2016). Self-regulation and beyond: Affect regulation and the infant–caregiver dyad. *Frontiers in Psychology*, *7*. 10.3389/fpsyg.2016.00889

Tremblay, R. E. (2003). Why socialization fails. The case of chronic physical aggression. In B. B. Lahey, T. E. Moffitt, & A. Caspi (Eds.), *Causes of conduct disorder and juvenile delinquency* (pp. 182–224). Guilford Press.

Ungar, M. (Ed.). (2021). *Multisystemic resilience: Adaptation and transformation in contexts of change*. Oxford University Press.

Ungar, M., Collin-Vézina, D., & Perry, B.D. (2021) Violence, trauma, and resilience. In R. Alaggia & C. Vine (Eds.) *Cruel but not unusual: Violence in Canadian Families*. Wilfred Laurier University Press

8 School experiences of children experiencing domestic violence

Sabreen Selvik[1] and Carolina Øverlien[2]

[1]*Assistant Professor, Oslo Metropolitan University, Norway*
[2]*Professor of Social Work at the Norwegian Centre for Violence and Traumatic Stress Studies*

Introduction

School is an arena both for education and for forming relationships with adults and peers. Peer relationships at school are particularly important for child and adolescent development (see e.g., Giordano et al., 2015) and future somatic and psychological outcomes. For children experiencing domestic violence (DV), school has repeatedly been recognised as an important arena, one of the few where their home situation can be recognised and reported to authorities (Münger & Markström, 2019; Lloyd, 2018; Chanmugam & Teasley, 2014; Øverlien, 2015; Nordtveit, 2016). In addition, school has been identified as an important arena for violence prevention and intervention work (Stanley et al., 2015a,b; Ellis & Thiara, 2014; Eriksson et al., 2013). At the same time, the role of schools in the lives of children experiencing DV has been described by researchers such as Eriksson et al. (2013) as "a neglected area of research."

Alongside parents, teachers have a vital role as one of the very few outlets through which children and adolescents can disclose their experiences of DV and thereby receive the help they need to end their experiences of violence and rebuild their sense of security (Nikupeteri et al., 2015). Furthermore, teachers are the professional group in society that meet and interact with children daily. For some children, teachers might be the only adults, besides their parents, with whom they routinely interact because severely controlling families may isolate children from the outside world (Mullender et al., 2002; Øverlien, 2012). As school attendance is mandatory, the classroom setting is one of the few places where a violent home situation can be identified.

However, children who experience DV learn very early on that violence and abuse is the family's or the abuser's secret. Due to feelings of shame, self-blame, fear and loyalty to their parents, many may refrain from sharing their experiences with friends or adults in their environment (Morrison, 2016; Eriksson et al., 2013). Refraining from disclosure may also relate to a fear of child protection services, of being separated from mothers or siblings, or worry that the police will place their abusing parent in jail (Øverlien, 2012).

Therefore, early pupil-teacher experiences can have a lasting impact, not only on the educational and work choices children will make as adults but

DOI: 10.4324/9781003124634-11

also on their decisions about disclosure (Arai et al., 2019; Morrison, 2016; Sunde & Raaheim, 2009). Nevertheless, teachers still report struggling in their encounters with this group of children (Selvik & Helleve, 2023; Münger & Markström, 2018; Alisic, 2012). For some children experiencing DV, partial or complete school absence or change of schools are an inevitable consequence of their physical and mental reactions to the violence and residential instability (Bracewell, 2020; Selvik, Raaheim & Øverlien, 2017). Some children may experience having to flee from the abuser with their non-abusive parent and seek emergency shelter: with a trusted friend, at a domestic violence refuge, or at a confidential address assigned by the police (Hamby, 2017; Chanmugam, 2009). Others may be placed by child protection services in foster homes away from their abusive parents (Backe-Hansen, Havik, Backer & Grønningsæter, 2013). Some may choose to skip school and stay at home to safeguard their non-abusive parent and younger siblings (Øverlien, 2015). Yet others may struggle to keep up with their schoolwork and choose to drop out (Frederick & Goddard, 2010). Thus, school experiences may vary depending on the complexity of each child's situation.

This chapter reviews existing research on the impact of DV on children's schooling and school experiences. With the help of the voices of children we have interviewed in our studies, we will explore their perspectives on school attendance and absence, their experiences of "coming and being" at school and their experiences of teacher recognition and school strategies. A concluding discussion addresses their rights to education, to attend school and pursue schooling, to learn, to feel safe at school and to receive help.

Domestic violence: Impact on schooling

The impact of domestic violence (DV) on children's social, emotional development and mental wellbeing is well documented (Arai et al., 2019; Stanley, 2011; Øverlien, 2010). The impact of experiences of DV on children's schooling, however, has been less investigated. Most children experiencing DV report social and academic challenges at school (Chanmugam & Teasley, 2014; Huang & Mossige, 2012). A meta-analysis by Fry et al. (2018) on the relationship between childhood violence and educational outcomes shows that children who experienced any form of violence had a 13% predicted probability of not graduating from school. This is highly problematic, as education is understood to be a central component of resilience and overcoming adversities (Nordtveit, 2016). Put bluntly, education can be a ticket out of adversity. Hence, every effort should be made, for children in difficult life situations, to facilitate and provide opportunities for continued schooling despite a problematic home situation. However, this effort must be on children's own terms. In other words, it must be adapted to their needs, and based on an open dialogue with the goal of rebuilding their sense of security and wellbeing in school.

School attendance and absence

Complete or partial physical absence from schooling is an inevitable experience for many children experiencing domestic violence and can result in negative social and academic consequences, both short- and long-term. "Linda," age 13, ran home during every lunch break to check on her abused mother. She often threw food in the toilet and claimed she had thrown up so that she would be allowed to stay home from school. "Sara," age 16, was not able to attend school at all. She had missed a great deal of school, not only during her two refuge stays with her mom and siblings but also prior, when her family had had to move on short notice to temporary accommodations far from her school before they settled into a new apartment. Sara described her lack of school attendance during her stays at refuges in different cities as follows:

> ... we [the family] got to that house [temporary place] and then I couldn't get my homework done, I missed a lot of school. There was no peace in the house [the new apartment] and there was a lot of [school] absence. Then suddenly we had to move to refuge 1 in city 2. And then we couldn't go out of the door because it wasn't safe. They [the refuge employees] said we just had to stay inside, and when we did go [out] someone drove us all the way up to the [refuge] door while we sat [in the car] and then they drove us back and forth. No school! And then after we were there for almost two weeks I think, not sure ... at refuge 1... ... we moved to city 3 and then we came here to refuge 2 ...

As the cases of Linda and Sara show, children can experience school absences both while living at home with the abuser and when living at a refuge for abused women. According to statistics collected annually in Norway, more than one third of all children living with their mothers in Norwegian refuges experience gaps in schooling. For some children, schooling comes to a complete stop when moving to the refuge, while for others, schooling is sporadic. Of those children who continue their schooling, only 60% can stay in the same school as before the move. Refuges most commonly report that the reason for this is security: it is too dangerous to allow the child to leave the refuge, or to continue in the same school. Other reported reasons are difficulties with transportation or a long school commute (Bufdir.no).

Learning can become difficult with knowledge gaps related to unsynchronised teaching because of school absence (as in Linda's case) or having to move multiple times to escape violence and thus be abruptly forced to change or miss school (as in Sara's case). It is unsurprising, therefore, that children may struggle with *mental capacity fatigue* which can act as a temporary barrier to learning and cause educational gaps in their matrix of knowledge. "Sjur" age 9, made two stays at a refuge for abused women. He struggled with schoolwork. When interviewed, he said his teacher had asked him "to concentrate a little more about doing things [classwork] and let my thoughts come at home ... not at school." He had earlier told his teacher about his parents' fighting. Even one year after he had stopped living with the abuser, he mentioned that often at school he could not stop his thoughts from drifting to "how they [his parents] used to quarrel in the evenings" (Selvik et al., 2017, p. 11). Many children like Sjur experience an absence of "mental capacity" because they have flashbacks to the violence, not only while they are experiencing DV but also long after they move to a safe environment and may need referral to specialised services. In many of these cases, children begin to struggle in school, experience failure and eventually drop out (Fry et al., 2018; Koutselini & Valanidou, 2014).

However, different children are affected differently, and some succeed academically despite their experiences of DV (Coohey et al., 2011). Some may even excel at school and find pleasure in school activities helping them to forget their troubled experiences at home (Selvik, 2020). They may also perceive doing well at school as a way to gain control over their lives (Mullender et al., 2002).

Experiences of "coming and being" at school

In Selvik and Thjømøe (2021), children differentiated between coming to and being at school. All children felt positively about *coming* to school because it gave them a sense of continuity. "Peter," age 11, who had made five moves to a refuge for abused women and was able to continue attending his regular school, said, "It's good to be there [school] ... It was like nothing was changing." Children also acknowledged that school activities provided an arena to forget outside things and offered a return to normality. Children experiencing DV often report experiencing school as a safe and secure place, a shelter away from home (Buckley et al., 2007) and a respite from violence (Eriksson et al., 2013). They also see school as a place where they can escape their situation (Mullender et al., 2002), or as a method to get away from their troubles at home (Chanmugam, 2009). School is also referred to as a free zone, an arena where they can forget, a place for therapeutic friendships and play and a place of belonging (Selvik, Raaheim & Øverlien, 2017; Selvik, 2020).

However, school may also evoke experiences of frustration, anxiety and pain that last through the educational years and even into adult life (Peterson, 2014). At school, children may experience a continuous fear of abduction or harm by the abuser or may often feel the need to hide their home experiences of violence by telling "white lies" (Buckely et al., 2007). School may also provide a stage where parental conflicts are played out (Eriksson et al., 2013). Children may experience feelings of discomfort when they are not sure who at school knows about their home situation (Selvik et al., 2017). In Nielsen (2015), young women aged 16–20 years who experienced DV reported feelings of otherness and alienation at school. In these young women, these feelings were related to low academic achievement, general unhappiness and experiencing bullying at school. Their home situation clearly impacted their ability to concentrate in class, but this was not addressed at school. On the contrary (and similarly to Sjur, earlier), these young women's teachers asked them to leave their troubles where they belonged, i.e., at home, so that they could concentrate in school. Consequently, their daily school experience became difficult, as they experienced social and academic exclusion and were themselves considered the problem. According to Selvik and Thjømøe (2021), school may resemble a *stressful continuity* if children experience *being* at school as overloading. This may be compounded by unsynchronised teaching because of school absence and change, indecisive teacher communication when addressing their experiences of violence and difficulties in making and maintaining friendships.

Experience of teacher recognition

In several studies, children experiencing DV identify their teachers as their closest contact at school (Selvik, 2020; Øverlien, 2015; Frederick & Goddard, 2010). Children experiencing DV also report paying close attention to teachers' actions and reactions to their home experiences (Selvik et al., 2017; Øverlien, 2012; 2015). Indecisive communication and reaction by teachers—simply in terms of what they did or did not do—may impact these children's perceptions of their home situation, the seriousness of their experiences and their choices about disclosure (Morrison, 2016). For example, 'Simon', age 12, explained how he finally disclosed to his teacher the violence and abuse occurring in his home after a long period of keeping it secret:

Simon:	*I talked to my teacher, and he arranged so I could talk to the school nurse.*
Interviewer:	*Oh okay, so what did you tell him?*
Simon:	*I told him about things that had happened.*
Interviewer:	*And why did you tell him?*
Simon:	*Because he saw, he saw that something was wrong with me.*
Interviewer:	*Okay, so he asked you?*
Simon:	*Yes, like, 'Has something happened'? And I always answered no. But then one day I just couldn't keep it all in.*
Interviewer:	*So he kept asking?*
Simon:	*Yes, he continued and continued. Until I broke down. He asked me every time he thought I looked worried and sad, he saw that something wasn't right. He asked me over and over again, 'What's going on Simon, do you want to talk to me' [in a soft voice].*

Simon explains that his teacher "saw" him and didn't give up. His teacher's soft and sensitive approach led Simon to disclose the violence at home and created an opportunity for him to finally get help. According to Nikupeteri,

Tervonen and Laitinen (2015), teachers play an important role in helping children reconstruct and strengthen their sense of safety and security. Simon's teacher offered Simon safety, thus strengthening his "opportunity to tell" (Madison, 2016). In other cases, negative experiences at school may be provoked when children's reactions to their experiences of DV are misunderstood, ignored or simply unnoticed by their teachers. Drawing on observations made by children of teachers' reactions to their experiences of violence, Selvik et al. (2017) identified five different ways in which teachers recognised and acknowledged situations of domestic violence. Informal recognition, the teacher acknowledged the child's circumstances in one-on-one conversation. In practical recognition, the teacher silently guided the child through extra new routines. In forced recognition, the child informed the teacher about the home situation (as Sjur did in the example earlier). In third party recognition, children became aware of their teachers' recognition through third-party conversations with other school staff. Finally, coincidental recognition occurred unintentionally through everyday conversations with the teacher. Based on their observations, children reasoned to themselves in a variety of ways about what prevented teachers from talking to them about their experiences. Some children believed the teacher did not perceive their experiences of DV as serious enough, or thought the teacher was simply unwilling to talk to them. Others thought that teachers had no time to spare for such a conversation. Few children understood that teachers did not talk to them because the children were talking to adults working in other services.

School strategies

Children who experience DV learn early in life that their home experience is the family's secret (Callaghan et al., 2016; Mullender et al., 2002). Accordingly, they learn to deal on their own with their DV experience and reactions at home, preschool, school and leisure activities. Earlier research reveals how sensitive children are towards teachers' reaction to their experiences of DV (Chanmugam & Teasley, 2014; Frederick & Goddard, 2010; Buckely et al., 2007). When teachers intentionally or unintentionally misunderstand children's behaviour, some children may develop strategies to regain a normal school day: one that is safe, worry-free, playful and educational. Their strategies often involve gaining feelings of safety, keeping their experiences a secret, dealing with painful thoughts and releasing feelings of stress and anxiety (Øverlien, 2015; Buckely et al., 2007). "Camilla," age 9, had experienced four refuge stays in two different cities. Her first stay lasted for one year and took place during her last year of preschool. At school she experienced flashbacks of the violence and memories of many painful thoughts. These could occur anywhere, at any time in school. Here, Camilla describes a way that she gained control over these painful memories during class:

Interviewer:	... ... *I wonder if it happens [you get painful memories] in the middle of class ... suddenly you get some [painful] memories... ... What do you do then?*
Camilla:	*If I was in class?*
Interviewer:	*Yes.*
Camilla:	... ... *if I was finished with an assignment, then I would have asked the teacher if I could get another assignment. Learning and thinking gets rid of painful thoughts.*

For children like Camilla, focusing on schoolwork was a strategy to shift their attention from painful chains of thought: what Selvik (2020) calls "recreational learning." This strategy may be low effort, since it is based on a strength they already have (excelling at schoolwork): a personal protective factor. Performing well in school, however, can also mean that teachers are less likely to see underlying difficulties, especially when no "obvious" worries can be identified. Thus, these children risk going through school unnoticed and without receiving needed professional help. Children like Camilla may experience being "invisible and unnoticed" throughout their school years (Natland & Rasmussen, 2012).

Nevertheless, children are creative beings and sometimes find ways to cope using the fewest resources possible. One example is using their imagination to cognitively construct a safety plan of how the adults at school will protect them if the abuser approaches them at school. Selvik (2020) calls this strategy "imaginative safety." Other children in the same study used 'healing talks': i.e., they shared their thoughts and experiences with close friends who listened to them and offered advice. These talks seemed to have a therapeutic effect and were described by Camilla as giving her "psychological answers" on how to deal with her painful thoughts. Other children used "physical activity"—for example, running around the schoolyard—and "divertive play"—socially interacting with friends through play at breaktimes to divert painful chains of thought. Many also felt the need to keep their DV experiences secret and thus dealt with curiosity from classmates using "creative explanations" (Selvik, 2020).

On the one hand, not all children are aware of their strategies or able to communicate them. For these children, talking to their teachers about their difficulties and the strategies they are using to deal with them may not only encourage their awareness of their strength but also increase their resilience against their diverse experiences of DV. Such teacher-child *resilient conversations* are also important to follow up the strength and functionality of the children's strategies. Some children, for example, continuously find new strategies when old ones do not work, and in the long run such processes may exhaust children's capacities. On the other hand, not all children are able to develop strategies, and some may experience difficulties hiding their reaction to DV at school.

Discussion

The children's voices in this chapter speak not only of their difficulties and needs at school but also of the school's importance as an intervention arena that can provide children with different alternatives for dealing with and exposing their experiences of DV. For example, the strategies developed by the children in Selvik (2020), were established merely through attending school, playing with friends and engaging in schoolwork and activities. These school activities apparently influenced the children's abilities to deal with their difficult circumstances. School also provides a place where children can air their reaction to their experiences of DV and thereby a chance for them be noticed and notified. The voices heard here also highlight the inevitable role of teachers in accommodating their needs, providing safe platforms for disclosure, offering places where they can process their reactions and communicating information about various support agencies.

The right of children to education is highlighted in article 28 of the United Nations Convention on the Rights of the Child (UNCRC, 1989). It obligates States Parties to "… recognise the right of the child to education … with a view to achieving this right progressively and on the basis of equal opportunity" (p. 9). Article 28 requires states to provide compulsory, free-of-charge primary education, make available different forms of secondary education, make higher education accessible and take measures to encourage regular attendance at schools and work to reduce drop-out rates. Although the convention has been ratified by 193 countries, unfortunately, the right to education has still not been fully secured for children experiencing DV. Even in countries like Norway, where primary and secondary schooling are compulsory and the UNCRC was not only ratified in 1991 but also incorporated into the Norwegian Human Rights Act of 2003 (Act of 1st August, 2003 nr. 86), an abuser's right to privacy can take precedence over a child's rights to protection and education. For example, children who are forced into confidential accommodation such as abused women's refuges are sometimes unable to attend school, mostly for safety and security reasons (Selvik & Øverlien, 2015; Chanmugam, 2009; Mullender et al., 2002). From a legal point of view, this can result when their civil rights, such as their right to education and to a life without violence and maltreatment (Article 19), are not highlighted and emphasised when protection measures are chosen. In other words, the children's rights are sacrificed for the abuser's right to due process protections (Selvik & Thjømøe, 2021; UNCRC, 1989).

In order to safeguard educational rights for children experiencing DV and allow them to benefit from school as an intervention arena, it is essential to provide access to a safe school (Article 3) and a stable and safe home environment (Article 24) that helps them develop and reach their potential (Article 27) and to accommodate their needs. It is also essential to provide these children with their right to disclose, as stated in the UNCRC (1989) Articles 12 and 13, by offering them opportunities to tell that are suitable for their age, needs and developmental pace. These articles underscore that children do not have a responsibility to disclose experiences of DV, but they do have the right to be provided with opportunities to do so at school. By doing so, children are then provided with the opportunity to regain their ability to learn through providing them with an education that develops their personality, talent and mental and physical abilities to their fullest potential (Article 29) and thereby gain access to their right to learn and pursue schooling. Understanding and accommodating children's needs can also help indicate whether they need further support from specialised agencies, thereby securing their right to receive help (Article 39). However, schools and teachers cannot safeguard all these rights for children without the involvement and cooperation of other agencies (Article 36), including the police and child protection or other specialised services.

Many texts on schooling and children experiencing domestic violence conclude that schools are making insufficient efforts and school personnel need to step up their game. We can imagine that this is rather daunting for school personnel. Therefore, it is very important to convey that the issue of children experiencing domestic violence and their right to schooling along the same lines as other children, is a shared responsibility. Schools need sufficient resources to be able to address and respond to their children's needs, for example in the form of more school counsellors and more continuing education time for personnel. They need the opportunity to develop actions in cooperation with domestic violence refuges, social services and other agencies. This calls for governments to prioritise domestic violence, allocate resources to schools and strengthen laws and policies concerning schools' abilities to safeguard and support their students.

References

Arai, L., Heawood, A., Feder, G., Howarth, E., MacMillan, H., Moore, T. H. M., Stanley, N., & Gregory, A. (2019). Hope, agency, and the lived experience of violence: A qualitative systematic review of children's perspectives on domestic violence and abuse. *Trauma, Violence, and Abuse*, OnlineFirst, 1–12. 10.1177/1524838019849582

Alisic, E. (2012). Teachers' perspectives on providing support to children after trauma: A qualitative study. *School Psychology Quarterly*, *27*(1), 51–59. 10.1037/a0028590

Backe-Hansen, E., Havik, T., & Backer Grønningsæter, A. (2013). Fosterhjem for barns behov. Rapport fra et fireårig forskningsprogram [Foster home for children's needs. Report from a four-year research program]. Report 16: NOVA. Obtained from: http://www.kineo.nu/skolfam/moodle/pluginfile.php/42/mod_resource/content/1/Norsk%20Novarapport_Sammen%20For%20Laering.pdf

Bracewell, K., Larkins, C., Radford, L., & Stanley, N. (2020). Educational opportunities and obstacles for teenagers living in domestic violence refuges. *Child Abuse Review*, *29*(2), 130–143. 10.1002/car.2618

Buckley, H., Holt, S., & Whelan, S. (2007). Listen to me! Children's experiences of domestic violence. *Child Abuse Review: Journal of the British Association for the Study and Prevention of Child Abuse and Neglect*, *16*(5), 296–310. 10.1002/car.995

Bufdir.no. https://ny.bufdir.no/

Callaghan, J. E., Alexander, J. H., Sixsmith, J., & Fellin, L. C. (2016). Children's experiences of domestic violence and abuse: Siblings' accounts of relational coping. *Çlinical Child Psychology and Psychiatry, 21*(4), 649–668. 10.1177/13591 04515620250

Chanmugam, A. G. (2009). *Perspectives of young adolescent and mother dyads residing in family violence shelters: A qualitative study using life story methods.* The University of Texas at Austin.

Chanmugam, A. & Teasley, M. L.. (2014). *What should school social workers know about children exposed to adult intimate partner violence?* National Association of Social Workers. 10.1093/cs/cdu023

Coohey, C., Renner, L. M., Hua, L., Zhang, Y. J., & Whitney, S. D. (2011). Academic achievement despite child maltreatment: A longitudinal study. *Child Abuse & Neglect, 35*(9), 688–699. 10.1016/j.chiabu.2011.05.009

Ellis, J., & Thiara, R. K. (Eds.). (2014). *Preventing violence against women and girls: Educational work with children and young people.* Policy Press.

Eriksson, M., Bruno, L., Näsman, E. (2013). *Domestic violence, family law and school: Children's right to participation, protection and provision.* UK: Palgrave Macmillan.

Fry, D., Fang, X., Elliott, S., Casey, T., Zheng, X., Li, J.,... ... & McCluskey, G. (2018). The relationships between violence in childhood and educational outcomes: A global systematic review and meta-analysis. *Child Abuse & Neglect, 75*, 6–28. 10.1 016/j.chiabu.2017.06.021

Frederick, J., & Goddard, C. (2010). 'School was just a nightmare': Childhood abuse and neglect and school experiences. *Child & Family Social Work, 15*(1), 22–30. 10.1111/j.1365-2206.2009.00634.x

Giordano, P. E., Kaufamn, A. M., Manning, W. D., & Longmore, M. A. (2015). Teen dating violence 3: The influence of friendships and school context. *Sociological Focus, 48*(2), 150–171. 10.1080/00380237.2015.1007024

Huang, L., & Mossige, S. (2012). Academic achievement in Norwegian secondary schools: The impact of violence during childhood. *Social Psychology of Education, 15*(2), 147–164. 10.1007/s11218-011-9174-y

Hamby, S. (2017). On defining violence, and why it matters. *Psychology of Violence, 7*(2), Apr 2017, 167–180. 10.1037/vio0000117

Koutselini, M. & Valanidou, F. (2014). Children living with violence against their mothers:The side effects on their behaviour, self-image and school performance. *Pedagogy, Culture & Society, 22*(2), 213–231. 10.1080/14681366.2013.815259

Lloyd, M. (2018). Domestic violence and education: Examining the impact of domestic violence on young children, children, and young people and the potential role of schools. *Frontiers in Psychology, 9*, 2094. 10.3389/fpsyg.2018.02094

Madison, D. S. (2016). Narrative poetics and performative interventions 1. In *Qualitative inquiry and the politics of evidence* (pp. 221–249). Routledge.

Mullender, A., Hauge, G., Imam, U., Kelly, L., Malos, E., Regan, L. (2002). *Children's perspectives on domestic violence.* London: Sage Publications.

Morrison, S. E. (2016). *Legal disclosure of childhood sexual abuse: What can professionals tell us?* (Doctoral dissertation, University of Glasgow).

Münger, A. C., & Markström, A. M. (2018). Recognition and identification of children in preschool and school who are exposed to domestic violence. *Education Inquiry, 9*(3), 299–315. 10.1080/20004508.2017.1394133

Münger, A. C., & Markström, A. M. (2019). School and child protection services professionals' views on the school's mission and responsibilities for children living with domestic violence–tensions and gaps. *Journal of family violence, 34*(5), 385–398. 10.1007/s10896-019-00035-5

Natland, S., & Rasmussen, M. (2012). "Jeg var ganske usynlig-": sju ungdommer om sine grunner for å avbryte videregående utdanning. "I was quite unnoticeable": seven youths about their reasons for interrupting secondary education]. *Fontene Forskning [Fontene Research], 1*, 4–18.

Nikupeteri, A., Tervonen, H., & Laitinen, M. (2015). Eroded, lost or reconstructed? Security in Finnish children's experiences of post-separation stalking. *Child Abuse Review, 24*(4), 285- 296. 10.1002/car.2411

Nielsen, A. (2015). *Ett liv i olika världar: Unga kvinnors berättelser om svåra livshändelser* [A life in different worlds: Young women's stories about difficult life events] (Doctoral dissertation, Umeå Universitet).

Nordtveit, B. H. (2016). *Schools as protection: Reinventing education in contexts of adversity*. Springer.

Øverlien, C. (2012). *Vold i hjemmet: Barns strategier [Domestic violence—children's strategies]*. Oslo: Universitetsforlaget.

Øverlien, C. (2010). Children exposed to domestic violence: Conclusions from the literature and challenges ahead. *Journal of Social Work, 10*(1), 80–97. 10.1177/14 68017309350663

Øverlien, C. (2015). *Ungdom, vold og overgrep. Skolen som forebygger og hjelper [Youth, violence and abuse—school as a preventer and helper]*. Oslo: Universitets forlaget.

Peterson, D. A. (2014). *An exploration of children's perspectives of their school experiences: A mixed methods research study*. Sam Houston State University.

Selvik, S. , & Thjømøe, C. (2021). Children fleeing domestic violence to emergency accommodations: Education rights and experiences. *Journal of Family Violence, 36*(8), 1003–1015. 10.1007/s10896-021-00287-0

Selvik, S., & Helleve, I. (2023). Understanding teachers' uncertainty in encounters with pupils with experiences of domestic violence. *Scandinavian Journal of Educational Research, 67*(4), 650–662. 10.1080/00313831.2022.2042845

Selvik, S., Raaheim, A., & Øverlien, C. (2017). Children with multiple stays at refuges for abused women and their experiences of teacher recognition. *European journal of Psychology of Education, 32*, 463–481. 10.1007/s10212-016-0302-0

Selvik, S., & Øverlien, C. (2015). Children with multiple stays at Nordic refuges for abused women: Conclusions, challenges, and causes for concern. *Nordic Social Work Research, 5*(2), 98–112. 10.1080/2156857X.2014.982158

Selvik, S. (2020). School strategies of children with multiple relocations at refuges for abused women. *Scandinavian Journal of Educational Research, 64*(2), 227–241. 10.1 080/00313831.2018.1539032

Stanley, N. (2011). *Children experiencing domestic violence: A research review*. Dartington: Research in practice.

Stanley N., Ellis J., Farrelly N., Hollinghurst S., & Downe S. (2015a). Preventing domestic abuse for children and young people: A review of school-based interventions. *Children and Youth Services Review, 59*, 120–131. 10.1016/j.childyouth.2015.10.018

Stanley, N., Ellis, J., Farrelly, N., Hollinghurst, S., Bailey, S., & Downe, S. (2015b) Preventing domestic abuse for children and young people (PEACH): A mixed knowledge scoping review. *Public Health Research, 3*, 7, http://www.journalslibrary. nihr.ac.uk/phr/volume-3/issue-7#abstract

Sunde, E., & Raaheim, A. (2009). Jeg hadde en dårlig lærer. En undersøkelse av skoleerfaringer blant mannlige arbeidstakere med kort utdanning ["I had a bad teacher" - An examination of school experiences among male workers with short education]. *Norsk Pedagogisk Tidsskrift, 93*(5), 356–367.

UNCRC. (1989). Obtained from: http://www.ohchr.org/en/professionalinterest/pages/crc.aspx

9 Barriers to help-seeking from the victim/survivor perspective

Elizabeth Bates, Julie Taylor, and Elizabeth Harper

University of Cumbria, UK

Introduction

The wider domestic abuse (DA) literature includes a wealth of evidence that indicates the negative impact of growing up in a home where there is violence and abuse. Historically, children living in these environments were positioned at the margins (Taylor, 2019), described as "witnesses" of this abuse rather than victims which carried the implication of them being passive in experiencing the abuse in the home (e.g., Callaghan & Alexander, 2015; Callaghan et al., 2017) with significant impact on their access (specifically the lack of) to help and support (Callaghan et al., 2018). Recognition of their victim status is an important gateway into being able to get support from DA agencies. It is positive to see this change has been reflected in the new Domestic Abuse Act that has been developed and introduced in England and Wales over the last couple of years; indeed, the Domestic Abuse Act (2021) makes explicit reference to children as victims if *"they see, hear, or experience the effects of the abuse ... ."*

This change in status from "witness" to "victim" means children and young people should have greater access to support, yet we know there exists a range of barriers that prevent them from doing so. The aim of this chapter is to briefly review some of the literature on the barriers children and adolescents face in help-seeking and reporting their experiences. This will then include new data that has explored the personal, social and structural level challenges that children face when seeking help. These barriers and potential sources of support are examined in the context of current policy and practice. We further draw upon data that has explored children's retrospective experiences of growing up in a home where there was DA and explores the barriers they faced in help-seeking and their help-seeking responses. This chapter draws on the data of Taylor et al. (2022) which is also discussed in Chapter 3.

Barriers to help-seeking for domestic violence and abuse

Much of the research exploring the impact of exposure to DA on children has focused on their outcomes; for example, there is evidence of their increased risk of experiencing other life adversities (e.g., Holt et al., 2008), experiencing

DOI: 10.4324/9781003124634-12

behavioural problems and self-regulation difficulties (e.g., DeVoe & Smith, 2002), the negative emotional impact (Thornton, 2014) and experiencing trauma symptomology (e.g., Ghasemi, 2009). Other research has focused on exposure to DA as an adverse childhood experience (ACE) and its associated negative outcomes (e.g., McGavock & Spratt, 2017), and its function as part of the intergenerational transmission of abuse (e.g., Ehrensaft et al., 2003). Whilst obviously this work presents valuable insights into the experiences and impacts for child victims, it persists in positioning children as passive rather than active social agents within not only the family but also with respect to their later life choices. For further discussion of this research see Chapter 2 of this volume for a review and chapters 3 and 10 for further discussion of the impact on children.

There has been a dearth of literature in this important area, with little exploration of the specific barriers children face when help-seeking or disclosing after exposure to DA. Wider child abuse disclosure literature points to shame, self-blame and fear as being significant barriers to help-seeking (e.g., Alaggia et al., 2019) as well as indicating the importance of a person to trust and those who are confident to ask directly (e.g., Brennan & McElvaney, 2020). From the DA literature, we know that the failure to ask and hear the accounts of children and young people in the context of DA is even more impactful because of their experience of abuse in the home; these are "voices already silenced by violence and coercion in the family" (Callaghan et al., 2017, p.3371). Furthermore, Øverlien and Hydén (2009) stress the importance of seeing each child as an agent within a context and relational situation.

DA victimisation has been described as a "stigmatised identity" status (Overstreet & Quinn, 2013; p.3) and we know that children are aware of the stigma associated with violence in the home (Stanley et al., 2012). Overstreet and Quinn (2013) produced a model of stigmatisation comprised of three factors stigma internalisation, anticipated stigma and cultural stigma. These factors are used to explain how stigma creates barriers to help-seeking for victims of DA. The stigma extends from recognising the experience as DA through to making decisions to disclose and choose support. Stigma internalisation refers to the internalised negative beliefs about DA victim status and anticipated stigma is concerned with ruminations about what will happen when others find out about the abuse. Cultural stigma refers to negative cultural beliefs and stigma about DA that delegitimises people experiencing the abuse. Their model has been applied to other so called "hidden" groups including male victims of female perpetrated DA (see Taylor et al., 2022).

Whilst not explicitly applied to child victims of DA, we can see evidence that aligns to the different forms of stigma within the research literature. For example, evidence of a lack of trust in adults (Callaghan et al., 2017) could reflect anticipated stigma and an awareness that their voices might not be heard in the "adult world" (ibid). This example resonates with the description of cultural stigma. Shame and anticipatory stigma have been linked as barriers to help-seeking for child sex abuse victims (Kennedy & Prock, 2018). Children fear not being listened to or believed and they fear reprisals when disclosing any abuse (e.g., Halvorsen et al., 2020). One barrier to help-seeking can be whether the violence and abuse crosses the boundary of what is perceived by the recipient as "normal" (e.g., McCleary-Sills et al., 2016). This is particularly pertinent when thinking about children whose benchmark for normal is often limited to their own direct experiences within their early years.

Children's retrospective accounts: Barriers to help-seeking

We now draw on data from a recent study that qualitatively examined children's retrospective experiences of living in a home where there was DA. The sample consisted of 114 respondents (with 105 completing all questions) and was made up of those identifying as male (21.9%), female (77.1%) and non-binary (1%). There was an age range of 18 to 67 with an average age of 37.45. The survey asked about their experiences of DA including who was the perpetrator(s) and victim(s), what behaviours occurred, how they responded, as well as experiences at school and seeking support/disclosing about the abuse. The data discussed in the following is focusing on the disclosure and seeking of support to examine barriers experienced.

Experiences of domestic abuse

Participants described a range of DA that was experienced within the home including verbal, physical, sexual and psychological abuse. Perpetrators included fathers, stepfathers, mothers, stepmothers and there were also clear bidirectional abuse patterns seen where people were both perpetrators and victims of the abuse.

Participants described the behaviour they had seen:

> … mother was a verbally, emotionally and occasionally physically violent person. Not only to me but also to her husband and son. Decades of shrieking, screaming, slaps, scratching, put-downs, sneers, belittling… … I hated her for what she did to the others I loved. (Participant 22)
>
> Violence, alcohol abuse, binge drinking. Violence from both mum and stepdad not just stepdad. (Participant 69)

Some participants also described the way this abuse continued after the end of the relationship:

> Coercive control on a regular basis up until the age of 13 when the relationship broke down. Continued coercive control during contact visits. Witnesses incidents of physical violence around the time of relationship breakdown- hitting, punching etc. (Participant 1)

Participants also alluded to the longevity of the abuse and the environment and atmosphere that was created within the home:

> My mum went through domestic abuse for just over ten years. My father was an incredibly violent man who did not hide his abuse from me and my brother. We lived in a dangerous home environment. (Participant 6)

These experiences had a significant impact on participants, both as children and into adulthood and adult intimate relationships. For a more detailed discussion of the experiences of DA, see Chapter 3.

Disclosing the abuse

When asked if they told anyone about the abuse that was happening in their home, 64.8% (n=68) said no. Their reasons included shame, fear, there being no one to tell and not recognising it as abuse. For example, a number of participants described that they did not realise this was not normal behaviour within a family:

> I didn't know it wasn't normal or acceptable at the time. That was just how it was at home - I had no way of knowing that wasn't how everyone else's home life was. … I didn't know what it was or what constituted domestic violence so there was nothing to tell. (Participant 23)

Fear was driving motivation for a number of participants, fear of consequences as well as fear of the abusive parents. One participant described being fearful of their father, and this was exacerbated by the fact he was in the police:

> I was too scared of my dad and of becoming homeless. Not to mention he was in the police. (Participant 53)

For those who did not disclose, the lack of intervention from those who were aware reinforced a belief that nothing would or could be done:

> My entire family knew it was happening and did nothing, what could a child do? (Participant 83)
> I always wished the authorities or teachers would recognise something was wrong but they never did so I guess I felt if they didn't recognise it then it wasn't so bad. (Participant 99)

In their research, Callaghan et al. (2017) delineate the theme of "being" silenced or "choosing" silence. They describe the active way in which some children make this choice and "self-silence." For example, Taylor (2019) described participants in their adult female offending sample reflecting on their retrospective experience of abuse, saying that they stayed quiet at school, trying to go unnoticed so they could keep the abuse at home secret. This self-silencing could have a negative impact later in life (Clarke & Wydall, 2015). In Overstreet and Quinn's (2013) model, this could be seen as stigma internalisation and reflecting the internalised nature of the negative beliefs about the abuse.

Of the 35.2% who said yes to disclosing, different disclosure targets were identified, for example teachers, friends and other family members.

> Teachers at school, friends and their parents. And, no, I didn't receive any help beyond an acknowledgement that this is a difficult thing to live with. (Participant 25)
>
> I told my friend as she witnessed what had happened and she was petrified so I had to explain that it was 'normal' and to stay in my room and not move. (Participant 33)

There was a common theme that despite sharing this information, there was no intervention or change:

> I told school friends, but nothing came of it. I also told various CAMHS professionals what was going on at home but they didn't say anything I attempted to hint towards the abuse to teachers, but they didn't seem to pick up on the hints. (Participant 50)

For some they felt they were actually blamed for their experience and for disclosing:

> No. I was called a dirty slut & a liar. Eventually the police put me in care where I was told I'd be dead in a few years and I was a waste of money feeding as I'd never amount to anything. The care staff said I must have done something to lead my dad & his friends on. I wanted to die. (Participant 31)

This represented the potential cultural stigma that was experienced as part of their disclosure (Overstreet & Quinn, 2013). Where there was little action, or there was a sense of responsibility imbued on the participants, they recognised why this may impact on others not reporting; one participant had a similar experience where they disclosed but nothing was done:

> … trouble is with family is they want to believe everything is lovely and saying it isn't destroys their sense of close, family safety. Guess this is why people don't believe people who say they experienced abuse - it undermines their own sense of intimate safety. Or reminds them of things that they felt weren't right but buried deep and have ignored for years. (On the other hand tough shit! Abuse should be reported, believed and stopped). (Participant 32)

Previous research indicates that should victims not be taken seriously on initial disclosure that this will adversely impact any future help-seeking, this specifically includes children (e.g., Clarke & Wydall, 2015). It is less clear at this point in the literature how these negative disclosures may impact on psychological wellbeing though (e.g., Overstreet & Quinn, 2013).

There was an overwhelming theme in the narratives that disclosing was rarely followed by additional help or was not perceived to improve how they were feeling. This was not all participants though; some did report that their disclosure had resulted in positive change.

> Yes I received support to help me learn to cope with the after affects the violence had on me mentally. (Participant 44)
>
> which we then went to the police and to an organisation which provided me and my family with counselling. (Participant 52)

There was no significant gender difference in terms of the decision to disclose ($\chi^2(2) = 5.69$, $p = .058$) although the figures point to the fact men were reporting less than would be expected by chance. There is evidence within the wider DA literature that men are less likely to disclose than women and that they face numerous barriers to help-seeking (e.g., Taylor et al., 2022) and that boys can be less likely to disclose child sex abuse (e.g., Alaggia et al., 2019).

Did anyone intervene?

We asked participants "Could you describe any instances when somebody asked you if everything was ok at home or indicated that they suspected that you were living in a violent and abusive home?." The responses indicated that 53.3% (n=56) of participants had never been asked about it. In some cases, this was despite them feeling that people were aware:

> Everyone knew but for some reason nothing was done. It's kinda weird to think that social workers weren't called. (Participant 20)

The fact people knew but did not ask or intervene served to further reinforce the shame and stigma that was felt by participants. This is a reflection mirrored in Taylor's (2019) participant accounts where adults reflect on the paradox between being clear many adults knew but also being threatened with further abuse if they talked. One participant in this study "Josie" said: *"he said he would know if I talked … and he would kill me."* which further represents a family pressure to maintain silence about the violence (e.g., Callaghan et a., 2017).

For those who reported having been asked, this was commonly by teachers or friends/family. This was then sometimes followed by action:

The nurse got the Police twice (once when I was hospitalised from violence and once when my mam was in intensive care) but in the 70's police wouldn't take action without a statement from my mum which she wouldn't give. (Participant 73)

For others however, their answers were not followed up on or any further action taken with the knowledge:

Yes – teachers, grandmother, aunts all asked but when told the truth were embarrassed by it and did nothing. That was actually harder. We were told to make sure we looked after our mother too. (Participant 85)

This points to discussion in the wider literature where children and young people find themselves adopting an adult role to protect themselves and others (e.g., Stanley et al., 2012; Clarke & Wydall, 2015)

The lack of intervention for this participant and the impact of being assigned a responsibility to protect the adult was clearly experienced by this participant as an additional burden. Others were asked but hid the abuse:

I remember being asked what happened to my mums face and I reiterated the lie I was told to tell people, that she had fell over his big boots. (Participant 15)

This reinforces the narrative that children are decision makers when living through their abusive home lives (Callaghan et al., 2017) and they are very much active not passive in these situations (Taylor, 2019). Management of disclosure is an important and powerful coping strategy for children (Callaghan et al., 2017). Øverlien and Hydén (2009) asserted that there is never an absence of action for children, they always "do" something during the violence which could also be seen within the frame of *the action of apparent inaction* around help-seeking.

Alternatively, participants described recognising that questions may be coming and so distanced themselves from the possibility:

I also had an English teacher who questioned me in subtle ways. She was gradually building that trusting relationship, but I pulled back. I was 14 and not used to someone showing any kind of care towards me. I started bunking her lessons too. (Participant 70)

Participants described here that as children they were either known to be in an abusive home and nothing was done, or they were directly asked and more often than not, no action was taken to protect them. Where research and practice are encouraging victims to overcome barriers to seek help, this was not positively reinforced by the behaviour of adults at the time. Many children avoid drawing attention to themselves or their family's problems (Callaghan et al., 2017).

Support

When asked if they were aware as children of any support available 76.19% (n=80) said no, or that there was not any at the time. Those that were aware of some pointed to Childline and the NSPCC, but many did not call:

> I was aware of the existence of the NSPCC but thought that was for children who were being severely abused and neglected and didn't think that was me. (Participant 50)
>
> I knew about ChildLine. I didn't know if what I was experiencing was bad enough (ads were very dark and had very small children in them. I wasn't living on a wooden floor under the stairs) Plus it was part of my mother's taunts "go on then ring ChildLine!" "Do you think they have time to deal with you?" "They'll send you off to a care home where it will be worse! (Participant 32)

We asked participants what support they would recommend or children and young people who are currently living in a violent and abusive home. Many responses involved providing a safe space and opportunity to disclose:

> Someone to talk to who doesn't just push the responsibility back onto the child not to antagonise them. (Participant 4)
>
> Someone to talk to who is independent of school and parents. (Participant 8)
>
> Find a person who you can speak to. Have champions for children that allow them to speak confidentially without being in a school environment. (Participant 28)

Others suggested more formal services such as

> Restorative programmes like Choices for Change from Restorative Change. (Participant 34)
>
> Counselling or a psychologist. (Participant 44)

Some participants felt school related support and action would be effective:

> School safeguarding leads recognising and taking seriously any possible behaviours that could be related to abuse. (Participant 70)
>
> After school clubs that have a safe space for children, schools to actively have checks in place for kids, checking attendance and checking up on it, available counselling, staff to be proactive in seeing dirty clothes, foul smells, anxieties to be checked up on not scolded and punished by teachers for being off school or late. (Participant 102)

There were also many calls for wider awareness raising and education about the issue for both children and those who may be able to support them:

I think it's all about teaching children about healthy relationships. (Participant 16)

Awareness raising in school in vital - nobody ever spoke about DA at all in school - I didn't know the term until I was much older. (Participant 36)

These recommendations from participants fit with the previous literature that points to a number of factors which have been important working with children disclosing any type of abuse including maintaining agency through facilitating safe self-expression (Callaghan et al., 2017), giving children permission *not* to talk in recognition of their experience and how they may be suspicious and experience a great deal of mistrust of adults (Kroll, 2004). Brennan and McElvaney (2020) list six facilitators of disclosing abuse and three are particularly pertinent ones here which include access to someone to trust, realising it is not normal and being directly asked.

Summary of findings

This chapter explored the barriers to help-seeking for children and young people who were exposed to DA and included analysis of retrospective accounts of adults who reflected on their experiences of DA as children. We have seen across these accounts several barriers that were influential in their childhood experiences; the influence of the attitudes and responses of adults was prominent amongst these, alongside a lack of awareness about available or appropriate support.

Implications and recommendations

Supporting recommendations of previous research (e.g., Callaghan et al., 2017), there is a need to ensure that professionals and practitioners value the accounts of children and young people and afford them the same credibility we would afford adult victims. Indeed, many of the recommendations come from participants themselves in terms of how we can improve service availability and responses. The participants support previous suggestions (e.g., Kroll, 2004) in recommending the importance of trusted, reliable people for children to confide in, specifically those outside the family and those who may be trusted.

Evidence suggests that some of the barriers police and other service have in working with children in this context can be related to a lack of knowledge or skills (e.g., Saxton et al., 2020) or barriers in meeting their needs relating to institutional or operational level demands (e.g., Clarke & Wydall, 2015) This is particularly relevant when other evidence suggests that sometimes straight talking is effective to get over the barriers or the "taboo" (Kroll, 2004). Only a small percentage of victims of crime seek help formally with many more using informal sources. Ten years ago they called for more research to explore this but there is still very little contemporary work in this area and even less looking at children's experiences (McCart et al., 2010). Indeed, there have been calls for more child and family friendly police and criminal justice services (Finkelhor et al., 2001). It is essential we engage and intervene as early as possible to ensure children get access to this support and to prevent the possibility of future revictimization as adolescents and adults (Kennedy & Prock, 2018).

At this stage it is important to consider further complexity issues such as intersectionality and indeed the importance of professionals listening, taking them seriously and validating their accounts (Stanley et al., 2012). The effects of culture and context are important factors across the help-seeking pathway from identifying the problem through to engaging with service providers (Cauce et al., 2002). Similarly, evidence suggests socio-economic status (SES) impacts how children seek help in the classroom (Calarco, 2011). Developing our understanding of the barriers to help-seeking helps us understand how to serve and support those who currently appear to be underserved (Srebnik et al., 1996). Indeed, barriers for help-seeking are often "multi-scalar (individual-, interpersonal-, and structural-level)" (Planey et al., 2019; p.190). As with much of the women's literature (e.g., Fugate et al., 2005), we know that many children in the current study report not being aware of the support available. We recommend addressing these key aspects highlighted through the literature and the narratives of participants.

References

Alaggia, R., Collin-Vézina, D., & Lateef, R. (2019). Facilitators and barriers to child sexual abuse (CSA) disclosures: A research update (2000–2016). *Trauma, Violence, & Abuse, 20*(2), 260–283. 10.1177/1524838017697312

Brennan, E., & McElvaney, R. (2020). What helps children tell? A qualitative meta-analysis of child sexual abuse disclosure. *Child Abuse Review, 29*(2), 97–113. 10.1002/car.2617

Calarco, J. M. (2011). "I Need Help!" social class and children's help-seeking in elementary school. *American Sociological Review, 76*(6), 862–882. 10.1177/0003122411427177

Callaghan, J.E.M., & Alexander, J.H. (2015). Understanding agency and resistance strategies (UNARS): *Children's experiences of domestic violence. Report,* University of Northampton, UK.

Callaghan, J. E., Alexander, J. H., Sixsmith, J., & Fellin, L. C. (2018). Beyond "witnessing": Children's experiences of coercive control in domestic violence and abuse. *Journal of Interpersonal Violence, 33*(10), 1551–1581. 10.1177/0886260515618946

Callaghan, J. E. M., Fellin, L. C., Mavrou, S., Alexander, J., & Sixsmith, J. (2017). The management of disclosure in children's accounts of domestic violence: Practices of telling and not telling. *Journal of Child and Family Studies, 26*(12), 3370–3387. 10.1007/s10826-017-0832-3

Cauce, A. M., Domenech-Rodríguez, M., Paradise, M., Cochran, B. N., Shea, J. M., Srebnik, D., & Baydar, N. (2002). Cultural and contextual influences in mental health help seeking: A focus on ethnic minority youth. *Journal of consulting and clinical psychology, 70*(1), 44.

Clarke, A., & Wydall, S. (2015). From 'Rights to Action': Practitioners' perceptions of the needs of children experiencing domestic violence. *Child & Family Social Work, 20*(2), 181–190. 10.1111/cfs.12066

DeVoe, E. R., & Smith, E. L. (2002). The impact of domestic violence on urban preschool children: Battered mothers' perspectives. *Journal of Interpersonal Violence, 17*(10), 1075–1101. 10.1177/08862605-0201710-04

Domestic Abuse Act. (2021). Domestic Abuse Act 2021. Retrieved from: https://www.legislation.gov.uk/ukpga/2021/17/contents/enacted

Ehrensaft, M. K., Cohen, P., Brown, J., Smailes, E., Chen, H., & Johnson, J. G. (2003). Intergenerational transmission of partner violence: A 20-year prospective study. *Journal of Consulting and Clinical Psychology, 71*(4), 741–753. 10.1037/0022-006X.71.4.741

Finkelhor, D., Wolak, J., & Berliner, L. (2001). Police reporting and professional help seeking for child crime victims: A review. *Child Maltreatment, 6*(1), 17–30. 10.1177/1077559501006001002

Fugate, M., Landis, L., Riordan, K., Naureckas, S., & Engel, B. (2005). Barriers to domestic violence help seeking: Implications for intervention. *Violence against Women, 11*(3), 290–310. 10.1177/1077801204271959

Ghasemi, M. (2009). Impact of domestic violence on the psychological wellbeing of children in Iran. *Journal of Family Studies, 15*(3), 284–295. 10.5172/jfs.15.3.284

Halvorsen, J. E., Solberg, E. T., & Stige, S. H. (2020). "To say it out loud is to kill your own childhood."–An exploration of the first person perspective of barriers to disclosing child sexual abuse. *Children and Youth Services Review, 113*, 104999. 10.1016/j.childyouth.2020.104999

Holt, S., Buckley, H., & Whelan, S. (2008). The impact of exposure to domestic violence on children and young people: A review of the literature. *Child Abuse & Neglect, 32*(8), 797–810. 10.1016/j.chiabu.2008.02.004

Kennedy, A. C., & Prock, K. A. (2018). "I still feel like I am not normal": A review of the role of stigma and stigmatization among female survivors of child sexual abuse, sexual assault, and intimate partner violence. *Trauma, Violence, & Abuse, 19*(5), 512–527. 10.1177/1524838016673601

Kroll, B. (2004). Living with an elephant: Growing up with parental substance misuse. *Child & Family Social Work, 9*(2), 129–140. 10.1111/j.1365-2206.2004.00325.x

McCart, M. R., Smith, D. W., & Sawyer, G. K. (2010). Help seeking among victims of crime: A review of the empirical literature. *Journal of Traumatic Stress: Official Publication of The International Society for Traumatic Stress Studies, 23*(2), 198–206. 10.1002/jts.20509

McCleary-Sills, J., Namy, S., Nyoni, J., Rweyemamu, D., Salvatory, A., & Steven, E. (2016). Stigma, shame and women's limited agency in help-seeking for intimate partner violence. *Global Public Health, 11*(1-2), 224–235. 10.1080/17441692.2015.1047391

McGavock, L., & Spratt, T. (2017). Children exposed to domestic violence: Using adverse childhood experience scores to inform service response. *British Journal of Social Work, 47*(4), 1128–1146. 10.1093/bjsw/bcw073

Överlien, C., & Hydén, M. (2009). Children's actions when experiencing domestic violence. *Childhood, 16*(4), 479–496. 10.1177/0907568209343757

Overstreet, N. M., & Quinn, D. M. (2013). The intimate partner violence stigmatization model and barriers to help seeking. *Basic and Applied Social Psychology, 35*(1), 109–122. 10.1080/01973533.2012.746599

Planey, A. M., Smith, S. M., Moore, S., & Walker, T. D. (2019). Barriers and facilitators to mental health help-seeking among African American youth and their families: A systematic review study. *Children and Youth Services Review, 101*, 190–200. 10.1016/j.childyouth.2019.04.001

Saxton, M. D., Jaffe, P. G., Dawson, M., Olszowy, L., & Straatman, A. L. (2020). Barriers to police addressing risk to children exposed to domestic violence. *Child Abuse & Neglect, 106*, 104554. 10.1016/j.chiabu.2020.104554

Srebnik, D., Cauce, A. M., & Baydar, N. (1996). Help-seeking pathways for children and adolescents. *Journal of Emotional and Behavioural Disorders, 4*(4), 210–220. 10.1177/106342669600400402

Stanley, N., Miller, P., & Richardson Foster, H. (2012). Engaging with children's and parents' perspectives on domestic violence. *Child & Family Social Work, 17*(2), 192–201. 10.1111/j.1365-2206.2012.00832.x

Taylor, J. C. (2019). Childhood experiences of domestic violence and adult outcomes: Where are we now: challenges, debates, and interventions? In *Intimate Partner Violence* (pp. 154–171). New York:Routledge.

Taylor, J. C., Bates, E. A., Colosi, A., & Creer, A. J. (2022). Barriers to men's help seeking for intimate partner violence. *Journal of Interpersonal Violence, 37*(19–20), NP18417–NP18444.

Thornton, V. (2014). Understanding the emotional impact of domestic violence on young children. *Educational and Child Psychology, 31*(1), 90–100. 10.53841/bpsecp. 2014.31.1.90

10 The journey towards recovery

Adults reflections on their learning and recovery from experiencing childhood domestic abuse

Angie Boyle
University of Cumbria

Introduction

This chapter is based on my research with adults who have experienced domestic violence and abuse (DVA) as children and young people (CYP) growing up in the UK. Studies exploring the impact of DVA on CYPs lives appear plentiful. For example, the effects of prolonged exposure to cortisol upon the unborn foetus causing delays in achieving developmental milestones, to young adults coping with impaired physical and/or mental health in response to increased levels of DVA induced stress and trauma (Carpenter & Stacks, 2009). Despite the accrual of an impressive body of literature in the field, much of it has focussed on negative outcomes, for example, impairments to the victim-survivor's adult psychosocial and/or physical self (O'Brien et al., 2013). With research indicating high levels of depression, anxiety and post-traumatic stress disorder (e.g., Anderson & Danis, 2006). Indeed Callaghan et al. (2016) refer to a range of studies that have found negative psychosocial effects such as mental ill health, risks of becoming a bully or being bullied, relationship "problems," lack of educational attainment and self-regulation difficulties. The literature tends to assume that following adverse circumstances; a child will "follow predictably negative trajectories" (Daniel, 2010, p. 232). The dominance of adversity-driven research, overwhelmingly quantitative in design, tends to exclude considerations of how people cope with DVA (Lepistö et al., 2010). There appears to be a dearth of research exploring the potential for victim-survivor growth following childhood DVA and research actively examining CYP's resistance to DVA in the home appears to be particularly scarce (Anderson & Danis, 2006).

Contemporaneous research exploring the contextual richness of CYPs experiences by drawing upon the lived experiences of research participants and the stories which they choose to tell from a strength-based perspective, does exist (Callaghan et al., 2015; 2016; Katz, 2015). However, whilst it is important to understand what is going on for CYP at the time abuse is occurring in order to understand their unique viewpoint, exploring how their early experiences of abuse have impacted upon them over the course

DOI: 10.4324/9781003124634-13

of their adulthood is equally important. However, this appears to be a neglected area of research. Research that has been carried out on adults' perceptions and accounts of the abuse they experienced as CYP is limited. Studies including participants 30 years of age and above is limited to a handful of studies for example, Anderson and Bang (2012) (USA); Evans et al. (2014) (USA); Futa et al. (2003) (USA); Gonzales et al. (2012) (USA); Miller-Graff et al. (2016) (Sweden) and O'Brien et al. (2013) (Australia).

Anderson and Bang (2012) researched the resistance and resilience strategies adopted by adult daughters of women who had experienced DVA. They drew on the experiences of 12 participants ranging in age from 22 to 54 years (M = 37). They found that acts of resistance to childhood experiences of abuse within the home evolved into strategies of resistance that the women were able to use throughout their adult lives. These strategies contributed to their resolve to break free from the cycle of violence. Various protective strategies were used to withstand and oppose their sense of powerlessness as a child enabling toleration of the oppressive and violent atmosphere within the home. They reported that these strategies helped them to deal with the effects of the abuse and protect themselves (Anderson & Danis, 2006). Moreover, these accounts may indicate that whilst there are undoubtedly negative experiences associated with experiencing DVA as children, there may also be unintended positive consequences.

Gonzales *et al.*'s (2012) research investigated adult men's resilience following childhood exposure to domestic abuse, they recruited 12 men aged between 25 and 70 years (No mean age was provided). Their participants reported several ameliorating factors in adulthood, for example, involvement in sports, meeting personal and professional goals and having supportive relationships. Resilience in adulthood was also found to be supported by additional factors such as being able to express oneself, having a space to retreat to when necessary and taking measures to protect themselves from the negative impact of abuse, for example, cutting off contact with the abusive parent (Gonzales et al., 2012).

Participants in the research undertaken by Miller-Graff et al. (2016) included 703 Swedish adults (20–24, average age being 21 years). Participants were asked to assess their exposure to violence, parental warmth in childhood and present-day mental health and wellbeing (Ibid.). They found that the experiences of living with DVA in childhood was mediated by the warmth of the child-parent relationship. What these studies indicate is that childhood experiences of DVA will differentially impact on adult lives depending on a number of factors. However, the research in this field is limited as O'Brien, Cohen and Pooley (2013) stated, very little is known about the potential longer-term effects that DVA in childhood may have on the adult self. Therefore, to encourage a reflexive and strengths-based approach which seeks to add to our understanding of people who have experienced DVA, I adopted a Narrative Enquiry technique. The selection of narrative enquiry reflects the importance I have attached to capturing the rich contextual detail from participants' retrospective accounts.

Method

Narrative Enquiry is particularly suited to exploring "the spaces where untold stories lurk" (Speedy, 2008, p.22). The voices of adults who experienced domestic abuse and violence whilst growing up has been a neglected area within research receiving little attention and Speedy (2008) asserts that narrative enquiry methods can aid the exploration of people who live at the *margin of their own lives.* In other words, the interpretivist research design and methodology respect the told story and its teller. Narrative enquiry enables researchers to respect participants' experience and in so doing offers opportunities to reveal knowledge, often made invisible. In particular, knowledge about the factors that have influenced participants who experienced DVA as children as they have navigated their lives.

Domestic violence and abuse research largely fails to involve the children and young people themselves in research which pertains to their experiences. Portraying CYP's experiences of DVA as passive observers fails to examine the damaging aspects of their experiences by largely focusing on the views and opinions of other people, with very little research directly asking children about their own experiences (Callaghan & Alexander, 2015).

This phenomenon, that I refer to as the "mothers and others" approach, is reflective of research that garners the views of caregivers (typically the "mothers") or the professionals they have been involved with (including teachers, social workers, health professionals and police, in other words, the "others"). However, when both children and parent/s are interviewed children often report different experiences of domestic abuse than their parents (Sullivan et al., 2002). Whilst including the views of people around the child can provide additional insights and perspectives, this should not be at the expense of hearing the direct account from the CYP themselves. The central role of the person at the heart of the research is referred to by Mason (2018) as the "knower." She states that *"knowers" are centrally implicated in the production of knowledge* (Mason, 2018, p. 220). In other words, the research participant is the site of knowledge, and their contribution should be integral to the process, not incidental to it.

When engaged with research in an under-researched area such as the experience of adults who lived with domestic abuse whilst they were growing up, the research process should be mindful of how marginalised their voices have been. Batsleer (2011) refers to these marginalised voices as "newly emerging voices' – as their experiences have, largely, been excluded and unheard before. The ability of qualitative research to question traditional methods of what constitutes knowledge and how this can be presented enables these "newly emerging voices' to create different spaces and *"enable a different relationship than those of established hierarchies of social and symbolic power'* (Batsleer, 2011, p. 43). Considering how power is enacted within research is vital. The inevitable power differential between the researcher and the researched (Butler, 1990) can be balanced to an extent, by qualitative research methods which enable participants to unfold and *"describe their experiences as they perceive them, not through the researcher's preconceived notions about what their worlds are like"* (Miner & Jayaratne, 2014, pp. 303–4). For participants who have been subject to controlling and abusive environments in the past, as in my research, and have often had views imposed upon them, been told what to think, when to speak et cetera, qualitative research can facilitate a less rigid and unstructured approach which seeks to validate their experiences (Speedy, 2008).

My research consisted of a qualitative open-ended survey which included a request for participants to indicate if they wished to volunteer for a follow-up interview. Eighteen of the 26 survey participants elected to participate in a follow-up interview. The mean age of the participants was 47 years.

The narrative analysis was conducted using the combined approach of a thematic, structural and performative analysis approach to as discussed by Bengtsson and Andersen (2020). The thematic element being concerned with the participants' story in its entirety (What is the story about? What themes arise?) and the structural analysis focusing on the sections of the story and how these are organised into the narrative being presented (Bengtsson & Andersen, 2020). Finally, the performative analysis examines the wider social context in which the story is recounted (Ibid.).

Findings and Analysis

The analysis revealed that all participants reported experiencing direct and indirect abuse as CYP, the negative implications of which often manifested in their teens and early adult lives. However, my participants identified a process of re-evaluation later in life, a reflective process that prompted a change in understanding and behaviour. From the stories of my participants, I have proposed a 5-Stage Framework for Redefining the Past (for adults who experienced DVA as CYP). Whilst progression through the various stages was experienced in order of the sequence listed below by participants, I anticipate that further testing of this framework might find certain stages overlap or repeat.

Framework Stages

1 Childhood Experience
2 Impact
3 Catalyst for Change
4 Self-development
5 Redefining the Past

Stage 1: Childhood experience

Direct abuse of participants in childhood

As discussed widely in the recent literature (e.g., Callaghan et al., 2015; Taylor, 2019) and in the recent legal changes in the UK (Domestic Abuse Act, 2021) my findings support the victim status of children who grow up in homes where DVA is present. For example, participants described abuse such as:

- **Emotional** – being shouted at, screamed at, told you are unwanted, threatened.
- **Financial** – experiencing poverty, lack of access to food or warmth, deprivation.
- **Physical** – being punched, assaulted, dragged, beaten, hit with a belt, headbutted.
- **Sexual** – being raped and sexually assaulted, being pimped out for sex, witnessing sexual assault or rape, forced to engage in sex acts, punished using sexually degrading acts, being photographed, or watched.
- **Psychological** – being isolated and feeling imprisoned, threats to self or others, made to feel ashamed, threats of suicide.
- **Coercive Control** – being intimated, threatened, controlled, restriction of movement/activities, destroying property, constantly watched, or monitored.

Abuse between parents: Experiences from childhood

Of all those who disclosed the abuse dynamic in the parental relationship, 100% identified a main perpetrator/victim-survivor dynamic. Sixty-nine percent of participants indicated that their father/stepfather was abusive to their mothers and 27% that their mother perpetrated the abuse to their father. Only one participant did not indicate which parent was abusive to whom. The abuse included coercive controlling behaviour, emotional, psychological, physical, sexual and financial abuse.

The participants described seeing and/or hearing the following examples of abuse:

- Rape and sexual assault
- Having to physically restrain a parent from jumping out of a window
- Witnessing a parent being physically beaten and injured
- Stabbed
- Seeing a parent attacking another family member in front of you

I've witnessed him [Dad] punching my brother so hard that he left the ground and hit the door of the living room which came off its hinges. (Participant 26)

They were regular [incidents of abuse] between Mam and stepdad, and stepdad and older sibling. These were physical whereby stepdad would beat Mam up and rape her then he would wait for my sister to come home and smack her head from the walls and kick her in the belly before pushing her down the stairs. (Participant 19)

These accounts support Callaghan et al. (2015) who contests the notion that children and young people are "exposed" in a passive sense but rather, they live with it and experience it directly, just as adults do.

Coping responses

However, participants were also able to describe a range of coping responses which helped to ameliorate the abuse experienced at home. These included:

• Engaging in activities and hobbies
• Managing or adapting their responses to suit the situation
• Engaging with support networks
• Envisioning rescuing the abused parent
• Being driven to achieve as a means of escaping the abuse

These findings were consistent with previous research, the children and young people adopt coping and survival strategies such as sourcing a safe space to retreat to and having an adult they could trust. These strategies were reported to serve as a buffer to help combat the negative impacts of dealing with the abuse (e.g., Anderson & Danis, 2006; Callaghan et al., 2016; Gonzales et al., 2012; O'Brien et al., 2013).

The second stage of the framework, *Impact*, explores how their childhood experiences were often played out in risk taking behaviours.

Stage 2: Impact

Participants clearly reflected upon a stage spanning their adolescence to early adulthood in which they engaged in risk taking behaviours as a means of escaping the reality of their situation at home and the impact it had on them. For some this led to seeking love and connections in unlikely places, for example, drug and/or alcohol abuse (see earlier) but for other participants, it came in the form of cutting or attempts to commit suicide:

> During my teenage years I did cut myself and try to kill myself on numerous occasions the cutting was about feeling physical pain rather than so much mental and emotional pain the physical pain was easier to deal with and sometimes I had just had enough I constantly had like a horror film playing in my head of all the bad things I'd seen heard and had done to me and I felt I couldn't carry on anymore. (Participant 17)

Other participants described how living with domestic abuse at home affected their ability to engage in healthy and respectful intimate relationships/friendships with people outside of the home:

> I found it hard to trust for several years until approximately the age of 25. I was extremely anxious when around loud noises and in larger groups of people. I found it difficult to commit to friendships, jobs, and other commitments as I didn't understand the logistics behind them all. (Participant 24)

The first two stages reflect both witnessing and experiencing abuse in childhood, however according to participants, there is a point at which things may change. The third stage reflects this, referred to as the Catalyst for Change, it is characterised by the exploration of the reasons change is deemed necessary.

Stage 3: Catalyst for change

Major life events often proved to be the catalyst for change promoting a period of reflection and of piecing the past together. Participants talked about a moment of realisation kicking in when the behaviour of the abusive partners they were living with were impacting upon their children:

> I had always said if I was physically hurt then I would leave and I did the day he assaulted me in front of our then 8-year-old daughter. (Participant 5)
>
> I married a man and he abused me for 18 years, but I had no idea how serious it was because my life was easier than my childhood it was when he threatened to kill my 8-year-old that I woke up after eighteen years. We fled. (Participant 13)

For others, change seemed to occur due to running out of the energy it took to mask the dissonance and feelings of disconnection from the world around them:

> I wasn't eating, I wasn't sleeping, and I was just partying all the time and then it just got to a point where I was just enough is enough ... I needed to go through that to get through the chaos to find my rock bottom because the only way was up from there ... I literally had nothing left in my body and my soul and my mind to give. I'd done everything that I could to destroy myself. (Participant 4)

The response to the catalyst, whatever form that took, was the beginning of a journey of self-development.

Stage 4: Self-development

The fourth stage describes a period of self-development, of finding some way to cast off the shadow that their experiences from living with domestic violence and abuse and dealing with the negative aftereffects had caused. For some this took the form of learning to love their own bodies:

> Do not underestimate the value of learning to dance, and own your own body in beautiful, independent and creative ways. It engages the whole body and quiets & focusses the mind to the moment. (Participant 14)

Others persisted with the uncomfortable feeling of navigating change and finding something that worked for them:

> That period of wobbliness and fragility went on for a long time ... but through that fragility I was always striving to get better, to feel better, to understand, to move on ... it felt for a while that I kept falling apart and things would be ok and it would come back and haunt me and I'd fall apart again and that went on for a while, and it happened a few times and it could have broken me I suppose but I kept striving. (Participant 1)

Taking up interests and activities that previously would have been denied to them and looking after their health and wellbeing in a compassionate and self-caring manner enabled others to cope:

> [Having] Therapy, learning how to assert boundaries without being reckless or an arsehole. Replacing self-harm with self-care. Reading, reading different perspectives on social interactions and power. Feminism. Learning about where patriarchal bullshit comes from. (Participant 14)

Stage 5: Redefining the past

> There does feel like a before and after person, that there was a very definitive moment you know, in all of it where I thought 'I can't play this game anymore ... and I've got to do something about it'. (Participant 1)

In terms of a positive recovery, the ability to be able to move forwards without feeling the need for forgiveness, either towards themselves and one or both parents, was a recurrent theme. Being able to process "*and understand without needing to 'forgive or reconcile'*" (Participant 14) the abusive parent appeared integral:

> For a long time, I was preoccupied by received wisdom about it all being my fault, about abused people going on to abuse, and about forgiveness

being the only answer (that last one tortured me for ages!), but I kept facing my demons until I found ways to evolve them into learning, strength and understanding. (Participant 1)

Participants acknowledged that they had been able to redefine the past *because of*, not despite, their earlier experiences of DVA. They describe having an increased awareness of other people's emotions, internal strength and resilience:

My experiences have been difficult but also from a toxic situation has come real resilience which is something I would not change now I am at this point in my life. (Participant 24)
I am stronger now I wouldn't let anyone bully me or anyone else for that matter. I can empathise with many people and situations due to my childhood experiences. I want to be a social worker to make a difference to people's lives. (Participant 17)
I believe I am quite intuitive with people's feelings and needs. I spent years of my life trying to interpret early signs and reading body language and as a result I can get quite intense gut feelings in reading situations. I am able to intensively reflect on experiences and feelings which has been useful as well as detrimental. (Participant 3)

Reaching the fifth stage of the framework, Redefining the Past was apparently a consequence of the previous stages. It was not age dependent in my sample, with participants from their thirties to seventies all describing having gone through the same stages. What did differentiate participants was the timing of their transition through the stages.

I wouldn't have described my home life as abusive until the last couple of years when I've had a better understanding of control. (Participant 15)
I didn't know it was abuse but I felt unhappy at home. Everything revolved around keeping dad happy. I remember him getting up in the morning and rampaging round the house "cleaning up", which involved throwing our belongings away in bin bags. (Participant 16)

Commonalities included being reflexive and having taken time to work through and come to terms with their story.

Hanging onto things that have happened in the past is just going to get you stuck, just going to depress you even more. To live in your past, it's quite sad, isn't it? You know, not everyone has the power to move on from that … it takes a lot of fight and a lot of reflection, and I suppose love as well. For yourself and for them other people even when you want to hate. (Participant 6)
8 or 10 years ago I wouldn't have even acknowledged that was wrong … at that time it was too painful to reflect … I was just emotionally raw;

I was like a raw nerve all the time. Everything hurt, everything hurt, like personally hurt, simple things, like day-to-day things, if you knocked something off there'd be a full-scale eruption rather than just it's just bloody milk! [laughs] I was literally crying over spilt milk. (Participant 4)

Conclusion

This research found that CYP who are subject to DVA in their formative years' experience it in a multisensory way: they see it, hear it and experience the aftermath (Øverlien & Hydén, 2009). DVA does not only occur in the lives of the adult victims but it also takes place in the lives of the children also. Research on how individuals have interpreted their survival, and the strengths that led to that survival, have often been obscured in previous literature. The importance of my research has been about facilitating adults who experienced DVA in their childhood to tell us, from their own perspective, how it was for them. Portraying CYPs experiences of DVA as passive observers without coping mechanisms, negates and actively ignores their strategies for survival, rendering them invisible. Callaghan et al. (2016, p. 101) referred to this state of invisibility and argued that the victim-survivors' ability to articulate their experiences *"reminds us that the abuser has sought to obliterate the embodied subject, but that they have survived."* The participants whose voices we have heard in this chapter have worked hard at surviving. The direction of the research gaze has been reversed and they have been able to take centre stage. Recognition of their capacity for agency and the role that they play in DVA contexts positively contributes to discussions about being able to regain power, autonomy and self-belief and offers hope to counteract some of the negative dialogue about how CYP are impacted upon in the literature.

I will end with an insight from a woman in her 50's:

I have a beautiful healthy relationship, I've had a really successful career, and I absolutely don't believe that people with difficult childhoods will automatically become hopeless adults with crappy lives and miserable ever afters. (Participant 1)

References

Anderson, K. M., & Bang, E.-J. (2012). Assessing PTSD and resilience for females who during childhood were exposed to domestic violence. *Child & Family Social Work, 17*, 55–65. 10.1111/j.1365-2206.2011.00772.x

Anderson, K. M., & Danis, F. S. (2006). Adult daughters of battered women. *Affilia, 21*(4), 419–432. 10.1177/0886109906292130

Batsleer, J. (2011) Voices from an edge. Unsettling the practices of youth voice and participation: Arts-based practice in The Blue Room, Manchester Pedagogy. *Culture and Society, 19*(3), 419–434. ISSN 1468-136

Bengtsson, T. T., & Andersen, D. (2020). Narrative analysis: Thematic, structural, and performative. In M. Jarvinen & N. Meyer (Eds.), *Qualitative Analysis: Eight Approaches for the Social Sciences*, pp. 265–282. Sage.

Butler, J. (1990) *Gender Trouble: Feminism and the Subversion of Identity*. New York: Routledge.

Callaghan, J.E.M. and Alexander, J.H. (2015). *Understanding Agency and Resistance Strategies: Children's Experiences of Domestic Violence Report*. Northampton. Retrieved from www.unars.co.uk.

Callaghan, J. E. M., Alexander, J. H., Sixsmith, J., & Fellin, L. C. (2015). "Beyond "witnessing": Children's experiences of coercive control in domestic violence and abuse". *Journal of Interpersonal Violence, 33*(10), 1551–1581. 10.1177/0886260515618946.

Callaghan, J. E. M., Alexander, J. H., Sixsmith, J., & Fellin, L. C. (2016). Children's experiences of domestic violence and abuse: Siblings' accounts of relational coping. *Clinical Child Psychology and Psychiatry, 21*(4), 649–668. 10.1177/1359104515620250

Carpenter, G. L., & Stacks, A. M. (2009). Developmental effects of exposure to intimate partner violence in early childhood: A review of the literature. *Children and Youth Services Review, 31*(8), 831–839. 10.1016/j.childyouth.2009.03.005

Daniel, B. (2010). Concepts of adversity, risk, vulnerability and resilience: A discussion in the context of the "Child Protection System." *Social Policy and Society, 9*(2), 231–241. 10.1017/s1474746409990364

Evans, S. E., Steel, A. L., Watkins, L. E., & DiLillo, D. (2014). Childhood exposure to family violence and adult trauma symptoms: The importance of social support from a spouse. *Psychological Trauma: Theory, Research, Practice, and Policy, 6*(5), 527–536. 10.1037/a0036940

Futa, K. T., Nash, C. L., Hansen, D. J., & Garbin, C. P. (2003). Adult survivors of childhood abuse: An analysis of coping mechanisms used for stressful childhood memories and current stressors. *Journal of Family Violence, 18*, 227–239.

Gonzales, G., Chronister, K. M., Linville, D., & Knoble, N. B. (2012). Experiencing parental violence: A qualitative examination of adult men's resilience. *Psychology of Violence, 2*(1), 90–103. 10.1037/a0026372

Katz, E. (2015). Recovery-promoters: Ways in which children and mothers support one another's recoveries from domestic violence. *British Journal of Social Work, 45*(suppl 1), i153–i169. 10.1093/bjsw/bcv091

Lepistö, S., Åstedt-Kurki, P., Joronen, K., Luukkaala, T., & Paavilainen, E. (2010). Adolescents' experiences of coping with domestic violence. *Journal of Advanced Nursing, 66*(6), 1232–1245. 10.1111/j.1365-2648.2010.05289.x

Mason, J. (2018). *Qualitative Researching* (2nd ed.). Sage.

Miller-Graff, L. E., Cater, Å. K., Howell, K. H., & Graham-Bermann, S. A. (2016). Parent–child warmth as a potential mediator of childhood exposure to intimate partner violence and positive adulthood functioning. *Anxiety, Stress, & Coping, 29*(3), 259–273. 10.1080/10615806.2015.1028030

Miner, K., & Jayaratne, T. (2014). Feminist survey research. In Hesse-Biber, SJ Feminist research practice a primer, 296–329.

O'Brien, K. L., Cohen, L., Pooley, J. A., & Taylor, M. F. (2013). Lifting the domestic violence cloak of silence: Resilient Australian women's reflected memories of their childhood experiences of witnessing domestic violence. *Journal of Family Violence, 28*, 95–108. 10.1007/s10896-012-9484-7

Överlien, C., & Hydén, M. (2009). Children's actions when experiencing domestic violence. *Childhood, 16*(4), 479–496. 10.1177/0907568209343757

Speedy, J. (2008). *Narrative Inquiry & Psychotherapy.* Basingstoke: Palgrave Macmillan.

Sullivan, C. M., Bybee, D. I., & Allen, N. E. (2002). Findings from a community-based program for battered women and their children. *Journal of Interpersonal Violence, 17*(9), 915–936. 10.1177/0886260502017009001

Taylor, J. (2019). Child experiences of domestic violence and adults outcomes: Where are we now: challenges, debates and interventions. In E. Bates & J. Taylor (Eds.), *Intimate Partner Violence: New Perspectives in Research and Practice.* Routledge.

Part III

Insights from practice

11 Negotiating power, ethics and agency

Working towards centralising children's voices in the DVA intervention evidence base

Tanya Frances[1] *and Grace Carter*[2]

[1] *The Open University*
[2] *University of Coventry*

Background

Extensive international evidence acknowledges that children's experiences of DVA can have adverse impacts on their physical and mental health, quality of life, social development and educational attainment (Evans, Davies & DiLillo, 2008; Fowler & Chanmugam, 2007; Holt, Buckley & Whelan, 2008; Howarth et al., 2016; Kitzmann, Gaylord, Holt & Kenny, 2003; Radford et al., 2013; Wolfe, Crooks, Lee, McIntyre-Smith & Jaffe, 2003). Whilst a large body of literature has explored the negative implications of children experiencing DVA and positions children as "damaged," some studies have identified that factors such as supportive peer and family relationships and children's coping skills can promote resilience (Callaghan & Alexander, 2015). Studies that have involved directly speaking to children show that children find creative and agentic ways of coping in light of experiencing DVA, even if these coping strategies are perceived by others as "dysfunctional" (Callaghan & Alexander, 2015; Cooper & Vetere, 2008; Katz, 2016; Swanston, Bowyer & Vetere, 2014; Ugazio, 2013).

Children's experiences of DVA have been defined as a form of child maltreatment (MacMillan et al., 2009) requiring a healthcare and societal response (Howarth et al., 2016). In the UK, the DVA sector continues to be one of the hardest hit by austerity (Sanders-McDonagh, Neville & Nolas, 2016; Vacchelli, Kathrecha & Gyte, 2015), and there are still significant gaps and barriers to service access and provision for children (Action for Children, 2019). Our focus in this chapter is on developing the evidence base to inform such service provision. Although there are different types of services or interventions that aim to prevent DVA or the negative outcomes associated with experiencing DVA, the backdrop of this chapter is in relation to "late" or "tertiary" services which support children who have already experienced DVA (Howarth et al., 2016).

DOI: 10.4324/9781003124634-15

Intervention effectiveness

There has been increasing demand for interventions to be underpinned by robust evidence in order to reduce and prevent DVA (Gondolf, 2012). Against a backdrop of competing for diminishing resources, statutory services, third sector and nongovernmental organisations need to demonstrate evidence of intervention effectiveness and cost-effectiveness in order to secure funding to support the commissioning and delivery of interventions (Downes, Kelly & Westmarland, 2014). Traditionally, randomised controlled trials have been seen as the "gold standard" to demonstrate intervention effectiveness with quantitative outcome measures being used to provide "hard" evidence.

Reviews of DVA intervention evaluation studies have examined the international evidence to identify which types of interventions are effective for supporting children who have experienced DVA (British Columbia Centre of Excellence for Women's Health-BCCEWH, 2013; Graham-Bermann, 2000; 2001; Graham-Bermann & Hughes, 2003; Howarth et al., 2016; Rizo, Macy, Ermentrout & Johns, 2011; Romano, Weegar, Galllitto, Zak & Saini, 2019). Despite interventions for children being recommended, we still know little about how and why such interventions work and how children experience these interventions.

Howarth et al. (2016) asserted that confidence in drawing conclusions about intervention effectiveness was limited mainly because of the methodological limitations associated with quantitative evaluation studies. For example, evaluation studies often compared pre- and post-quantitative intervention outcomes without further follow-up points. Furthermore, evaluation studies have often defined the "success" of an intervention using a narrow set of health-oriented outcomes and inconsistent tools which limits cross-study outcome comparisons. In light of this, Howarth et al. (2015; 2016) recommended that a Core Outcome Set should be developed for future DVA intervention trials to explore a broader range of key outcomes which were important to intervention stakeholders and the use of consistent tools for outcome measurement.

Whilst synthesising findings from studies or trials of interventions would provide useful information on intervention efficacy, relying solely on quantitative outcomes alone is problematic as they do not explain why some individuals might benefit from an intervention and why others do not, or why some children might complete an intervention whilst others discontinue. We argue that qualitative intervention studies are critical for informing the content, delivery and provision of support so that it is more effective, acceptable and accessible and of higher quality, particularly for marginalised or hard-to-reach groups (Dixon-Woods, Agarwal, Jones, Young & Sutton, 2005).

Evaluation studies have traditionally been adult informed. However, a growing number of researchers have directly involved children as research advisors and active participants in developing, piloting and evaluating DVA interventions (rather than relying only on adult by-proxy evidence), using qualitative research methods (Barter et al., 2015; Beetham, Gabriel & James,

2019; Callaghan & Alexander, 2015; Carter, 2018; Houghton, 2015; 2017; Pernebo & Almqvist, 2016). Whilst demonstrating intervention effectiveness is important, the current evidence base, which relies heavily on quantitative outcomes reported by adults, is inconclusive about what interventions are effective. Outcomes-based evidence (i.e., the "consequences" of living with DVA) still tends to be privileged amongst practitioners, academics and in public discourse (Överlien & Holt, 2017). Additionally, a reduction in symptoms/disorder outcomes remains the main currency of intervention effectiveness underpinning the DVA evidence base for children (Howarth et al., 2016). Unsurprisingly, this tends to categorise children's outcomes and overlooks evidence based on children's lived experiences (Houghton, 2015).

Centralising children's voices in the intervention evidence base

Children are typically less represented in DVA research, due to assumptions that their age is synonymous with vulnerability and a need to be protected from things that might be upsetting to talk about (Eriksson & Näsman, 2012; Åkerlund & Gottzén, 2017). Whilst these are important considerations, we argue that it is necessary to treat children as competent, active agents and meaning-makers, who are able to tell their own stories and contribute in meaningful ways to knowledge construction (Eriksson & Näsman, 2012; Tisdall, 2017). What follows in this chapter, is some of our reflections on conducting two studies independently, that had some shared aims (Beetham, Gabriel & James, 2019; Carter, 2018). We interviewed children aged 7–12 in the UK about their experiences of participating in group programmes for children affected by DVA. For this chapter, we consider our data as blended and draw on our data as a whole dataset. We highlight themes of agency and choice, and we draw on some examples where the research interview itself can act as a space for negotiation of agency.

Children's recovery narratives

Whilst outcome measures are an important part of evaluating service-effectiveness and client outcomes (Howarth et al., 2016), we draw attention to their limitations, in particular, the limiting recovery narratives that are produced in contexts where outcome measures risk being the sole measurement of a child's recovery. The dominance of a narrow set of health, behaviour or "wellbeing" oriented outcomes as the main currency of intervention effectiveness can communicate a particular set of messages about recovery from DVA. In our research, we found that such messages about recovery can be limiting for those who participate in interventions and tell their recovery stories. For example, Sophie, on being asked about how she felt when the group ended, reflected:

when I graduated I felt happy and I didn't want to leave … but I have got my book and my pen and now I can just write. (Sophie)

Additionally, Jo reflected on her improved confidence:

Jo: *She made me more confident. Helped me talk to people in school without being shy.*
Interviewer: *yeah, so helped you talk to new people and make new friends?*
Jo: *yeah cos sometimes I used to be really shy.*
Interviewer: *Has that changed now?*
Jo: *mhmm a lot.*

Further, Penny explained that she had befriended an animal puppet at the intervention and the facilitators gave Penny the animal puppet to keep. Penny shared that even ten months after the intervention finished, she continued to talk to her puppet about her feelings, which made a positive difference to her life beyond the intervention itself:

I always whisper to it to him about how I feel about dad. (Penny)

Sophie, Jo and Penny told versions of their recoveries that ended in happiness and improved confidence. These experiences of feeling better at the end of a programme are important to acknowledge. However, these are also versions of recovery that may be considered "desirable" outcomes, when considered in the context of what a "successful" recovery looks like. We do not suggest that these improvements and experiences are not true, but we would like to consider how these kinds of linear versions of recovery are constructed. From our experience, we recognise that outcomes measures can restrict the space in which children are invited to express their "recovery" and this can overlook what is meaningful to them. Furthermore, it also shapes recovery into a particular narrative which assumes recovery is the same for everyone.

Agency and choice in service contexts

Children's agency in DVA contexts is a relatively widely explored issue in recent years, with researchers arguing that children are not simply passive witnesses to domestic abuse, but they are active agents in their lives, and thus, children are directly involved and affected by domestic abuse (Callaghan, Alexander, Sixsmith & Fellin, 2016; Swanston, Bowyer & Vetere, 2014; Vetere & Cooper, 2005). However, in relation to children's recoveries and children's participation in DVA interventions, the concept of agency has not been explored in as much depth. Our research shows that agency and choice should be central in both how children participate in interventions and in how children are invited to share their views and feedback about the service they have participated in.

Children we interviewed spoke about several positive aspects of their participation, such as making new friends, having fun and learning more about their emotions. They also spoke about aspects of the process of their participation where their choice and power had been constrained. For example, when developing a "Top Tips" poster (Beetham et al., 2019) for adults working with children who have experienced DVA, children stated that they did not wish to be "treated like babies," showing that having a sense of personal power is a relational issue and it is central to how children experience intervention and recovery. Furthermore, children reported that they were glad that they had gained an understanding of DVA through the intervention and that being young should not prevent them from having a choice about accessing knowledge:

Even if they're young I think they should know, like what's going on between their mum and dad … At least they wouldn't have to grow up like I wonder what domestic abuse was … at least they can grow up to know what it actually was. (Cinderella)

Sophie also spoke about having choices about participating:

My mum made me come … I just wanted to see what it was like yeah, but I wanted to go see some friends and stuff, after school and stuff. I wanted to skip some to see my friends, but my mum said no you have to go every week like every other person like every after school club, you've got to go. I was like uuuuurgh mummy. (Sophie)

Sophie expressed that whilst she was glad that she attended the group and that it had "changed [my] life," she also explained that being able to make choices about attending to enable her to attend in her "own time" would have been better and more empowering.

If it was like in school times or something, and we could go when we wanted to go. If we were in lessons and we wanted to go, we could just say erm, I need to go to the group. Like so we could come in our own time … it isn't good when people force you to go, is it? (Sophie)

Children were keen to express that they still had fun and that participating in the groups was a very positive experience. Cinderella reflected on the impact of a group activity that she had engaged with in the intervention. Her experience of fun through the activity made the key message more memorable.

The volcano helped me to not hold my emotions in … it was basically telling us if we didn't tell people like how we feel about stuff that's basically what would happen inside our heads and it will all come out at once like if you're angry and sad … even though it was fun I still remember the meaning of it. (Cinderella)

Children also expressed coexisting stories of significantly constrained and limited opportunities for them to experience a sense of personal power and agency and a meaningful choice about participation. Children made references throughout interviews about not having information beforehand and not knowing what to expect *("we could have had a show around as a starter to see where we were going to be and who were were going to be with ... I'm really excited now but then I was nervous as well" (Jo))* and, for Sophie, feeling "forced" to go.

For some children, their understanding of the intervention developed over time:

> *Well I seriously thought I was going to walk into a bunch of people going, [hands closed like praying] "we will love today" ... About half the way through and I was like, I actually understand why I've got to be here now, I understand what's the point in it... but at first I'd didn't actually want to know about it. (Cinderella)*

Agency in research interviews

Our interviews with children have shown that agency and choice in the context of participating in an intervention or accessing a service is an issue that is central to their recovery experience. However, we also draw attention to our interactions with children within the research interview context. We share the following examples to demonstrate that a research interview or any interaction with a child can act as a space for negotiation of agency.

When inviting Cinderella to take part in the research interview, she expressed that she simply wanted to have an "adult" conversation and rather than engaging in other creative methods that may be perceived as "child friendly." From our experience, we have learned that we cannot assume we know how children will want to articulate their experiences and we should not impose what we think is appropriate. This has presented a challenge to us as we consider the extent to which children's voices shape how researchers and practitioners invite children to share their views on intervention development and evaluation.

In another research interview, Kwaii-Chan wanted to show the researcher her pets during the interview at various junctures. This meant that the "flow" of the interview itself felt interrupted but the dialogue between child and researcher continued. The interview was an opportunity for Kwaii-Chan to share what was important with the researcher and to invite them to be part of this:

Kwaii-Chan: *You're not allergic to hamsters are you?*
Interviewer: *No.*
Kwaii-Chan: *Mmm can I get her?*

Kwaii-Chan: *You can stroke her if you like.*

Interviewer: *Can I stroke her? Shes very soft.*
Kwaii-Chan: *Very very soft.*

The interviews with Liam and Jack took place in their school. Before the interviews began, they were keen to show the researcher around the school. These "show and tell" walks around the school acted as a relational space where the children were "in charge" and the researcher was in a new and unfamiliar place. These interactions offered time and space to settle into time together and negotiate agency in ways that transgressed typical adult-child power relations, particularly in school settings. This "setting up" of the interview relational space seemed to soften the boundaries around how other aspects of the interview were negotiated, such as children choosing whether they answered questions or not and how to jointly manage time. The next extract from the interview with Liam shows a negotiation of questions and the management of time:

Interviewer: *what do you think… has anything changed in your life since coming to the group?*
Liam: *hmmmm.*
Interviewer: *tricky one?*
Liam: *mmm. How long is it until 2 o clock?*
Interviewer: *well we only have about 10 minutes but we can finish now if you like? Are we ready to finish now?*
Liam: *no.*
Interviewer: *we're not ready to finish now?*
Liam: *no – we can finish at break time at 2. In infants we used to have 2 break times but now we have three.*

In this instance, the dialogue with Liam above shows a careful negotiation of talk and time within an interview context. It could be viewed that Liam did not wish to or feel able to answer the question that the researcher wanted to ask "neatly," about what had changed in his life since coming to the group. Instead, he shifted the focus, and, perhaps jumping to assumptions, the interviewer asked if it was a tricky question. Liam then shifted the focus, taking "control" of the interview space, by asking about when the interview would end, but ensuring that it did not end at a time that would be disruptive to the routine of school lessons and break times.

Similarly, the interview with Jack also shows a negotiation of time and agency. The interview had been arranged by teachers, without directly seeking Jack's approval for the date and time, even though it had been expressed to the school that it was important to check Jack was happy with the arrangements. It emerged during the interview that Jack seemed to be missing playing football at break time, and whilst he wanted to participate in the interview, he did not want to miss break time.

Interviewer: *There are still a few things for us to have a chat about, but I know you want to go play football now at break time. Shall we have a chat another day or do you want to leave it?*
Jack: *yeah tomorrow?*
Interviewer: *we might have to look a little bit at times. Maybe after half term?*
Jack: *Thursday?*
Interviewer: *Hmm why don't you tell me what days are good and what lessons you don't want to miss?*
Jack: *ermmm Thursday.*

This negotiation with Jack does reveal something about the possibilities for negotiating choice and agency with children, even in contexts such as schools where adult-child power relations are typically power over, rather than power-shared.

These examples from our interviews would not usually be drawn on in reports or publications, and they are not typically extracts that would be considered as "data." They may even be parts of interview transcripts that researchers may remove because they do not explicitly address the research questions, are part of rapport-building, are deemed "irrelevant" or disrupt the flow of the interview. In our experience, we have learned from what emerged through these negotiations. We have learned that agency and choice are not only central to children's participation in DVA services, but also as DVA researchers, children showed us that it is also necessary to stay open to these negotiations, in order to meaningfully commit to listening to what children want to say.

Discussion and recommendations

Whose voices count?

Foundational to this chapter, is a question of whose voices count in the evidence base underpinning interventions to support children. As we have argued, children's voices should carry significant weight but remain largely absent. This is problematic given that those who have experienced violence and abuse have already lived in and through dynamics of subordination and disempowerment. Adult-child power relations play a part in shaping whose voices "count" and carry epistemological weight (Burman, 2017). Assumptions that children lack capacity, maturity and rationality shape a landscape in which their voices and experiences are taken less seriously and carry less weight (Burman, 2017; James & Prout, 2015). This kind of adult-centric knowledge production in the development of the intervention evidence base is problematic, and we point to the need to pay careful attention to how we attend to the expertise that children can offer about their own lives.

Recovery from DVA can be shaped by several factors and cannot be measured by a reduction of symptoms alone. We argue that a sole focus on outcomes in the evidence is problematic as it overlooks children's lived experiences and academics, practitioners and intervention stakeholders have a responsibility to challenge the structures which are set up to privilege particular kinds of "gold standard" evidence (e.g., "objective" and categorical). We recommend that there is value in generating a Core Outcome Set if meaningful outcomes and the tools that measure them are informed by children and if outcome reporting is not solely reliant on adults' voices.

"Trauma informed" practice and shared power

"Trauma informed care" has become a mainstreamed concept (Reeves, 2015), particularly in light of ACE and resilience agendas (Finkelhor, 2018; Leitch, 2017). However, this does not minimise the importance of exploring how issues of power, autonomy and agency can be worked with meaningfully and in a trauma-sensitive way with children affected by DVA. We suggest that closely attending to power and relationships, maximising autonomy and agency and working towards "power sharing" rather than "power over" (Elliott, Bjelajac, Fallot, Markoff & Reed, 2005; Kulkarni, 2019) relations are fundamental in research and service contexts. These are core for facilitating a space in which children can meaningfully engage with their recovery process and articulate their experiences.

In the context of working with children who have experienced DVA, we draw attention to Judith Herman's work on trauma recovery, in particular, her articulation that "no intervention that takes power away from the survivor can possibly foster recovery, no matter how much it appears to be in her immediate best interest" (Herman, 1992, p. 133). Facilitating personal empowerment is not simply about getting informed consent from children, and it is not about the act of asking children about their preferences. Children we spoke to showed that experiencing a sense of personal agency and power is a nuanced relational issue and not something we can "give" by offering a set of choices. Our findings show that children have the capacity to make informed choices about their participation in research and in services and that they welcome information and knowledge about this beforehand in a way that meets their individual needs. Furthermore, children do recognise when this does not happen and can articulate the impact this has on them and their experience of recovery.

Critical reflexivity

We have explored the multiple ways that children can express what is meaningful to them in ways that go beyond our particular outcome measures if we encourage and facilitate space for that and if we are willing to listen. We have highlighted the need for children's voices to be attentively listened to and acted upon in the development of interventions for children affected by DVA. We recommend that academics, practitioners and intervention stakeholders take a critically reflexive position in asking questions about their methods, recruitment practices, listening practices and evaluation measures.

Such questions may include: what action are we willing to take in light of what children deem important? How willing and able are we as adult researchers and practitioners to listen to all of what children communicate and their multiple ways of expressing themselves? How can we attend to power dynamics that shape **how** we invite children, **who** we invite and **how** we listen to them and put into action what we find?

Conclusion

When we first started conducting research with children who had experienced DVA, we knew little about what recovery looked like from their viewpoints. By children having the space to articulate what was important to them, we learned invaluable lessons about negotiating power, choice and agency and these lessons continue to challenge us. We hope that our experiences might help transform the current intervention evidence base to one that authentically centralises the voices of children.

References

Action for Children. (2019). *Patchy, Piecemeal and Precarious: Support for Children Affected by Domestic Abuse.* London.

Åkerlund, N., & Gottzén, L. (2017). Children's voices in research with children exposed to intimate partner violence: A critical review. *Nordic Social Work Research, 7*(1), 42–53. 10.1080/2156857X.2016.1156019

Barter, C., Stanley, N., Wood, M., Aghtaie, N., Larkins, C., Øverlien, C., ... Lesta, S. (2015). *Safeguarding Teenage Intimate Relationships (STIR): Connecting online and offline contexts and risks.* Retrieved from: http://stiritup.eu/wpcontent/uploads/2015/06/STIR-Exec-Summary-English.pdf

Beetham, T., Gabriel, L., & James, H. (2019). Young children's narrations of relational recovery: A school-based group for children who have experienced domestic violence. *Journal of Family Violence*, 1–11. 10.1007/s10896-018-0028-7

British Columbia Centre of Excellence for Women's Health (BCCEWH). (2013). *Review of Interventions to Identify, Prevent, Reduce and Respond to Domestic Violence.* Retrieved from: https://www.nice.org.uk/guidance/ph50/resources/review-of-interventions-toidentify-prevent-reduce-and-respond-to-domestic-violence2

Burman, E. (2017). *Deconstructing Developmental Psychology* (3rd ed.). London: Routledge.

Callaghan, J. E. M., & Alexander, J. H. (2015). *Understanding Agency and Resistance Strategies: Final Report for the European Commission.* Northampton: University of Northampton. 10.13140/RG.2.1.2509.2324

Callaghan, J. E. M., Alexander, J. H., Sixsmith, J., & Fellin, L. C. (2016). Children's experiences of domestic violence and abuse: Siblings' accounts of relational coping. *Clinical Child Psychology and Psychiatry, 21*(4), 649–668. 10.1177/1359104515620250

Carter, G. J. (2018). *Developing the Intervention Evidence Base for Children and Young People Who Have Experienced Domestic Violence and Abuse* (Unpublished doctoral thesis), University of Liverpool, Liverpool.

Cooper, J., & Vetere, A. (2008). *Domestic Violence and Family Safety: A Systemic Approach to Working with Violence in Families*. Chichester: Wiley and Sons.

Dixon-Woods, M., Agarwal, S., Jones, D., Young, B., & Sutton, A. (2005). Synthesising qualitative and quantitative evidence: A review of possible methods. *Journal of Health Services Research & Policy*, *10*(1), 45–53. 10.1177/135581960501000110

Downes, J., Kelly, L., & Westmarland, N. (2014). Ethics in violence and abuse research – A positive empowerment approach. *Sociological Research Online*, *19*(1), 1–13. 10.5153/sro.3140

Elliott, D. E., Bjelajac, P., Fallot, R. D., Markoff, L. S., & Reed, B. G. (2005). Trauma-informed or trauma-denied: Principles and implementation of trauma-informed services for women. *Journal of Community Psychology*, *33*(4), 461–477. 10.1002/jcop.20063

Eriksson, M., & Näsman, E. (2012). Interviews with children exposed to violence. *Children & Society*, *26*(1), 63–73. 10.1111/j.1099-0860.2010.00322.x

Evans, S. E., Davies, C., & DiLillo, D. (2008). Exposure to domestic violence: A meta-analysis of child and adolescent outcomes. *Aggression and Violent Behaviour*, *13*(2), 131–140. 10.1016/j.avb.2008.02.005

Finkelhor, D. (2018). Screening for adverse childhood experiences (ACEs): Cautions and suggestions. *Child Abuse & Neglect*, *85*, 174–179. 10.1016/J.CHIABU.2017.07.016

Fowler, D. N., & Chanmugam, A. (2007). A critical review of quantitative analyses of 205 children exposed to domestic violence: Lessons for practice and research. *Brief Treatment and Crisis Intervention*, *7*(4), 322–344. 10.1093/brieftreatment/mhm01

Gondolf, E. W. (2012). *The Future of Batterer Programs: Reassessing Evidence-Based Practice*. Boston: Northeastern University Press.

Graham-Bermann, S. A. (2000). Evaluating interventions for children exposed to family violence. *Journal of Aggression, Maltreatment, & Trauma*, *4*(1), 191–215. 10.1300/ J146v04n01_09.

Graham-Bermann, S. A. (2001). Designing intervention evaluations for children exposed to domestic violence: Applications of research and theory. In S. A. Graham-Bermann & J. L. Edleson (Eds.), *Domestic Violence in the Lives of Children: The Future of Research, Intervention, and Social Policy* (pp. 237–267). Washington: American Psychological Association.

Graham-Bermann, S. A., & Hughes, H. M. (2003). Intervention for children exposed to interparental violence (IPV): Assessment of needs and research priorities. *Clinical Child and Family Psychology Review*, *6*(3), 189–204. 10.1023/A:1024962400234

Holt, S., Buckley, H., & Whelan, S. (2008). The impact of exposure to domestic violence on children and young people: A review of the literature. *Child Abuse & Neglect*, *32*, 797–810. 10.1016/j.chiabu.2008.02.004

Herman, J. L. (1992). A syndrome in survivors of prolonged and repeated trauma. *Journal of Traumatic Stress*, *5*(3), 377–391.

Houghton, C. (2015). Young people's perspectives on participatory ethics: Agency, power and impact in domestic abuse research and policy-making. *Child Abuse Review*, *24*(4), 235–248. 10.1002/car.2407.

Houghton, C. (2017). Voice, agency, power: A framework for young survivor's participation in national domestic abuse policy-making. In S. Holt, C. Øverlien, & J. Devaney (Eds.), *Responding to Domestic Violence - Emerging Challenges for Policy,*

Practice and Research in Europe (pp. 77–96). Philadelphia: Jessica Kingsley Publishers.

Howarth, E., Moore, T. M., Shaw, A. G., Welton, N. J., Feder, G. S., Hester, M., … Stanley, N. (2015). The effectiveness of targeted interventions for children exposed to domestic violence: Measuring success in ways that matter to children, parents and professionals. *Child Abuse Review, 24*(4), 297–310. 10.1002/car.2408

Howarth, E., Moore, T. H., Welton, N. J., Lewis, N., Stanley, N., MacMillan, H., …Feder, G. (2016). Improving outcomes for children exposed to domestic violence (IMPROVE): An evidence synthesis. *Public Health Research, 4*(10), 1–342. 10.3310/phr04100

James, A., & Prout, A. (2015). *Constructing and Reconstructing Childhood: Contemporary Issues in the Sociological Study of Childhood* (2nd ed.). New York: Routledge.

Katz, E. (2016). Beyond the physical incident model: How children living with domestic violence are harmed by and resist regimes of coercive control. *Child Abuse Review, 25*(1), 46–59. 10.1002/car.2422

Kitzmann, K. M., Gaylord, N. K., Holt, A. R., & Kenny, E. D. (2003). Child witnesses to domestic violence: A meta-analytical review. *Journal of Consulting and Clinical Psychology 17*(12), 339–352. 10.1037/0022-006X.71.2.33

Kulkarni, S. (2019). Intersectional trauma-informed intimate partner violence (IPV) services: Narrowing the gap between IPV service delivery and survivor needs. *Journal of Family Violence, 34*(1), 55–64. 10.1007/s10896-018-0001-5

Leitch, L. (2017). Action steps using ACEs and trauma-informed care: A resilience model. *Health & Justice, 5*(1), 5. 10.1186/s40352-017-0050-5

MacMillan, H. L., Wathen, C. N., Barlow, J., Fergusson, D. M., Leventhal, J. M., & Taussig, H. N. (2009). Interventions to prevent child maltreatment and associated impairment. *The Lancet, 373*(9659), 250–266. 10.1016/S01406736(08)61708-0

Øverlien, C., & Holt, S. (2017). Including children and adolescents in domestic violence research: When myths and misconceptions compromise participation. In S. Holt, C. Øverlien, & J. Devaney (Eds.), *Responding to Domestic Violence - Emerging Challenges for Policy, Practice and Research in Europe* (pp. 97–112). Philadelphia: Jessica Kingsley Publishers.

Pernebo, K., & Almqvist, K. (2016). Young children's experiences of participating in group treatment for children exposed to intimate partner violence: A qualitative study. *Clinical Child Psychology and Psychiatry, 21*(1), 119–132. 10.1177/1359104514558432

Radford, L., Corral, S., Bradley, C., & Fisher, H. L. (2013). The prevalence and impact of child maltreatment and other types of victimization in the UK: Findings from a population survey of caregivers, children and young people and young adults. *Child Abuse & Neglect, 37*(10), 801–813. 10.1016/j.chiabu.2013.02.00

Reeves, E. (2015). A synthesis of the literature on trauma-informed care. *Issues in Mental Health Nursing, 36*(9), 698–709. 10.3109/01612840.2015.1025319

Rizo, C., Macy, R., Ermentrout, D., & Johns, N. (2011). A review of family interventions for intimate partner violence with a child focus or child component. *Aggression and Violent Behaviour, 16*(2), 144–166. 10.1016/j.avb.2011.02.004

Romano, E., Weegar, K., Galllitto, E., Zak, S., & Saini, M. (2019). Meta-Analysis on interventions for children exposed to intimate partner violence. *Trauma, Violence & Abuse*, 1–11. 10.1177/1524838019881737

Sanders-McDonagh, E., Neville, L., & Nolas, S.-M. (2016). From pillar to post: Understanding the victimisation of women and children who experience domestic violence in an age of austerity. *Feminist Review, 112*(1), 60–76. 10.1057/fr.2015.51

Swanston, J., Bowyer, L., & Vetere, A. (2014). Towards a richer understanding of school-age children's experiences of domestic violence: The voices of children and their mothers. *Clinical Child Psychology and Psychiatry, 19*(2), 184–201. 10.1177/1359104513485082

Tisdall, E. K. M. (2017). Conceptualising children and young people's participation: Examining vulnerability, social accountability and co-production. *International Journal of Human Rights, 21*(1), 59–75. 10.1080/13642987.2016.1248125

Ugazio, V. (2013). *Semantic Polarities and Psychopathologies in the Family: Permitted and Forbidden Stories.* London: Routledge.

Vacchelli, E., Kathrecha, P., & Gyte, N. (2015). Is it really just the cuts? Neo-liberal tales from the women's voluntary and community sector in London. *Feminist Review, 109*(1), 180–189. 10.1057/fr.2014.38

Vetere, A., & Cooper, J. (2005). *Domestic Violence and Family Safety.* In J. Cooper & A. Vetere (Eds.). London: Whurr Publishers Ltd. 10.1002/9780470713112

Wolfe, D. A., Crooks, C. V., Lee, V., McIntyre-Smith, A., & Jaffe, P. G. (2003). The effects of children's exposure to domestic violence: A meta-analysis and critique. *Clinical Child and Family Psychology Review, 6*(3), 171–187. 10.1023/A:1024910416164.

12 How children talk about domestic abuse in the home

Insights for practitioners

Samuel Larner[1] *and Mark McGlashan*[2]

[1]*Manchester Metropolitan University*
[2]*Birmingham City University*

Introduction

Few scholars would dispute the central role of children's voices in research exploring their experiences of living in homes with domestic abuse,[1] both to gain their insight into how they understand their problems (Øverlien, 2010) and to recognise the importance of their individual experiences (Swanston et al., 2014). As Callaghan et al. (2017a) argue, children must not be seen as passive witnesses. However, gaining access to those crucial voices is fraught with problems. First, on a methodological level, simply gaining access to children for participation in research can be very difficult (Øverlien, 2010). Second, children can be distrusting of adults and their responses to disclosures, which constitutes a significant barrier to disclosing being a witness to, or victim of, domestic abuse (Callaghan et al., 2017b). As such, it is unsurprising that children more commonly disclose to a same-aged peer: they are more likely to disclose to a friend rather than a close or familiar adult (Howell et al., 2014).

Due to the challenges of working with children described earlier, we have insufficient understanding of domestic violence from the child's perspective, particularly as told in an authentic context, free from power dyads or fear that the disclosure might lead to unwanted action being taken. Indeed, the knowledge that has been accrued has largely been derived from retrospective semi-structured interviews with adults who were victims as children (Callaghan et al., 2015; Naughton et al., 2019; Stanley et al., 2012). Whilst such an approach provides a safe space for researcher and participant to collaboratively explore their ideas, they are situated within a context that may influence participant responses and are reliant on the adults having accurate recollection of the events and their experiences. The current state of knowledge largely reflects adults' memories of experiences of domestic abuse, rather than their experiences in the moment.

Further, many children are recruited to participate in such interviews through treatment and intervention programmes or through their residence at refuge homes (Izaguirre & Cater, 2018; Ornduff & Monahan, 1999; Peled, 1998), meaning that the children who constitute such samples do not represent

DOI: 10.4324/9781003124634-16

participants at the most vulnerable point of disclosure: they will have been well informed about the wrongful actions of the aggressor, which may have affected their willingness to talk. The content and structure of their narratives are unlikely to be in their rawest, most authentic form and the children's thoughts and feelings about domestic abuse will, in many cases, have been shaped and re-framed to some extent. Moreover, studies of participants which focus pre-dominantly on children of refugee backgrounds, whilst providing valuable and necessary insight into their particular experiences, perhaps do not represent broader experiences of other children in the community (Swanston et al., 2014). Naughton et al. (2019) offer a notable exception with none of their 14 parti-cipants having undergone specific treatment for exposure to domestic violence; that said, 12 of the 14 participants did disclose that they had received treatment for mental health conditions (although no link between the mental health treatment and domestic violence is stated or implied by Naughton et al. (2019)).

To overcome some of the limitations of previous research and to more accurately capture the experiences of children who live in homes where domestic abuse has occurred, the present research attempts to capture the voices of children at the point of informal disclosure to unknown peers: specifically, through their posts to an asynchronous online support forum. For this purpose, our data came from Childline[2] message boards. By working directly with the words that children use in a naturalistic, non-experimental context that is in the moment rather than relying on self-reports, their voices may be more authentically represented. This chapter begins by exploring how data was captured and the way in which ethics were considered before re-porting the findings from an initial exploratory analysis focussing specifically on how children talk about their feelings. We conclude by highlighting the significance of our findings for practitioners involved in supporting children who have witnessed or been subjected to domestic abuse.

Data: A methodological challenge

Data were collected in late 2019 from Childline's online message boards.[3] Posts made to these message boards are organised around a set of broad **categories** that group together specific **topics** of discussion. For example, the message board **category** "bullying, abuse and keeping safe" subsumes the following **topics**:

• bullying and discrimination
• emotional abuse
• neglect
• online safety and cyber bullying
• physical abuse
• racism
• sexual abuse

The Childline message board provides a search function which enables users to search for and identify topics of interest through the selection of broad **categories** and subsidiary **topics** as well as through searching the message boards using specific **search terms**.

Regarding the present research, *domestic abuse* does not exist as either a **category** or **topic** on the message board, but reports of domestic abuse (henceforth, DA) are present in the Childline online message boards. Although many of the reports are framed as abuse, only a small minority directly refer to "domestic abuse" when reporting incidents of behaviour that characterise DA. Most reports do not, for example:

> I'm [Age] and I go to high school. My mum and I have been living with her abusive boyfriend for [X] years by now and honestly, it was terrible. Here is why:
> [...]
> -He took of my mums clothes and even called me to come into the room. He also pressures[4] her for sex.

That many reports do not contain the term "domestic abuse" presents both methodological and analytical challenges in terms of how to first identify and second interpret language related to DA in posts on the Childline message boards. Relatedly, and more problematically, that Childline lacks a board dedicated to the discussion of DA presents a potential barrier to accessing community advice on DA as a generalised **topic**. Simply searching "domestic abuse" in the hope that all posts referring to DA are returned is insufficient to discover the variety of ways in which DA is codified, reported and discussed in the message boards. This methodological challenge is identified by Callaghan et al. (2017b). Based on semi-structured interviews with 107 children aged 8–18 years from across the United Kingdom, Greece, Italy and Spain, Callaghan et al. (2017b) found that their participants "expressed caution, suspicion and distrust about disclosure" (p. 3375) and that they commonly used euphemisms and understatements to describe their experiences, rather than directly labelling what they experienced as *violence* (p. 3375). They conclude that for "fraught and difficult experiences like domestic violence, the available language for children to articulate their experiences can be very limited" (p. 3382).

In response, we took an approach to sampling that would enable us to capture as many reports as possible of DA whilst also attempting to mitigate researcher bias. Although researchers may have intuitions about the contents of reports, it is important that these intuitions do not bias the "shape" of the data or analysis. Therefore, rather than attempting to generate an exhaustive list of search terms that we think reports of DA might contain or collecting posts in boards **categories/topics** that we might suspect would refer to DA, we adopted a form of purposive sampling that aimed to identify as many posts referring to DA as possible by detecting which boards and topics *tend to* attract discussion of DA (which may be characterised by DA, abuse or violence in the home or "family violence"). Our sampling method thus began by identifying posts that matched searches containing combinations of (domestic OR home OR family) AND (abuse OR violence). Specifically:

- domestic AND abuse
- domestic AND violence
- home AND abuse
- home AND violence
- family AND abuse
- family AND violence

Search results enabled us to tabulate how resulting posts were distributed across different **categories** (Figure 12.1) and **topics** (Figure 12.2) and found that posts matching the earlier searches occurred most frequently in the message board **categories** *bullying, abuse and keeping safe* and *home and school* (Table 12.1; Figure 12.2) and, more specifically, within the **topics** *emotional abuse, sexual abuse, physical abuse* and *home and family* (Table 12.1; Figure 12.2).

Using this information about the distribution of posts that may contain reference to DA, we are able to make an educated guess that these topics tend to attract posts containing reference to DA but also acknowledge that the terminology of our search terms might not accurately capture all discussions of DA within these topics. As such, to analyse the potential variety of discussions of DA within these topics, we collected **all** posts made to the message board **topics** given in Table 12.1, resulting in a corpus containing data from **3,242** posts, which contain a total of **521,395** words (Table 12.2).

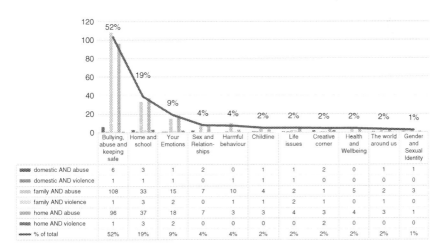

	Bullying, abuse and keeping safe	Home and school	Your Emotions	Sex and Relationships	Harmful behaviour	Childline	Life issues	Creative corner	Health and Wellbeing	The world around us	Gender and Sexual Identity
domestic AND abuse	6	3	1	2	0	1	1	2	0	1	1
domestic AND violence	1	1	1	0	1	1	1	0	0	0	0
family AND abuse	108	33	15	7	10	4	2	1	5	2	3
family AND violence	1	3	2	0	1	1	2	1	0	1	0
home AND abuse	96	37	18	7	3	3	4	3	4	3	1
home AND violence	1	3	2	0	0	0	0	2	0	0	0
% of total	52%	19%	9%	4%	4%	2%	2%	2%	2%	2%	1%

Figure 12.1 Post frequency by Childline message board category.

Figure 12.2 Post frequency by Childline message board topic.

Table 12.1 Distribution of posts matching search terms across different message board topics. Most frequent shown

Category	Topic	Number of posts	% of total number of posts
Bullying, abuse and keeping safe	Emotional abuse	98	24%
	Sexual abuse	59	14%
	Physical abuse	58	14%
Home and school	Home and Family	50	12%
Totals		**265**	**64%**

Table 12.2 Distribution of posts according to category and topic

Category	Topic	Size of sub corpus (posts)	Size of sub corpus (words)
Bullying, abuse and keeping safe	Emotional abuse	426	78,078
	Sexual abuse	725	128,048
	Physical abuse	256	36,485
Home and school	Home and Family	1,835	278,784
Totals		**3,242**	**521,395**

Ethical considerations

The message boards exist freely in the public domain and no barriers exist to prevent the data from being downloaded. All children posting to the Childline message boards do so anonymously. Indeed, Childline moderators review each individual post prior to publication to ensure that it does not contain personal information. This means that no identifying names, addresses, telephone numbers, e-mail addresses, place names or any other details which could potentially identify the children are posted. Furthermore, this chapter does not include any extensive direct quotation from the posts in which participants could potentially be identified. Where we do rely on direct quotation to illustrate a point, the smallest stretch of discourse is used, of course, avoiding anything that might provide contextual details particular to an individual (noting again that Childline moderates all content for this type of material specifically, so it is highly unlikely that there will be any identificatory material in the posts). The protocol of downloading social media data, provided that anonymity and respect are afforded to the participants, is widely documented in the corpus linguistics literature (Coles & West, 2016; Hardaker, 2013; Herring et al., 2002). This research is therefore fully compliant with the ethical standards and expectations of corpus linguistics research and full ethical approval was granted by the Faculty of Arts and Humanities Research Ethics Committee (Manchester Metropolitan University).

Table 12.3 Posts which directly reference "domestic abuse"

Left of keyword	KWIC	Right of keyword
and alone at the moment my child's dad has been	domestically	abusive to me and tried breaking into my parents garden
let me give you the run down my parents were	domestically	abusive and got divorced when I was 6 my dad
to what happened my primary school headteacher would put out	domestic	abuse helplines hoping my mum would call them I only
woman being hit by a man your first thought is	domestic	abuse but if you see a man being hit by
hitting yelling cops were called and i was nearly arrested	domestic	violence assault 4th degree my mom wouldn't speak to me
bit up and down she has been through a lot	domestic	abuse multiple times from different partners drug and alcohol abuse
part in a family where there is a history of	domestic	abuse but some people just don't listen learn or care
i had a bad childhood anyway i was sexually assualted	domestically	and emotionally abused and with being the older sister i've

Findings

As discussed earlier, challenges exist for the identification and interpretation of reports of DA in the message boards. That explicit, direct reference to DA in posts is rare and presents a challenge for analysis. When searching for direct reference to "domestic abuse" in the corpus described in Table 12.2, just nine posts were identified (0.28% of the corpus) of which eight referred directly to a form of DA as shown in Table 12.3. Following corpus linguistics conventions, the middle column shows the keyword in context (KWIC), i.e., the lemma *domestic**. The left column shows the words that immediately precede the KWIC and the righthand column shows the words that immediately follow the KWIC.

These reports include DA involving the respondent, reports of DA between parents, reports of child abuse and a single question about DA as a gendered phenomenon. To potentially capture reports of DA that do not include explicit reference, our analysis here first explores some quantitative linguistic findings on the corpus (see Table 12.2) before discussing the contents of the posts in more qualitative detail.

Quantitative linguistic analysis

Quantitative analysis begins here with an exploration of some frequent features of the texts. Table 12.4 gives 4 lists showing the top 30 most frequent words, lemma (dictionary headwords; the canonical form of a group of words), and variants of these lists which have had grammatically closed-class words, words that have restricted grammatical functions and limited semantic

Table 12.4 Top 30 most frequent words

Rank	Words			Words (stopwords removed)			Lemma			Lemma (stopwords removed)		
	Feature	Freq.	DocFreq.	Feature	Freq.	DocFreq.	Feature	Freq.	DocFreq.	Feature	Freq.	DocFreq.
1	i	28605	3131	just	3210	1657	i	28607	3131	mum	3231	1535
2	and	21805	3091	like	3006	1613	and	21805	3091	just	3211	1658
3	to	17222	3030	mum	2998	1483	to	17222	3030	get	3130	1736
4	my	16254	3020	know	2698	1696	my	16254	3020	like	3115	1641
5	me	12354	2779	really	2392	1404	me	12354	2779	know	2923	1763
6	the	8907	2547	feel	2364	1349	it	9056	2578	feel	2906	1531
7	a	7984	2557	dad	2235	1185	the	8907	2547	want	2656	1516
8	it	7091	2354	get	2181	1403	a	7986	2557	dad	2416	1231
9	but	6294	2473	im	2102	966	he	6561	1445	realli	2393	1405
10	he	6116	1402	want	2034	1283	but	6297	2474	go	2227	1319
11	was	5486	1731	dont	1493	821	was	5486	1731	im	2102	966
12	of	5093	2081	now	1451	1057	she	5481	1380	say	1909	1183
13	she	5079	1351	time	1419	1008	that	5148	2010	time	1820	1197
14	that	4829	1956	parents	1405	886	of	5093	2081	thing	1703	1101
15	in	4468	2043	can	1365	986	have	4546	2051	year	1692	1132
16	is	4391	2016	always	1347	885	in	4468	2043	make	1618	1072
17	so	4270	1991	go	1297	896	is	4391	2016	tell	1581	1051
18	have	4118	1956	told	1273	849	so	4270	1991	friend	1546	896
19	with	4010	1962	things	1258	869	with	4011	1962	parent	1534	943
20	for	3601	1843	said	1244	739	do	3990	2049	dont	1493	821
21	do	3508	1939	help	1241	941	for	3602	1843	now	1452	1057
22	this	3405	1763	even	1220	877	this	3405	1763	help	1395	1026
23	at	3365	1765	school	1215	770	at	3365	1765	think	1368	942
24	just	3210	1657	one	1173	856	mum	3231	1535	can	1367	988
25	her	3112	1124	tell	1100	812	just	3211	1658	alway	1350	887
26	like	3006	1613	got	1095	793	get	3130	1736	tri	1286	876
27	mum	2998	1483	never	1079	778	her	3122	1125	told	1273	849
28	on	2943	1673	think	1014	737	be	3117	1665	even	1254	894
29	when	2897	1623	friends	1008	689	like	3115	1641	school	1251	781
30	him	2863	1097	going	930	694	on	2943	1673	said	1244	739

content; also referred to as *stopwords* removed.[5] These lists are ranked by the frequency of the items in the *Feature* column and *DocFreq*, which shows how many texts a feature is distributed across.

The most frequent items in the words and lemma lists show a frequent use of personal pronouns (*I, my, me, he, she, her, him*), conjunctions (*and, but*) and articles (*a, the*), which are extremely common and well distributed across the corpus but do not reveal much (at the lexical level) about the topic of the posts being analysed. Other, more open-class words some of which are just as common and well distributed as pronouns, conjunctions and articles also appear to reveal some common topics of the posts in the corpus. Specifically, topics relating to relationships, including parents (*parents, mum, dad*) and *friends* and concerns relating to *school*, are some of the most common themes. Given the focus of this chapter on DA, we are unable to explore all of these topics but posts that focus on relations with and between *parents* may correlate broadly with discussions of DA in the posts from these message boards. As such, we focussed our discussion on only those posts that contained at least one reference to the lemma of both *mum* and *dad* in order to examine how children discuss relationships with and between these parents.

The more concentrated focus on posts referring explicitly to parents returned a smaller sample of 866 posts to work with (26.71% of the corpus). These 866 posts were manually read and all instances in which children expressed concern about some form of abuse or conflict between parents were selected, which resulted in a smaller set of 162 texts (henceforth, the DA corpus). Table 12.5 shows the top 100 frequently occurring words in the DA corpus, ranked by the frequency of the items in the *Word* column. The column labelled *Texts* indicates how many texts contain at least one instance of the *word* and the column labelled *Freq.* indicates how many instances of the word there are across the entire DA corpus.

There are many interesting aspects to the words that have been identified as occurring most frequently in the small DA corpus, as exemplified in Table 12.5. For instance, the first-person pronoun (*I*) indicates the personal nature of these disclosures and the references to *mum* (rank 9), *dad* (rank 12) and *parents* (rank 58) are to be expected since these posts were selected specifically for the reference to parents. Other words offer further opportunity for investigation such as *things* (rank 70) in terms of understanding what sorts of issues children are ambiguous or vague about (e.g., referring to specific events as *things*). Equally, *think* and *know* are interesting in terms of understanding what claims to knowledge children make about domestic abuse, and their opinions and *want* may provide insight into children's needs. However, one word that stands out as being particularly insightful, and which has support from the salient literature, is *feel* (which ranks at 51 and occurs 119 times across 67 texts). Naughton et al. (2019) carried out semi-structured interviews with 13 university students to understand how young people construct domestic violence and abuse in their families and how those constructions may affect the way they report their experiences. They found that participants constructed domestic violence and abuse as physical violence only

Table 12.5 The 100 most frequent words in DA corpus

N	Word	Texts	Freq.	N	Word	Texts	Freq.	N	Word	Texts	Freq.
1	I	156	1429	34	ABOUT	93	165	67	HOW	53	83
2	AND	160	1404	35	HAS	84	163	68	ARE	57	81
3	MY	160	1244	36	REALLY	90	161	69	NEVER	55	77
4	TO	156	1022	37	WHAT	100	157	70	THINGS	58	76
5	ME	138	586	38	BE	87	154	71	HELP	46	75
6	THE	136	568	39	NOT	85	150	72	GO	44	71
7	HE	101	479	40	DON'T	67	148	73	ONE	51	71
8	A	141	477	41	KNOW	83	147	74	YEARS	52	70
9	MUM	162	430	42	IF	74	143	75	THERE	50	68
10	BUT	136	394	43	LIKE	84	140	76	EVEN	50	66
11	IT	130	375	44	OR	79	134	77	GOT	48	66
12	DAD	161	366	45	WE	67	130	78	HOUSE	41	66
13	SHE	92	364	46	AS	65	128	79	OTHER	50	66
14	OF	120	318	47	GET	81	127	80	US	41	66
15	IS	116	310	48	ALL	80	124	81	BROTHER	37	65
16	THAT	114	282	49	UP	80	123	82	AM	43	62
17	WAS	92	269	50	I'M	68	122	83	ALSO	44	60
18	IN	116	265	51	FEEL	67	119	84	FROM	49	60

(Continued)

Table 12.5 (Continued)

N	Word	Texts	Freq.	N	Word	Texts	Freq.	N	Word	Texts	Freq.
19	HER	97	256	52	OUT	75	113	85	GOING	39	60
20	HAVE	115	251	53	BEEN	70	111	86	BEING	40	59
21	WITH	106	239	54	WANT	68	109	87	THEM	42	59
22	FOR	103	229	55	ALWAYS	70	108	88	STARTED	39	58
23	HIM	86	221	56	NOW	69	104	89	TOLD	37	58
24	SO	98	220	57	HAD	58	99	90	AN	44	57
25	DO	117	217	58	PARENTS	62	96	91	ANYTH-ING	47	57
26	AT	106	212	59	IM	45	95	92	BACK	41	57
27	THIS	104	208	60	WOULD	51	94	93	IT'S	35	57
28	#	87	203	61	DONT	46	90	94	ITS	38	56
29	JUST	95	190	62	HIS	43	90	95	MUCH	45	56
30	BECA-USE	86	185	63	TIME	72	87	96	THINK	40	56
31	WHEN	92	180	64	THEN	56	86	97	ANYONE	46	55
32	ON	99	171	65	YOU	34	84	98	DAY	39	54
33	THEY	71	171	66	CAN	62	83	99	OVER	37	54
								100	NO	38	53

and, in so doing, struggled to articulate the psychological aspects as a form of domestic violence and abuse. Furthermore, their analysis revealed that their participants normalised incidents and the behaviours that they had witnessed, meaning that it is harder for children to recognise that intervention is warranted. It seems then, that during research interviews at least, these young people struggled to articulate their feelings. Furthermore, Callaghan et al. (2017a) carried out an analysis of two case studies of interviews which explored the ways that siblings care for their brothers and sisters in families where domestic violence occurs. In one of the case studies, Callaghan et al. highlight that the 11-year-old child talked to her teddies about her feelings because there was no space within the family to talk about the domestic violence and abuse she was experiencing. They note that this is a "far from optimum way to express herself" (p. 20). Through an exploration of the word *feel*, it may be possible to better understand what children feel about their experiences of domestic violence. From the outset, however, we anticipate that the volume of examples will be few, so due caution will be exercised in interpreting and understanding our findings. We return to this matter in the conclusion.

What do children feel about domestic abuse?

For the purposes of this analysis, concordances[6] were extracted for the lemma *feel** (i.e., *feel, feeling, feelings*). Whilst *feel* occurred 119 times across 67 texts, the cumulation of *feel, feeling* and *feelings* generated 149 entries across 80 texts. Table 12.6 provides a list of the 100 most frequent words which collocate (co-occur) with *feel** in the DA corpus.

The same pattern as identified for Table 12.4 is evident for Table 12.6; that is, the prevalence of personal pronouns, conjunctions and articles. However, in terms of emotion terms, it is apparent that the emotions most frequently "felt" are negative, with *bad* being the most frequently expressed feeling (11 times across 9 texts) and words relating to loneliness (*alone, lonely*) being expressed 10 times across 9 texts. It is notable, however, that two positive terms are used in relation to feelings: *better* and *happy*. The following qualitative analysis explores how feelings are reported across the DA corpus.

There are 11 instances of children reporting feeling *bad* and these can be grouped into three types:

- other people exploiting the young person's feelings (n = 4)

  o e.g., *she has a go at me and tries to make me feel bad*

- the young person concerned with helping/protecting others (n = 5)

  o e.g., *my family aren't the most well off so now I feel really bad*

- the young person not getting support (n = 2)

  o e.g., *It makes me feel bad because I can't talk to anyone anymore*

Table 12.6 The 100 most frequent collocates of *feel** (emotions highlighted in red)

N	Word	Texts	Freq.	N	Word	Texts	Freq.	N	Word	Texts	Freq.
1	FEEL	67	119	35	DON'T	6	7	69	SOMETIMES	4	4
2	I	56	118	36	SHE	7	7	70	AT	4	4
3	AND	36	48	37	NOW	7	7	71	THOUGH	4	4
4	LIKE	26	35	38	MAKE	6	7	72	DEPRESSED	3	4
5	TO	22	33	39	JUST	7	7	73	DO	4	4
6	ME	21	27	40	I'M	4	7	74	BETTER	4	4
7	MY	17	19	41	IM	5	7	75	EVEN	4	4
8	#	9	16	42	BE	7	7	76	YOU	3	4
9	FEELS	14	14	43	ALONE	6	6	77	PEOPLE	4	4
10	BUT	13	14	44	AND	5	6	78	OTHER	4	4
11	FEELING	11	14	45	HAVE	6	6	79	ALL	4	4
12	THE	12	13	46	TO	5	6	80	FEELINGS	4	4
13	FOR	8	12	47	HE	5	6	81	TELL	3	3
14	THAT	9	11	48	REALLY	6	6	82	WHICH	2	3
15	SO	8	11	49	THEM	4	6	83	TO	2	3
16	IN	10	11	50	TALK	6	6	84	SINCE	3	3
17	BAD	9	11	51	GUILTY	4	5	85	SO	3	3
18	ABOUT	9	10	52	ONE	4	5	86	SHE	3	3
19	HE	9	10	53	DAD	4	5	87	SHOUTS	3	3

Rank	Word			Rank	Word			Rank	Word		
20	HER	7	9	54	MUM	5	5	88	MY	2	3
21	WHEN	7	9	55	THEY	4	5	89	TALKING	2	3
22	MAKES	9	9	56	ME	4	5	90	NO	3	3
23	IT	8	9	57	BEING	5	5	91	STILL	3	3
24	IT	7	8	58	IS	5	5	92	IT'S	3	3
25	THIS	7	8	59	IF	5	5	93	ALWAYS	3	3
26	HOW	7	8	60	NOT	5	5	94	CANT	3	3
27	OF	7	8	61	WAY	4	5	95	ANYONE	3	3
28	AS	7	8	62	AND	5	5	96	I	3	3
29	A	8	8	63	LONELY	3	4	97	BUT	3	3
30	WITH	6	8	64	LIKE	4	4	98	HAPPY	3	3
31	ALWAYS	7	8	65	NEVER	4	4	99	LIKE	2	3
32	BECAUSE	7	8	66	I	3	4	100	AROUND	2	3
33	HIM	6	8	67	ME	4	4				
34	CAN	7	7	68	SORRY	3	4				

Perhaps surprisingly, it is not necessarily the case that the domestic abuse itself directly makes children feel bad in this corpus; rather, their feelings are actively exploited by others (a sign of other forms of abuse, potentially) and that children feel bad because they cannot help and protect others, signalling their level of care and concern beyond how the situation affects them personally. Some examples reveal some concern for the abusive parent as illustrated in the following example where a father is abusive towards the mother: *most of us feel awkward talking to him (which I feel really bad about)*.

In terms of feeling *alone* and *lonely*, eight of the ten[7] examples state categorically that the children feel alone. They mention isolation and feeling that they have insufficient support: *He scares me sometimes. I feel alone, why won't my mum help me?* and *we have social workers and stuff but I feel like I'm alone in this world*. They report not being able to talk to anyone: *I have no one to talk to and feel completely alone* and grieving relationships they once had: *I feel so fucking lonely because I feel like I've lost her already and my dads never around*. In contrast to feeling *bad*, only one example expresses concern for other people's loneliness, offering to share her story so that other people *don't feel alone*.

Of the five instances of *guilt* and two instances of *guilty* identified in the corpus, two relate to feeling guilty about the abusive situation itself and specifically the young person's (perceived) role in the abuse: *I remember so much and I feel so guilty* and *I feel so guilty out what happened so i cannot tell her*. The remaining five instances express feeling guilt for other people's circumstances and concerns: *i feel guilty for being uncomfortable alone around him* (i.e., a concern for the abusive parent's feelings) and *I feel especially guilty as all of her money is being spent on my school fees* (i.e., guilt because of how a parent allocated limited financial resources).

From five instances of feeling *sorry*, one young person reports not wanting pity (*I have no one I can talk to without them feeling sorry for me*), two instances of feeling sorry for another person (e.g., *I do feel sorry for my mum*) and two instances of others feeling sorry for how the young person feels (e.g., in explaining why it's difficult to talk to others about their situation, the young person complains that the abusive parents' reactions are always *Im sorry that you feel this way about me* rather than *I'm sorry I make you feel this way*).

There are four instances of *depressed*: two children report feeling depressed because of other people's actions (*he is making me feel "low," "unwanted" and "depressed"* and *my mum has been really making me feel depressed and angry with myself*) and one occasion where it is the experience of domestic abuse itself causing the depression (*i always feel depressed, sad and anxious*). A further example reports a counsellor providing suggestions for how to feel less depressed.

Two words, *happy* and *better*, may suggest a more positive outlook and therefore need to be considered. There are three instances of feeling *happy*. However, in each of the examples of *happy*, that feeling is negated (*I just feel*

I can never be happy, i feel like shes never happy with me, and *I dont feel happy anymore*). We can therefore state with some certainty (unsurprisingly) that children are not happy living in homes with domestic abuse. What about the situation getting *better*? There are just four examples: one is an instance of a mother using the term sarcastically to indicate it would be better for the child to move out if she's so unhappy, one young person asks for advice about how to make her parents feel better (*is there anything you can do to try to make them feel a bit better?*), one example is negated as with *happy* (*I just feel like nothing will get better*) and the final instance is more positive, in that the young person reflects on her father's behaviour: *He has been better lately and i feel relaxed more*). In other words, except for the last example, the use of *better* does not typically suggest that the young person is in a positive place.

These insights into feelings of *bad, alone, lonely, guilt, sorry* and *depression* highlight, unsurprisingly, the prevalence of negative feelings amongst children disclosing their experiences of living in a home with DA, but further reveal that many of the negative feelings are not the direct result of the domestic abuse, but rather a consequence of other people's actions or for a concern over other people. Furthermore, when positive feelings are described, they are typically negated, adding to the overwhelming tone of negativity in describing feelings. Bearing in mind the small size of the corpus, the fact that children who are directly experiencing domestic abuse express stronger consideration for others over themselves appears to be prevalent, which is testament to the altruism of these children. However, it may also raise concerns about whether these children are being supported sufficiently at this early point of disclosure with processing how the abuse affects them directly and how much of the emotional burden they assume. The children also use descriptions of feelings about DA to signal that other forms of abuse may be present. In relation to describing feeling *sorry* and *depressed*, some of the children were disclosing mental and emotional abuse directly perpetrated against them, within the wider context of DA.

Conclusions: Implications for practitioners

As we have stated throughout, the limitation of this study is the small corpus which has been used for analysis, and this was attributable to the difficulty with identifying message board posts related to DA, requiring us to develop a methodological approach for identifying reports of DA. We are confident that in identifying posts relating to *mum, dad* and *parent*, we have achieved this, but this does of course further delimit the scope of our investigation to only those reports by children of parental DA. Similarly, the analysis has been based on very small frequencies, so a good degree of caution must be expressed over the interpretation of our results. Nonetheless, this research has captured the voice of children at the height of their distress, making a confidential disclosure of domestic abuse anonymously to their peers. This provides the benefit of exploring what they feel at the precise moment of disclosure rather than relying on what they say they felt at a later point, when perhaps they have been more reflective or influenced by other events.

Our main finding is that children experiencing DA feel *bad, lonely, guilty, sorry* and *depressed.* We suggest that this will be unsurprising to practitioners. However, the insight gained from this analysis is in the words used by children to label these feelings. The somewhat generic but most frequently used term *bad* provides a platform on which practitioners may initiate deeper conversations to explore the root of this feeling in an attempt to help children demarcate what exactly they feel bad about, so that more meaningful support can be provided. The fact that some of the children in this sample are concerned with other people's feelings and circumstances, including the perpetrator's, often at the expense of their own feelings, legitimates practitioners' assumptions that children are very likely blaming themselves, even if children do not articulate this for themselves.

Notwithstanding the many possible barriers to children making disclosures of any form of abuse, the range of behaviours (and ways of talking about those behaviours) associated with DA discussed in the posts under study highlights the value of platforms such as the message boards provided by Childline as an important site for children to make disclosures of, and to seek advice on, experiences and behaviours witnessed in the home that they may not fully understand. However, the difficulty in finding a clear source of message board posts indicates that no clear outlet for discussing domestic abuse exists. Given that some of the children in this research have expressed the desire to talk to someone or more specifically that their feelings of loneliness were attributable to not having someone to talk to, suggests that a dedicated message board on the Childline website, to sit along the other categories and/or topics, may better facilitate requests for advice and the sharing of stories.

This of course speaks to the bigger issue that for all the children who use Childline message boards to discuss their experiences, there will be many more who do not. For such children, the feeling of loneliness and isolation will likely be higher if they have no other outlet for exploring their experiences and emotions. A more proactive approach to engaging at-risk children in difficult conversations may be beneficial since it shifts the burden away from the child having to initiate a conversation. However, such an approach may require reconsideration of how practitioners engage with children over safeguarding concerns. Of significance here is the fact that children's posts to a Childline message board do not (typically) constitute evidence in the way that a social worker or teacher talking to a child about safeguarding concerns likely will (Department for Education, 2020). This limits the extent to which some practitioners can have an informal conversation with a child about domestic abuse before their professional duty to make a formal referral is activated. Exploring further spaces and opportunities for children to talk informally about their experiences of domestic abuse may therefore be beneficial in helping them to understand their emotions. And of course, the fact that the children writing these posts were primarily disclosing to their peers is also significant: further research is needed into the changing dynamics between peer-to-peer disclosures and child-to-adult disclosures.

Whatever motivates children to disclose DA-related experiences, the findings in this chapter confirm previous findings (Callaghan et al., 2017a) that parental conflict and, indeed, abuse are oftentimes not talked about using the language of "domestic abuse." These findings might suggest that these experiences are not talked about by children as being forms of DA but may also suggest that children do not possess the language to fully articulate their experiences of DA. The findings from the work done here suggest that there may be a need for a specific space for children to report experiences of and seek help about DA, whether happening to them or others, as well as child-directed guidance on what may or may not constitute an instance of DA. Given that accounts of DA are often not described as DA and are reported alongside a variety of other issues being experienced by the child, implications may exist for practitioners in their being able to address and respond to reports of what a child might perceive to be DA but is not describing as such.

Notes

1 The term *domestic abuse* will be used throughout as a coverall term for all types of interpersonal violence and conflict (both verbal and non-verbal) that occurs within the home unless describing salient research where an alternative term is used (notably, *domestic violence*). The methods which drive our data collection do not allow us to use more nuanced terminology when describing our own data.
2 Childline is a free, confidential counselling and support service for young people in the UK aged up to 19 years old.
3 https://www.childline.org.uk/get-support/message-boards/
4 All extracts are reported faithfully including typographical errors as in the original. Where appropriate, we have redacted any potentially identificatory material such as the age of the child.
5 The reason for removing stopwords is to focus more directly on those less semantically restricted words in a corpus.
6 Citations of *feel* in the context in which they occur.
7 One example uses *alone* in the literal sense of not wanting to be *alone around* the abusive parent so has been excluded.

References

Callaghan, J. E. M., Alexander, J. H., Sixsmith, J., & Fellin, L. C. (2015). Beyond "witnessing": Children's experiences of coercive control in domestic violence and abuse. *Journal of Interpersonal Violence, 33*(10), 088626051561894. 10.1177/08862 60515618946

Callaghan, J. E. M., Alexander, J. H., Sixsmith, J., & Fellin, L. C. (2017a). Children's experiences of domestic violence and abuse: Siblings' accounts of relational coping. *Clinical Child Psychology and Psychiatry, 21*(4), 649–668. 10.1177/1359104515620250

Callaghan, J. E. M., Fellin, L. C., Mavrou, S., Alexander, J., & Sixsmith, J. (2017b). The management of disclosure in children's accounts of domestic violence: Practices of telling and not telling. *Journal of Child and Family Studies, 26*(12), 3370–3387. 10.1007/s10826-017-0832-3

Coles, B. A., & West, M. (2016). Trolling the trolls: Online forum users constructions of the nature and properties of trolling, *Computers in Human Behaviour, 60,* 233—244.

Department for Education (2020). *Keeping Children Safe in Education: Statutory Guidance for Schools and Colleges.* HM Government. https://assets.publishing. service.gov.uk/government/uploads/system/uploads/attachment_data/file/954314/ Keeping_children_safe_in_education_2020_-_Update_-_January_2021.pdf

Hardaker, C. (2013). "Uh … . not to be nitpicky,,,,,but … the past tense of drag is dragged, not drug.": An overview of trolling strategies. *Journal of Language Aggression and Conflict, 1*(1), 58–86. 10.1075/jlac 1 1 04har

Herring, S., Job-Sluder, K., Scheckler, R., & Barab, S. (2002). Searching for safety online: Managing "trolling" in a feminist forum. *The Information Society, 18*(5), 371–384. 10.1080/01972240290108186

Howell, K. H., Cater, Å. K., Miller-Graff, L. E., & Graham-Bermann, S. A. (2014). The process of reporting and receiving support following exposure to intimate partner violence during childhood. *Journal of Interpersonal Violence, 30*(16), 2886–2907. 10.1177/0886260514554289

Izaguirre, A., & Cater, Å. (2018). Child witnesses to intimate partner violence: Their descriptions of talking to people about the violence. *Journal of Interpersonal Violence, 33*(24), 3711–3731. 10.1177/0886260516639256

Naughton, C. M., O'Donnell, A. T., & Muldoon, O. T. (2019). Young people's constructions of their experiences of parental domestic violence: A discursive analysis'. *Journal of Family Violence, 34*(4), 345–355. 10.1007/s10896-018-0013-1

Ornduff, S. R., & Monahan, K. (1999). Children's understanding of parental violence. *Child and Youth Care Forum, 28*(5), 351–364. 10.1023/a:1021974429983

Øverlien, C. (2010). Children exposed to domestic violence. *Journal of Social Work, 10*(1), 80–97. 10.1177/1468017309350663

Peled, E. (1998). The experience of living with violence for preadolescent children of battered women. *Youth & Society, 29*(4), 395–430. 10.1177/0044118x98029004001

Stanley, N., Miller, P., & Richardson Foster, H. (2012). Engaging with children's and parents' perspectives on domestic violence. *Child & Family Social Work, 17*(2), 192–201. 10.1111/j.1365-2206.2012.00832.x

Swanston, J., Bowyer, L., & Vetere, A. (2014). Towards a richer understanding of school-age children's experiences of domestic violence: The voices of children and their mothers. *Clinical Child Psychology and Psychiatry, 19*(2), 184–201. 10.1177/ 1359104513485082

13 Psychological sequelae of witnessing intra-parental violence on children's development as individuals and (future) partners

Daniela Di Basilio

Ph.D., FHEA HCPC Registered Clinical Psychologist, The University of Manchester

Introduction

From birth, we show a propensity to learn from others, our caregivers in particular. Caregivers show us how to love, how to be loved and ultimately, what we can consider as 'love'. In a situation in which we are exposed to violence in our family context, we may learn to consider abuse as an acceptable component of our intimate relationships, or worse, as an integral part of them. The phenomenon accounting for the perpetration of violence against partners as being 'learnt' from previous generations is known as the 'intergenerational transmission of violence' (IGT) (Ehrensaft et al., 2003; Ehrensaft & Langhinrichsen-Rohling, 2022; Hou et al., 2016; Widom & Wilson, 2015). Practitioners, scholars and policymakers have often explained IGT using Social Learning Theory (SLT) (Anderson & Kras, 2005; Cochran et al., 2011; Kwong et al., 2003; Wareham et al., 2009).

This umbrella term encompasses different theories, whose common denominator is the idea that direct and/or indirect exposure to violence in the family of origin contributes to the formation of norms and beliefs regarding the appropriateness of violence against others, including partners. Well-known are, for example, Bandura's (1969; 1971; 1973) and Akers' (1973; 1998) SLTs, both emphasising the importance of observation and imitation: behavioural models can be learnt from early stages of life 'on a vicarious basis, through observation of other people's behaviour and its consequences for them' (Bandura, 1971, p. 2). Drawing upon SLT, the intergenerational model of violence suggests that children's direct experience of abuse, and/or the observation of violence between their parents, will increase their chances of developing an abusive relationship with their partners in adulthood. A consistent body of research has offered support to the IGT as a model explaining domestic violence (DV) perpetration and victimisation (Brownridge, 2006; Godbout et al., 2019; Hou et al., 2016; Kerley et al., 2010; Smith-Marek et al., 2015). Nevertheless, the IGT model as an explanation for DV is not exempt from criticism: if it is true that we 'learn to be violent', learning that DV is not acceptable (particularly if this

DOI: 10.4324/9781003124634-17

is learnt at a young age) should be enough to break the intergenerational cycle of abuse. In other words, teaching children that DV is to be avoided should prevent it from occurring in later stages of life, or at least should counteract the effects of DV exposure in the family of origin, reducing the severity of abuse perpetrated against partners. Yet, systematic reviews on the effectiveness of DV prevention programmes involving young people (e.g., De La Rue et al., 2014; Graham, 2021; Whitaker et al., 2006) concur to indicate that increased knowledge about violence may not be sufficient to prevent DV in adulthood.

This considered, we may need to look for an explanation of DV that has to do with a 'deeper' level of learning about oneself and others. Indeed, most of the learning processes occurring in childhood happen at an implicit, non-verbal level, particularly in the early stages of development (Ammaniti, 2018; Steele et al., 2008; Vallotton, 2008). The interactions with our caregiver's form affect-loaded representations of ourselves and others that scholars have referred to using different definitions, despite the remarkable similarities across them. One of the most notable conceptualisations of these internal representations derives from the work of John Bowlby, who drew from psychoanalytic concepts and cognitive theories to propose the concept of 'Internal Working Models' (IWMs; Bowlby, 1969; 1973; 1980). IWMs are experience-based representations of the self, attachment figures and the characteristics of our relationships with them. Once developed, they will provide a 'script' for our interactions with loved ones, that will inform and shape the relationships we will form throughout our life (Sherman et al., 2015; Waters & Waters, 2006). If we have experienced primary caregivers who were consistently available, warm and loving, we will be likely to have positive IWMs of ourselves and others, whilst having caregivers who were emotionally unavailable, insensitive, frightening or rejecting may lead us to consider other people as generally unavailable, unreliable or potentially dangerous (Fraley, 2002; Sutton, 2019; Thompson, 2021; Tougas et al., 2016). Together with information about others and what we can expect from them, the IMWs entail perceptions of ourselves, for example, as worthy of being loved, likely to be abandoned or at risk of being hurt or rejected (Cassidy, 2000). Research on adult attachment, pioneered by the work conducted by Cindy Hazan and Phillip Shaver (Hazan & Shaver, 1987; Shaver & Hazan, 1988; Shaver et al., 1988) suggested that different attachment configurations can emerge from the combination of positive and negative views of self and others. Their model encompassed three categories of adult attachment style: secure, anxious/ambivalent and avoidant. A few years later, their model was further elaborated by Bartholomew (1990) and Bartholomew and Horowitz (1991), who proposed a four-category classification of adult attachment that encompassed the categories of secure, preoccupied, dismissing-avoidant and fearful-avoidant attachment. These four categories are the result of the intersection between two main dimensions: the internal model of self (positive vs. negative) (Figure 13.1).

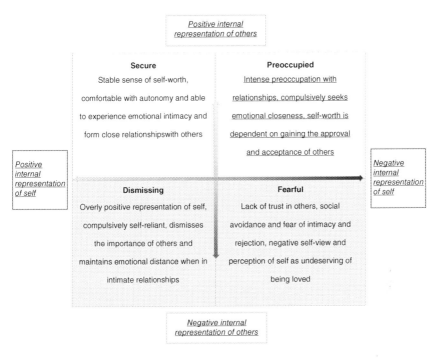

Figure 13.1 Categorisation of adult attachment proposed by Bartholomew and Horowitz (1991).

Secure individuals (positive models of the self and others) tend to have high levels of self-esteem and are likely to feel comfortable with intimacy and emotional closeness. *Preoccupied* individuals (negative model of the self but positive model of others) are characterised by a desire for closeness, a tendency to develop emotional dependence and an intense fear of abandonment. The distinctive features of the *dismissing-avoidant* pattern (positive model of self and negative view of others) include self-reliance, emotional withdrawal, discomfort with intimacy and tendency to down-play the importance of intimate relationships. Last, *fearful-avoidant* individuals (negative models of self and others) tend to avoid closeness due to fear of rejection, despite their yearning for intimacy and connection, thereby experiencing an insoluble conflict between the need to maintain a 'safe distance' from others and the desire to feel close to them.

The concept of IMWs highlight the direct influence that early experiences with caregivers can have on our identity as 'intimate partners' and offer a valuable explanation for the presence of the intergenerational cycle of abuse. first, it is important to consider that our IWMs are, indeed, *working*, i.e., far from being 'memories of the past', they bear an influence on our present choices and experiences. For example, they guide our expectations of how others will feel towards us and whether we can expect that they will be loving and caring or, instead, dismissive and rejecting. New information is 'filtered' by, and assimilated into, existing IWMs, meaning that our partners' behaviour is interpreted according to our pre-existing expectations. Second, our IMWs tend to remain coherent and resistant to change, as new information will undergo a process of 'accommodation' to 'fit into' existing frames of reference (Fraley & Shaver, 2000). For example, individuals with a fearful-avoidant attachment style may experience moments of deep emotional proximity with their partners but use violence to re-establish a distance from them when they start to perceive their partner's attachment needs, or their own, as overbearing. Dismissing-avoidant individuals may use violence to preserve their emotional autonomy and reinforce their 'boundaries', discouraging their partner from seeking intimacy or manifesting attachment needs (which tend to be perceived as threatening or intrusive). 'Preoccupied' individuals may remain in an abusive relationship due to the fear of losing their partner and may even selectively (albeit, at least partly, unconsciously) attract partners that have dominant traits. Indeed, partners with a propensity for coercion and control may be perceived – due to 'preoccupied' individuals' tendency to depend on their loved ones and compulsively seek their approval – as being 'reassuring' and therefore, desirable. These considerations find support in the plethora of studies on attachment and DV, whose results indicate that attachment styles and IWMs play an important role in both DV perpetration and victimisation (Allison et al., 2007; Gabbay & Lafontaine, 2017; Velotti et al., 2018).

When addressing the specific relationship between exposure to DV in childhood and later DV perpetration/victimisation, some have argued that attachment styles and IWMs may act either as 'mediators' or as 'moderators'. That is, they may account for the existence of a relationship between DV in childhood and in adulthood (mediating role), or they may influence the *strength* of this association (moderating role). For example, in a study involving 391 high-school students (52% girls; *M* age = 15.6, *SD* = 1.1 years), Grych and Kinsfogel (2010) found that in boys, attachment anxiety was a significant moderator of the association between exposure to violence in the family of origin and perpetration of dating violence. That is, there was a stronger link between having been exposed to DV in the family and perpetration of DV in male participants who scored higher on the 'attachment anxiety' dimension (as compared to the ones with lower scores). For girls, attachment avoidance, rather than anxiety, acted as a moderator of the association between intrafamilial DV and perpetration of abuse against partners, i.e., a strong positive association between DV in the family of origin and abuse against partners was identified in girls who were highly avoidant. Similar studies (Grady et al., 2018; Stover et al., 2018) concur to indicate that there is a complex interplay between the experience of family violence, the characteristics of cognitive and affective schemata and the propensity to use, or experience, abuse in intimate relationships.

This may, at least partly, explain why psychoeducational programmes and media campaigns have so far yielded no conclusive result in preventing domestic abuse (for a critical appraisal of the effectiveness of DV media campaigns, see for example, (Gadd et al., 2014; Keller et al., 2010)). Raising awareness on abusive dynamics and their risks does not seem to be enough to make a substantial difference in the fight to tackle DV. Indeed, some of the main psychological factors underpinning intra-couple abuse (cognitive-emotional schemata, sense of self and perceptions of others) are deeply embedded in one's psyche and, as a result, are likely to resist change. To effectively address IGT we would need to be able to produce a profound and substantial change in individuals' representations, at a cognitive, emotional and behavioural level. Cognitive change may be achieved, or at least pursued, via primary prevention and educational programmes, however, restructuring emotional and behavioural schemata may prove to be more challenging. This is because much of the emotional communication we share with our primary caregivers (and the learning processes that derive from it) take place at an 'implicit' (non-verbal) level (Dales & Jerry, 2008; Lamagna, 2011). Consequently, to change the IWMs underpinning the persistence of DV within and across generations, we would need to restructure both the accessible, explicit components of these IMWs and the more implicit, non-verbally encoded ones.

Bowlby (1980) had already proposed that IWMs operate primarily outside of our conscious awareness, but it was Allan Schore's seminal work *Affect Regulation and the Origin of the* Self (1994) that highlighted how our early experiences with significant others shape our ability to understand and regulate emotions, both at an explicit (conscious) level and implicit (subconscious) one. Schore's regulation theory (1994, 2003a, 2003b) postulates that the ability to understand, regulate and express emotions is central to human experience and that emotional regulation (ER) skills are developed via repeated positive mother-infant interactions. In line with this, he stated that: 'Attachment theory is essentially a regulatory theory and attachment can be defined as the interactive regulation of biological synchronicity between organisms' (Schore, 2000, p. 23). Progressively, this interactive regulation of synchronous mental and affective states will give rise to individuals' ability to autonomously regulate their own mental states. In particular, from a neurobiological perspective, 'attachment experiences shape the early organisation of right brain, the neurobiological core of the human unconscious' (Schore & Schore, 2008, p. 10). Support for this claim comes from the consistent evidence indicating that the right hemisphere is dominant in the storage of emotionally loaded, non-verbal, unconscious information (Gainotti, 2012; Joseph, 2013; Larsen et al., 2003). This also explains why brain damage affecting the right hemisphere can lead to deficits in emotional processing, for example, causing impaired perception of facial expressions of emotions (Charbonneau et al., 2003; Mandal et al., 1991), emotional distance and loss of empathy (Perry et al., 2001; Seeley et al., 2005; for a review, see also

Gainotti, 2019). This poses a dual problem: first, children exposed to DV are more at risk of developing insecure attachment styles and difficulties in emotional regulation (Howell, 2011; Martinez-Torteya et al., 2009) both acting as possible precursors to DV perpetration and/or and victimisation in adulthood (Bonache et al., 2019; Dutton & White, 2012). Additionally, most of their IWMs will be encoded in an implicit and procedural form, therefore guiding individual behaviours despite being inaccessible in a conscious, narrative form (Balbernie, 2001; Collins & Allard, 2008; Liotti, 2007).

This considered, how can we produce positive change in the IWMs of individuals who were exposed to family violence, to prevent the perpetuation of the cycle of abuse across generations? A possible way to achieve this goal could be represented by *corrective emotional experiences*, by engaging an individual's 'emotional core' changes may be produced in both the explicit and the implicit components of their IWMs. In Alexander and French's (1946) definition, these experiences occur when people are re-exposed to past situations that negatively affected them, but these are now faced under more favourable circumstances. The dissonance between individual expectations and lived experience gives rise to a drastic shift in previous conceptions (Lane, 2018; Zaccagnino et al., 2014). Consequently, the 'new experience' can be considered as 'corrective' as it creates new, long-lasting cognitive and affective representations that will influence the individual's subsequent behaviours (Brubacher, 2017; Lane, 2018). Corrective experiences can be provided in therapeutic settings, for example, by building a therapeutic alliance that provides a secure base for the client, which will gradually allow for the reparation of deficits in their emotion-regulating system and the acquisition of a more secure attachment style (Hill, 2015; Taylor et al., 2015). However, corrective experiences can also occur outside therapeutic settings, for example, when individuals with an insecure attachment style become involved in relationships characterised by stability and emotional closeness (Baldwin & Fehr, 1995; Davila & Cobb, 2004). This considered, it is argued that to effectively tackle the issue of IGT, professionals working with DV survivors and/or perpetrators should provide emotion-focused support, aimed at providing a 'right-brain-to-right-brain (…) transaction' (Schore, 2000, p. 46). Experiences of deep emotional connection with meaningful others (including professionals) can lead to a progressive reorganisation and restructuring of IWMs (Cobb & Davila, 2010; Gill, 2010), therefore, emotion-focused support could be beneficial to both victims and perpetrators to increase their emotion regulation abilities and modify the IWMs underpinning their use of violence and/or acceptance of the abuse. From a preventative perspective, involving children and young people (particularly if involved in violent family contexts) in attachment-restructuring, emotional regulation-focused interventions may be particularly beneficial. For example, there is emerging evidence that interventions improving parent-child attunement and parental affect regulation skills have the potential to enhance dyadic emotional communication and reduce child problematic (e.g., externalising) behaviour (Johnson & Lieberman, 2007; Siegel, 2013).

The combination of training of DV professionals on affect regulation interventions, children's school-led programmes and large-scale interventions to improve parental capacity to offer a secure base for younger generations, could represent an important contribution not only for the reduction in IGT rates but also for the creation of a more emotionally intelligent society.

References

Akers, R. L. (1973). *Deviant behaviour: A social learning approach.* Belmont, CA: Wadsworth.

Akers, R. L. (1998). *Social learning and social structure: A general theory of crime and deviance.* Boston: Northeastern University Press.

Alexander, F.G., & French, T.M. (1946). *Psychoanalytic therapy: Principles and applications.* Ronald.

Allison, C. J., Bartholomew, K., Mayseless, O., & Dutton, D. G. (2007). Love as a battlefield: Attachment and relationship dynamics in couples identified for male partner violence. *Journal of Family Issues, 29*(1), 125–150. 10.1177/0192513X07306980

Ammaniti, M. (2018) Implicit knowledge from infancy to the psychotherapeutic relationship: The contribution of Daniel Stern. *Psychoanalytic Inquiry, 38*(2), 138–147. 10.1080/07351690.2018.1405670

Anderson, J. F. & Kras, K. (2005). Revisiting Albert Bandura's Social Learning Theory to better understand and assist victims of intimate personal violence. *Women & Criminal Justice, 17*(1), 99–124. 10.1300/J012v17n01_05.

Balbernie, R. (2001). Circuits and circumstances: The neurobiological consequences of early relationship experiences and how they shape later behaviour. *Journal of Child Psychotherapy, 27*(3), 237–255. 10.1080/00754170110087531

Baldwin, M. W. & Fehr, B. (1995). On the stability of attachment style ratings. *Personal Relationships, 2,* 247–261. 10.1111/j.1475-6811.1995.tb00090.x

Bandura, A. (1969). Social–learning theory of identificatory processes. In D. A. Goslin (Ed.), *Handbook of socialization theory and research* (pp. 213–262). Chicago: Rand McNally & Company.

Bandura, A. (1971). *Social learning theory.* New York: General Learning Press.

Bandura, A. (1973). *Aggression: A social learning analysis.* Englewood Cliffs: Prentice–Hall.

Bartholomew, K. (1990). Avoidance of intimacy: An attachment perspective. *Journal of Social and Personal Relationships, 7*(2), 147–178. 10.1177/0265407590072001

Bartholomew, K., & Horowitz, L. M. (1991). Attachment styles among young adults: A test of a four-category model. *Journal of Personality and Social Psychology, 61*(2), 226–244. 10.1037/0022-3514.61.2.226

Bonache, H., Gonzalez-Mendez, R., & Krahé, B. (2019). Adult attachment styles, destructive conflict resolution, and the experience of intimate partner violence. *Journal of Interpersonal Violence, 34*(2), 287–309. 10.1177/0886260516640776

Bowlby, J. (1969). *Attachment and loss: Vol: 1. Attachment.* New York: Basic Books.

Bowlby, J. (1973). *Attachment and loss: Vol: 2. Separation: anxiety and anger.* New York: Basic Books.

Bowlby, J. (1980). *Attachment and loss: Vol 3. Sadness and depression.* New York: Basic Books.

Brownridge, D. A. (2006). Intergenerational transmission and dating violence victimization: Evidence from a sample of female University Students in Manitoba. *Canadian Journal of Community Mental Health*, *25*(1), 75–93. 10.7870/cjcmh-2006-0006

Brubacher, L. (2017). Emotionally focused individual therapy: An attachment-based experiential/systemic perspective. *Person-Centered & Experiential Psychotherapies*, *16*(1), 50–67. 10.1080/14779757.2017.1297250

Cassidy, J. (2000). Adult romantic attachments: A developmental perspective on individual differences. *Review of General Psychology*, *4*(2), 111–131. 10.1037/1089-2680.4.2.111

Charbonneau, S., Scherzer, B. P., Aspirot, D., & Cohen, H. (2003). Perception and production of facial and prosodic emotions by chronic CVA patients. *Neuropsychologia*, *41*(5), 605–613. 10.1016/s0028-3932(02)00202-6

Cobb, R. J. & Davila, J. (2010). Internal working models and change. Attachment theory and researhc in clinical work with adults. In J. H. Obegi and E. Berant (Eds.). *Attachment theory and research in clinical work with adults* (pp. 209–233). The Guilford Press.

Cochran, J. K., Sellers, C. S., Wiesbrock, V. & Palacios, W. R. (2011). Repetitive intimate partner victimization: An exploratory application of Social Learning Theory. *Deviant Behaviour*, *32*(9), 790–817, 10.1080/01639625.2010.538342.

Collins, N. L. & Allard, L. M. (2008). Cognitive representations of attachment: The content and function of working models. In: G. J. O. Fletcher & M. S. Clark (Eds.), *Blackwell handbook of social psychology: Interpersonal processes* (pp. 60–85). John Wiley and Sons.

Davila, J., & Cobb, R. J. (2004). Predictors of change in attachment security during adulthood. Adult attachment: Theory, research, and clinical implications. In W. S. Rholes, & J. A. Simpson (Eds.) *Adult attachment. Theory, research and clinical implications* (pp. 133–156). The Guilford Press.

Dales, S., & Jerry, P. (2008). Attachment, affect regulation and mutual synchrony in adult psychotherapy. *American Journal of Psychotherapy*, *62*(3), 283–312. 10.1176/appi.psychotherapy.2008.62.3.283

De La Rue, L., Polanin, J. R., Espelage, D. L., & Pigott, T. D. (2014). School-based interventions to reduce dating and sexual violence: A systematic review. *Campbell Systematic Reviews*, *10*(1), 1–110. 10.4073/csr.2014.7

Dutton, D. G., & White, K. R. (2012). Attachment insecurity and intimate partner violence. *Aggression and Violent Behaviour*, *17*(5), 475–481. 10.1016/j.avb.2012.07.003

Ehrensaft, M. K., Cohen, P., Brown, J., Smailes, E., Chen, H., & Johnson, J. G. (2003). Intergenerational transmission of partner violence: A 20-year prospective study. *Journal of Consulting and Clinical Psychology*, *71*(4), 741–753. 10.1037/0022-006x.71.4.741

Ehrensaft M.K., Langhinrichsen-Rohling J. (2022) Intergenerational transmission of intimate partner violence: Summary and current research on processes of transmission. In: R. Geffner, J. W. White., L. K. Hamberger, A. Rosenbaum, V.Vaughan-Eden & V.I. Vieth (Eds.) *Handbook of interpersonal violence and abuse across the lifespan* (pp. 2485–2509). Springer.

Fraley, R. C. (2002). Attachment stability from infancy to adulthood: Meta-analysis and dynamic modeling of developmental mechanisms. *Personality and Social Psychology Review*, *6*(2), 123–151. 10.1207/S15327957PSPR0602_03

Fraley, R. C. & Shaver, P. R. (2000). Adult romantic attachment: Theoretical developments, emerging controversies, and unanswered questions. *Review of General Psychology*, *4*(2), 132–154. 10.1037/1089-2680.4.2.132

Gabbay, N., & Lafontaine, M.-F. (2017). Understanding the relationship between attachment, caregiving, and same sex intimate partner violence. *Journal of Family Violence*, *32*(3), 291–304. 10.1007/s10896-016-9897-9

Gadd, D., Corr, M.-L., Fox, C. L., & Butler, I. (2014). This is Abuse ... Or is it? Domestic abuse perpetrators' responses to anti-domestic violence publicity. *Crime, Media, Culture*, *10*(1), 3–22. 10.1177/1741659013475462

Gainotti, G. (2012). Unconscious processing of emotions and the right hemisphere. *Neuropsychologia*, *50*(2), 205–218. 10.1016/j.neuropsychologia.2011.12.005

Gainotti, G. (2019). The role of the right hemisphere in emotional and behavioural disorders of patients with frontotemporal lobar degeneration: an updated review. *Frontiers in Aging Neuroscience*, *11*, Article 55. 10.3389/fnagi.2019.00055

Gill, S. (2010). The therapist as psychobiological regulator: Dissociation, affect attunement and clinical process. *Clinical Social Work Journal*, *38*(3), 260–268. 10.1007/s10615-009-0213-5

Godbout, N., Vaillancourt-Morel, M.-P., Bigras, N., Briere, J., Hébert, M., Runtz, M., & Sabourin, S. (2019). Intimate partner violence in male survivors of child maltreatment: a meta-analysis. *Trauma, Violence, & Abuse*, *20*(1), 99–113. 10.1177/1524838017692382

Grady, M. D., Yoder, J., & Brown, A. (2018). Childhood maltreatment experiences, attachment, sexual offending: Testing a theory. *Journal of Interpersonal Violence*, *36*(11–12), 088626051881426. 10.1177/0886260518814262

Graham, L. M., Embry, V., Young, B.-R., Macy, R. J., Moracco, K. E., Reyes, H. L. M., & Martin, S. L. (2021). Evaluations of prevention programs for sexual, dating, and intimate partner violence for boys and men: A systematic review. *Trauma, Violence, & Abuse*, *22*(3), 15248380198511S. 10.1177/1524838019851158

Grych, J. H., & Kinsfogel, K. M. (2010). Exploring the role of attachment style in the relation between family aggression and abuse in adolescent dating relationships. *Journal of Aggression, Maltreatment & Trauma*, *19*(6), 624–640. 10.1080/10926771.2010.502068

Hazan, C., & Shaver, P. (1987). Romantic love conceptualized as an attachment process. *Journal of Personality and Social Psychology*, *52*(3), 511–524. 10.1037/0022-3514.52.3.511

Hill, D. (2015). *Affective regulation theory. A clinical model*. New York, NY: W. W. Norton.

Hou, J., Yu, L., Fang, X., & Epstein, N. B. (2016). The intergenerational transmission of domestic violence: The role that gender plays in attribution and consequent intimate partner violence. *Journal of Family Studies*, *22*(2), 121–139. 10.1080/13229400.2015.1045923

Howell, K. H. (2011). Resilience and psychopathology in children exposed to family violence. *Aggression and Violent Behaviour*, *16*(6), 562–569. 10.1016/j.avb.2011.09.001

Johnson, V. K., & Lieberman, A. F. (2007). Variations in behaviour problems of preschoolers exposed to domestic violence: The role of mothers' attunement to children's emotional experiences. *Journal of Family Violence*, *22*(5), 297–308. 10.1007/s10896-007-9083-1

Joseph, R. (2013). *The right brain and the unconscious: Discovering the stranger within.* Springer.

Keller, S. N., Wilkinson, T., & Otjen, A. J. (2010). Unintended effects of a domestic violence campaign. *Journal of Advertising, 39*(4), 53–68. 10.2753/JOA0091-33673 90404

Kerley, K., Xu, X., Sirisunyaluck, B., & Alley, J. (2010). Exposure to family violence in childhood and intimate partner perpetration or victimization in adulthood: Exploring intergenerational transmission in urban Thailand. *Journal of Family Violence, 25,* 337–347. 10.1007/s10896-009-9295-7

Kwong, M. J., Bartholomew, K., Henderson, A. J. Z., & Trinke, S. J. (2003). The intergenerational transmission of relationship violence. *Journal of Family Psychology, 17*(3), 288–301. 10.1037/0893-3200.17.3.288

Lamagna, J. (2011). Of the self, by the self, and for the self: An intra-relational per spective on intra-psychic attunement and psychological change. *Journal of Psychotherapy Integration, 21*(3), 280–307. 10.1037/a0025493

Lane, R. D. (2018). From reconstruction to construction: The power of corrective emotional experiences in memory reconsolidation and enduring change. *Journal of the American Psychoanalytic Association, 66*(3), 507–516. 10.1177/000306511 8782198

Larsen, J.K., Brand, N., Bermond, B., & Hijman, R. (2003). Cognitive and emotional characteristics of alexithymia. A review of neurobiological studies. *Journal of Psychosomatic Research, 54,* 533–541. 10.1016/s0022-3999(02)00466-x.

Liotti, G. (2007). Internal working models of attachment in the therapeutic relationship. In P. Gilbert & R. L. Leahy (Eds.), *The therapeutic relationship in the cognitive behavioural psychotherapies* (pp. 143–161). Routledge/Taylor & Francis Group.

Mandal, M. K., Tandon, S. C., & Asthana, H. S. (1991). Right brain damage impairs recognition of negative emotions. *Cortex, 27*(2), 247–253. 10.1016/s0010-9452(13) 80129-3

Martinez-Torteya, C., Anne Bogat, G., Von Eye, A., & Levendosky, A. A. (2009). Resilience among children exposed to domestic violence: The role of risk and protective factors. *Child Development, 80*(2), 562–577. 10.1111/j.1467-8624. 2009.01279.x

Perry, R. J., Rosen, H. R., Kramer, J. H., Beer, J. S., Levenson, R. L. & Miller, B. L. (2001). Hemispheric dominance for emotions, empathy and social behaviour: Evidence from right and left handers with frontotemporal dementia. *Neurocase, 7*(2), 145–160. 10.1093/neucas/7.2.145

Schore, A. N. (1994). *Affect regulation and the origin of the self: The neurobiology of emotional development.* New York, NY: W. W. Norton

Schore, A. N. (2000). Attachment and the regulation of the right brain. *Attachment & Human Development, 2*(1), 23–47. 10.1080/146167300361309

Schore, A. N. (2003a). *Affect regulation and disorders of the self.* New York, NY: W. W. Norton.

Schore, A. N. (2003b). *Affect regulation and the repair of the self.* New York, NY: W. W. Norton.

Schore, J. R., & Schore, A. N. (2008). Modern attachment theory: The central role of affect regulation in development and treatment. *Clinical Social Work Journal, 36*(1), 9–20. 10.1007/s10615-007-0111-7

Seeley, W. W., Bauer, A. M., Miller, B. L., Gorno-Tempini, M. L.,Kramer, J. H., Weiner, M., et al. (2005). The natural history oftemporal variant fronto-temporal dementia. *Neurology, 64*, 1384–1390. 10.1212/01.WNL.0000158425. 46019.5C

Shaver, P. R., & Hazan, C. (1988). A biased overview of the study of love. *Journal of Social and Personal Relationships*, 5(4), 473–501. 10.1177/0265407588054005

Shaver, P. R., Hazan, C. & Bradshaw, D. (1988). Love as attachment: The integration of three behavioural systems. In R. J. Steinberg, & M. L. Barnes (Eds.), *The psychology of love* (pp. 68–99). Yale University Press.

Sherman, L. J., Rice, K. & Cassidy, J. (2015). Infant capacities related to building internal working models of attachment figures: A theoretical and empirical review. *Developmental Review, 37*, 109–141. 10.1016/j.dr.2015.06.001

Siegel, J. P. (2013). Breaking the links in intergenerational violence: An emotional regulation perspective. *Family Process*, 52(2), 163–178. 10.1111/famp.12023

Smith-Marek, E. N., Cafferky, B., Dharnidharka, P., Mallory, A. B., Dominguez, M., High, J., ... Mendez, M. (2015). Effects of childhood experiences of family violence on adult partner violence: A meta-analytic review. *Journal of Family Theory & Review*, 7(4), 498–519. 10.1111/jftr.12113

Steele, H., Steele, M., & Croft, C. (2008). Early attachment predicts emotion recognition at 6 and 11 years old. *Attachment & Human Development*, 10(4), 379–393. 10.1080/14616730802461409

Stover, C. S., Choi, M. J., & Mayes, L. C. (2018). The moderating role of attachment on the association between childhood maltreatment and adolescent dating violence. *Children and Youth Services Review, 94*, 679–688. 10.1016/j.childyouth.2018.09.011

Sutton, T. E. (2019) Review of attachment theory: Familial predictors, continuity and change, and intrapersonal and relational outcomes. *Marriage & Family Review*, 55(1), 1–22. 10.1080/01494929.2018.1458001

Taylor, P., Rietzschel, J., Danquah, A., & Berry, K. (2015). Changes in attachment representations during psychological therapy. *Psychotherapy Research*, 25(2), 222–238. 10.1080/10503307.2014.886791

Thompson, R. A. (2021). Internal working models as developing representations. In: R. A. Thompson, J. A. Simpson, & L. J. Berlin (Eds.), *Attachment: The fundamental questions* (pp. 111–119). The Guilford Press.

Tougas, C., Péloquin, K., & Mondor, J. (2016). Romantic attachment and perception of partner support to explain psychological aggression perpetrated in couples seeking couples therapy. *Couple and Family Psychology: Research and Practice*, 5(4), 197–211. 10.1037/cfp0000068

Vallotton, C. D. (2008). Signs of emotion: What can preverbal children "say" about internal states? *Infant Mental Health Journal*, 29(3), 234–258. 10.1002/imhj.20175

Velotti, P., Beomonte Zobel, S., Rogier, G., & Tambelli, R. (2018). Exploring relationships: A systematic review on intimate partner violence and attachment. *Frontiers in Psychology, 9*, Article 1166. 10.3389/fpsyg.2018.01166

Wareham, J., Boots, D. P. & Chavez, J. M. (2009). A test of social learning and intergenerational transmission among batterers. *Journal of Criminal Justice, 37*(2), 163–173. 10.1016/j.jcrimjus.2009.02.011

Waters, H. S., & Waters, E. (2006). The attachment working models concept: Among other things, we build script-like representations of secure base experiences. *Attachment & Human Development*, 8(3), 185–197. 10.1080/14616730600856016

Whitaker, D. J., Morrison, S., Lindquist, C., Hawkins, S. R., O'Neil, J. A., Nesius, A. M., ... Reese, L. R. (2006). A critical review of interventions for the primary prevention of perpetration of partner violence. *Aggression and Violent Behaviour, 11*(2), 151–166. 10.1016/j.avb.2005.07.007

Widom, C. S., & Wilson, H. W. (2015). Intergenerational transmission of violence. In J. Lindert & I. Levav (Eds.), *Violence and mental health* (pp. 27–45). Springer. 10.1007/978-94-017-8999-8_2

Zaccagnino, M., Cussino, M., Saunders, R., Jacobvitz, D., & Veglia, F. (2014). Alternative caregiving figures and their role on adult attachment representations. *Clinical Psychology & Psychotherapy, 21*(3), 276–287.

14 Responding to the mental health needs of children who experience domestic violence

Alexandra Papamichail[1], Ali Shnyien[2], Niamh Ingram[3], and Joshua Eldridge[4]
[1]*Clinical Psychologist, London, UK*
[2]*Clinical Psychologist and Professional Lead for Youth Justice and Pupil Referral Unit CAMH services at South West London and St George's NHS trust*
[3]*Senior Clinical Psychologist and CBT Lead within NHS Child and Adolescent Mental Health Services*
[4]*Clinical Psychologist and Service Lead for a CAMHS Education Wellbeing Service in Southwest London and St George's NHS trust*

Introduction

During the last three decades, research has demonstrated that children can be profoundly affected by IPV in a multitude of ways; this led to the recognition that children's experiences of IPV constitute a form of maltreatment (e.g., Macmillan et al., 2009). However, it is also important to note that not every child who has experienced IPV will require a specialist mental health response (Kitzmann et al., 2003), and helpful responses may vary depending on life stage and contextual circumstances. In many instances, natural support within the context of safe environments, generally secure attachment relationships and regulated social contexts can support healthy development and resilience (El-Sheikh et al., 2008; Minze et al., 2010).

The mental health impact of developmental trauma, specifically the experience of IPV can be multi-layered and complex. It can impact children themselves and the systems around them. Children who have experienced IPV can present with a broad range of cognitive, emotional and behavioural challenges that are often the catalyst for the young person and/or family's referral into services. These can include underlying difficulties with their identity and feelings of shame or self-blame, difficulties with emotion regulation, challenges with forming and maintaining healthy attachment relationships, which at different stages may create internal or external distress that may present in a variety of ways (Sternberg et al., 2006; Adamson & Thompson, 1998). These can include *'hyper-aroused presentations'* such as 'anti-social behaviours', hyperactivity, physical, verbal or emotional aggression and outwardly expressed dysregulated or risky behaviours; and/or *'hypo-aroused presentations'* including anxious, repetitive or controlling behaviours, withdrawn or dissociative behaviours, self-harm, self-

DOI: 10.4324/9781003124634-18

medication or destructive patterns (Van der Kolk et al., 2005; Treisman., 2016; Cook et al., 2005; Blaustein & Kinniburgh, 2018). Trauma Systems Theory (Saxe, Ellis & Brown, 2016) understands many of these presentations as 'survival strategies/states', which are broadly understood as responses organised in early childhood, designed to reduce the likelihood or extent of harm to the self and attachment figures that a child relies upon. These survival states can be developed within the context of IPV and can continue to be re-activated or triggered later in life in response to reminders or perceived threats. These states are now understood to be embedded within children's brains, bodies and nervous systems and linked to fragmented emotional, sensory and somatic memories of trauma (Van der Kolk et al., 2005; Porges, 2011).

Theories that have informed mental health responses to developmental and relational trauma, including IPV, commonly emphasise the 'bottom up' development of our brains. For instance, neurosequential models of the brain suggest that the least complex part of our brain (i.e., the survival brain; brainstem), which is responsible for basic regulatory functions and the fight, flight, freeze, collapse/dissociation response, develops first. Second, are our emotion and attachment systems (e.g., the emotional brain; the limbic system and the amygdala) and then later, the cortex (e.g., the reasoning and learning brain), which allows for emotional-regulation, inhibition and executive functioning, as well as our ability to predict the consequences of our actions, perspective take and think about our future self. Therefore, if a child is exposed to a home environment that is not safe from early development, the brain will adapt to enable the child to survive. It will strengthen connections between the brain and body that help them monitor, be prepared for and respond quickly to danger (e.g., vagal responses involved in flight, fight and freeze) and will prioritise these connections over the development of 'higher' regulating systems (Perry, 2006). This basis provides a foundation to informing and understanding mental health responses for children exposed to IPV, dependent on their experiences and the extent to which their 'survival brains' have had to become overactive/highly sensitive in comparison to the other parts.

It is also noted that whilst this chapter focusses on mental health responses where indicated, a holistic focus is often required. Many children and families exposed to IPV are at greater risk of exposure to multiple Adverse Childhood Experiences (ACEs). This can include but is not limited to parental mental health difficulties, parental substance misuse, experiencing sudden losses or disruptions in relationships to caregivers, in addition to possible wider exposure to poverty, social injustice and deprivation (Zarling et al., 2013). Multi-agency consideration and response to such wider environmental, social and family factors is essential to child outcomes and often indicated as a prerequisite or in conjunction with specialist mental health interventions. Whilst the evidence-base around mental health responses for children exposed to IPV is still developing, this chapter looks to review how research and theory can be synthesised to help create trauma-informed mental health responses that are attuned to pressing mental health needs.

Key principles of trauma-informed assessment and intervention

This section outlines some of the key principles used to guide trauma-informed assessment and intervention approaches.

Relationships are the foundation of trauma-informed care

Children operate within complex social systems. Those that have witnessed IPV may be dependent on others who have caused them harm, who have had limited ability to protect them, and who may be coping with their own trauma experiences. Therefore, building strong alliances within these systems, be it with parents, siblings, peers, teachers and social workers, is the foundation to any positive outcomes.

Exposure to stressors such as IPV during development can impair a child's ability to trust others, which is a key part of our capacity to learn from others in our social world (Fonagy & Allison, 2014; Bevington et al., 2017). As a result, a child who has experienced trauma can potentially reject information that does not fit with their existing and at one time functional and protective beliefs about the world (Treisman, 2016). For example, young people may hold beliefs including 'people are untrustworthy, dangerous/unsafe, and/or unpredictable'. This can present significant barriers to engagement and development of the therapeutic relationship within assessment and intervention (Treisman, 2016; Bevington et al., 2017).

Supporting engagement

AMBIT (Adaptive Mentalization Based Integrative treatment; Bevington et al., 2017) is a mentalisation based approach that can provide a helpful framework for supporting and engaging young people with histories of trauma. This includes consideration of how a worker and service are introduced, paying attention to who in the family and network are important to speak to and the cultural and social aspects of the family. It is important to think in advance about who a practitioner will be meeting with first, an initial discussion with the parent, or if a young person will be attending – who would be the best family member or professional to help transition them into a mental health support. Asking who are the most safe, trusted and important members of their network, who they feel 'gets' them. These safe figures can be crucial supporters of engagement and future work. Pulling together the system around a young person and understanding the often-varied goals of each member can help prioritise needs and support the practitioner to consider the child's goals, hopes, fears and expectations.

A further aspect of AMBIT influenced work is taking a *mentalising stance* (Bateman & Fonagy, 2016; Bevington et al., 2017) which includes cultivating not-knowing, curiosity and inquisitiveness. The worker holds that minds are not transparent to one another and act tentatively, putting forward ideas in a manner that allows for rebuttal and refinement, paying careful attention to the dynamics of power. Another aspect of this is encouraging collaboration, joint storytelling and the broadcasting of the worker's intentions and internal 'thinking' in an accessible way to the young person. This can be a powerful engagement tool for young people who may not have had experiences of being 'seen' and heard or of having an adult share what is happening in their own mind. The underlying message behind the workers communication should be '*I am interested in you, I cannot know your mind but I am here to listen and understand, and what you say is important and valuable to me*'.

Creating a safe therapeutic environment

In addition, attention should be paid to the setting, for example, ensuring adequate privacy, the opportunity to speak alone with the child away from identified perpetrator(s), involving safe family members and trusted professionals. Ideally, the worker should share with the young person the parameters, outline and intentions of their work, ensuring they are comfortable to continue and that their boundaries will be respected. This includes empowering the young person by offering them choices, for example, to terminate sessions and decline to answer any questions without difficulty. Useful questions to ask can include: *How will I know if things are not going well between us today? Would you be able to tell me, or shall we agree a signal? Is there anyone I should speak to who could tell me more about you?* It is also essential that all parties know and understand the boundaries of confidentiality, especially given the workers duty of care to report abuse.

Assessments and interventions need to match the child's survival states and their developmental stage

The Neurosequential model of therapeutics (Perry, 2006; Barfield et al., 2012) provides a framework for selecting and sequencing interventions based on the child's developmental age, which parts of their brain are the most active (survival/emotional/limbic or reasoning/cortical brain) and to what extent the bottom-up development of the brain has been nurtured. Determining this is therefore a vital part of assessment and intervention.

Trauma Systems Theory (Saxe et al., 2016) puts the family environment and young person each on a continuum from distressed/unsafe to regulated/safe. One end of this continuum are environments where caregivers can protect children from threats/danger and be part of a treatment team helping children regulate. The other end is an environment where caregivers are causing harm to the child, are unable to protect them from actual threats and are unavailable to help them regulate due to their own mental health or emotional needs. A child's survival strategies are also on a continuum of how present and dangerous they are to the young person and others. It is the interaction of the child's social environment and the severity of their survival states that guides the treatment goals and interventions. Therefore, assessments and interventions will look different for each family depending on what they have experienced and their current resources.

Shame-influenced responses to the mental health needs of children who have experienced IPV are common and can act as a barrier to treatment

Shame can also adversely influence engagement and professional mental health responses with children and families who have experienced IPV. Awareness of this can support organisations, teams and individual practitioners to respond to a child and family from a trauma-informed framework.

It is recognised that shame, the unbearable sense within the child or parent, that they are 'bad', 'a failure', 'deserving' or 'responsible' for any harm that is inflicted, is commonly hidden but present amongst family members where domestic violence has been experienced (Deblinger & Runyon, 2005). When activated, shame can lead to a wide range of cognitive and behavioural patterns in families, which can risk being mirrored in organisational and practitioner responses. Unnoticed, this can potentially lead to disengagement, loss of team and network cohesion, professional burnout, deskilling and loss of creative and collaborative mental health responses (Sweeney, Clement, Filson & Kennedy, 2016; Daniels & Robinson, 2019; Bevington et al., 2017; Treisman, 2021).

Common shame-influenced responses

Shame can become activated at any stage of assessment or intervention. 'Stuckness' in progress or repeat presentations are common triggers. Practitioners may also mirror this 'stuckness' in their own work, experiencing repetitive self-critical thoughts alongside a sense that they are unable to meet the needs of the child or family. This can be accompanied by urges to dismiss/ reject, blame or become punitive with the family or network as they defend against shame, adopting a sense of sole responsibility for a family's needs may also arise, risking the practitioner entering a sole 'rescuer' position (Treisman, 2016; Daniels & Robinson, 2019). The child or family may also be labelled as 'not engaging' or 'hard to reach', when in fact they are often utilising strategies that have served to keep them afloat amongst past or current traumatic environments.

Alternative responses to shame

Critically, a key role for mental health professionals can be monitoring to what degree shame is influencing responses within themselves, the family or the network. It is important for all practitioners to recognise that they can help to coordinate and be a part of a collaborative multi-agency trauma-informed mental health response. This acknowledges that a single worker cannot meet all the needs of the child and family independently, but that they can provide support in the short or longer term, appreciating service strengths and parameters whilst thinking creatively about what is possible. Therefore, maintaining reflection on evoked feelings in the clinician or system and how these may reflect patterns in the family system, can provide access to alternative responses to shame-based cognitions. This awareness can support practitioners to connect with the child and family's strengths, traumas and attachment histories facilitating collaborative, empathic and validating responses that listen out for stories of resilience and explore how children and families can live fulfilling lives alongside their trauma (Treisman, 2016; 2021).

It is important to highlight that in order to support these processes and maintain a professional network's ability to work effectively with trauma embedded structures such as reflective practice (Kurtz, 2019; Treisman, 2021), clinical/reflective supervision (Sweeney et al., 2016; Knight & Borders, 2018; Treisman, 2021), psychologically-informed case consultation (Sweeney et al., 2016; Bevington et al., 2017; Snodgrass & Selman, 2019), trauma-informed managerial practices (Treisman, 2021), continued professional development and training (Layne et al., 2011; Berger & Quiros, 2016; Treisman, 2021) and the prioritisation of staff wellbeing (Sweeney et al., 2016; Treisman, 2021) are vital.

Assessments with children and families who have experienced IPV

Before meeting with the family – advance considerations

For mental health provisions to incorporate the principles of trauma-informed care into their service designs requires organisation and planning before seeing any referred child. Although it may be a child that is identified for mental health assessment in the context of IPV, practitioners should consider in advance the potential un-referred needs of family. This is because family members typically adopt varied emotional and behavioural responses to trauma (e.g., externalising and internalising behaviours).

Holding in mind the current reasons for a referral can also provide important insights. Young people's mental health concerns stipulated in a referral are commonly a response to current or re-triggered survival states. Their distress may indicate that IPV is occurring at home, or that they have detected a risk to family safety. This can include perpetrators of IPV re-initiating contact, a new partner or a family system change. Practitioners should take consideration of safeguarding needs prior to meeting with a young person or family for initial consultation.

Lastly, knowledge of local and national resources for parental/adult mental health, trauma and complex trauma services, IPV charities and third sector organisations providing mentoring, peer support and citizens/housing advice are invaluable resources.

Conducting assessments

Research indicates that adults with mental health needs describe an absence of professional enquiry about their histories of IPV and associated traumas during their contacts with healthcare systems (e.g., Rivett et al., 2006; Read et al., 2018). It is imperative that mental health practitioners build their skill in terms of being able to sensitively and confidently explore child and family domestic violence histories at a developmentally appropriate level. Standardised trauma-screening questionnaires can be used to assist this and have been shown to increase rates of child and family disclosure (Cusack et al., 2004). These can be particularly beneficial when referrals or case histories indicate presentations consistent with exposure to IPV or associated traumas (Van der Kolk et al., 2005; Treisman, 2016; Cook et al., 2005; Blaustein & Kinniburgh, 2018).

Providing opportunities for children and families to disclose IPV through both verbal and non-verbal means is arguably essential to formulating mental health needs and coordinating collaborative care plans based on shared understanding. Without which, there is a risk of mental health services disassociating young people's distress from their past and recent lived experiences. Diagnoses, therapies or medication may then be applied without an appreciation of context. Together, this can risk denying young people's lived experiences and a missed opportunity to recognise trauma-influenced responses. While there can also be a need to explore neurodevelopmental or other difficulties, the same curiosity and time should be spent exploring the impact of trauma and how this can go hand-in-hand with neurodevelopmental conditions.

'Mapping the terrain': The assessment process

The table that follows (Table 14.1) can be used to support workers in 'mapping the terrain' of a child's experience and gathering of relevant information from the family and professional network, including goals and priorities for assessment and a sense of the child position and perspective of the network. There are several comprehensive resources that can be looked to for further detail (The National Child Traumatic Stress Network, 2018; Treisman, 2016; 2017; Saxe et al., 2016; Blaustein & Kinniburgh, 2018).

A note on formulation

Utilising the information gathered, a 'map' or 'formulation' of the terrain can begin to develop, however, this should not be static or time limited but evolving and dynamic. It should shift as new information arises and interventions are tried, and it must be built collaboratively with the young person, family and system. This can take many forms from more formal reports and written documents to visual and creative 'maps' as well as verbal narratives and stories shared by the network, family and young person.

Sequencing interventions for children and young people who have experienced IPV and the systems around them

Interventions may be guided by how protective and secure the child's social environment is and how harmful their survival strategies or states are to their

Table 14.1 Assessment domains and factors for consideration

Domain	Factors & questions to consider

Developmental trajectory	• *Pre- and post-natal:*
	  • Were there significant stressors (e.g., domestic violence) during pregnancy?
	  • What were the hopes/expectations for this child?
	  • Was the pregnancy planned? How did the family system change on their birth?
	  • Was there substance use during pregnancy?
	  • What was the nature/quality of the parent's attachment to the child?
	• *Milestones and social, emotional and developmental needs:*
	  • Did the child meet their milestones?
	  • How were their physical (sleeps, shelter, safety etc.), relational (warmth, attunement, responsive, regulating etc.), cognitive (stimulation, reflection, communication, understanding etc.) and security (predictability, structure, boundaries etc.) needs met?
	• *Developmental delays/learning difficulties & disabilities/Speech language and communication needs/ neurodevelopmental conditions:*
	  • Have these been assessed or explored?
	  • Are there any concerns regarding this in the network?

Familial and systemic	• *The systems functioning and responses to trauma:*
	  • Who is in the family?
	  • General mental health, coping strategies, conflictual & supportive relationships, family patterns of communication, relevant family history & trauma and family experiences of guilt, shame and other strong emotions.
	  • What areas would the family like assistance with?
	• *Parenting or care experience:*
	  • Who is the primary caregiver, has this changed over time? What is home like?
	  • If the child is in care what is the history of this, their transitions, separations and losses?
	  • How are rules/boundaries negotiated in the family?
	• *Identity and cultural factors:*
	  • What is the family's cultural identity & does this differ between members?
	  • What language do they use to define this?
	  • How does the young person see their position in the family and culture?
	  • What are the shared beliefs, values and stories within this family/network?

(Continued)

Table 14.1 (Continued)

Domain	Factors & questions to consider

	• How is the young person constructing their identity in response to this?
	• *Relationships:*
	  • Who is important to the child?
	  • Why and what needs do they meet?
	  • What losses have they experienced and what positives?
	  • How have their interpersonal and social skills developed?
	  • What have they learned about how it is to 'be' in relationships?

Trauma	• *Exposure:*
	  • What age were they when the violence/trauma began and/or ended? Is this still ongoing?
	  • What was the nature/duration and frequency?
	  • How was it 'found out/disclosed'?
	  • How does the child now feel towards those who took part?
	  • How has the child understood the 'why' and made sense of/drawn meaning from this experience?
	• *Coping:*
	  • What is the child's experience of shame, guilt, anger, sadness and other strong emotions?
	  • How has the child learned to manage these?
	  • What is the child's relationship to their body like?
	  • What beliefs about themselves, others and the world have they internalised from the experiences?
	  • What strategies did the child use to survive and how do these manifest now?
	• *Triggers/reminders:*
	  • Many children especially younger may not be able to name their own triggers and drawn connections between them and their internal experiences and behaviour, therefore it is important to draw information from adults in the child's life about patterns and responses.
	  • What reactions are triggered by interaction with people, places, objects or situations?
	  • What physical experiences may trigger trauma responses e.g., sound., smells, sights and internal physical or body states?
	  • What responses are common for this child e.g., dissociation, controlling behaviours, externalising behaviours, internalising behaviours?

Presenting difficulties and impact	• *Define:*
	  • What is the presenting problem?
	  • Who defines it and what are the multitude of perspectives on it?

Table 14.1 (Continued)

Domain	Factors & questions to consider

	• How long or frequently has it been occurring?
	• What does it look and feel like?
	• What are the exceptions (e.g., when/where/with who it does it not happen/ when are things better)?
	• Are there patterns in its occurrence or non-occurrence?
	• *Impact:*
	  • What is the impact of the difficulty?
	  • On the child, the family and the network?
	  • Consider areas like sleep, appetite, social and school life, mood, self-care, relationships, self-worth and self-esteem.
	• *Meaning:*
	  • What does the young person understand about the difficulty?
	  • What meaning do they draw from it?
	  • What might the underlying communication or function of the problem?
	  • How does this fit with the child and networks narratives?

Education	• *Performance:*
	  • Academically, socially, behavioural, emotionally. Is this different to other settings?
	• *Additional needs:*
	  • Cognitive and executive functions. What support is provided in school?

Resilience factors	• What are the talents, strengths, skills, interests and areas of creativity in the family and young person? • What are the protective and resilience factors? What have the family and child navigated already? How did they survive? • Consider spirituality and religious beliefs as well as other culturally specific areas of meaning. • What community and social support is available? • What motivates and gives hope to the young person? What are their ambitions and interests?
Risk factors	• Consider the three pillars of risk assessment namely, risk to self, risk to & from others and risk to the worker. • What safety plans and risk assessments are in place? How are these checked and monitored? Are they working? What is the young person's view of these?
Goal setting	• What are the young persons and family's goals for treatment and support? How do they see them being completed? What are the priories and who holds these? What are the differences?

physical and emotional safety. There are several approaches to child trauma which hold this sequencing at their foundation (e.g., The Neurosequential Model of Therapeutics; Perry, 2006; Barfield et al., 2012; The Trauma Recovery Model; Skuse & Matthew, 2015; Trauma Systems Theory; Saxe et al., 2016; Attachment, Regulation & Competency Framework; Blaustein & Kinniburgh, 2018).

Often families, professionals and sometimes the young person themselves, can hold beliefs that the solution for a child who has experienced IPV is trauma therapy. However, healing from these experiences requires time and the careful sequencing of trauma-informed interventions. For some young people, it may take years before they are able to engage in trauma processing therapies, based on the needs and resources of the system around them. For others, they may find ways outside the therapy room to make sense of these experiences and their hopes for future life. This section illustrates what trauma interventions might look like and provides a guide for sequencing interventions and supporting networks to work creatively together towards a family's unique goals.

The survival brain: Safety-based interventions

The goal here is to create a 'safe enough' environment that the young person can begin accessing high-level brain functioning that is required for processing trauma. In this context, 'safe enough' means that caregivers and the network can protect the child from threats and stimuli that trigger survival responses, and they can help the child regulate their survival states. Young people still in unsafe environments and/or in survival states such as fight, flight and freeze (dissociation) may struggle to access memories, belief systems, thoughts and feelings as they are hijacked by their 'survival brain'. It would be ineffective and at worst, harmful, to engage in trauma reprocessing therapies without this basic level of safety.

Furthermore, in the presence of violence in the home, preventing a young person from 'completing' their trauma responses can truncate trauma processing in the brain (Corrigan, 2014). Examples of truncation can include preventing fight (e.g., shouting, screaming, smashing objects) and flight (leaving the home or staying in their room) responses, denying a child control over their immediate environment and not providing support when a child communicates a need. Over time truncation can trigger young people into more harmful survival states, for example, high levels of vigilance, dissociation, self-harm and suicidal thinking associated with post-traumatic stress disorder and depression (Porges, 2011; Corrigan, 2014). In fact, knowledge of this truncation process can help us understand why young people may experience these mental health symptoms i.e., because of repeated exposure to violence from which they could not fight, flee or receive help. This can help us develop creative interventions that allow young people to fulfil these natural bodily responses to trauma in a safe way. The tables that follow (Tables 14.2 and 14.3) offer practitioners a sample of what interventions might look like at this stage.

Table 14.2 Questions for practitioners engaging in safety-based interventions

Helpful questions for practitioners during this stage
• What does the child's behaviour tell me about how safe they are feeling?   • Are there any actual and/or current threats to the child's sense of safety?   • Are there particular stimuli in the child's environment that trigger them to be in survival states?   • Are these removable or are they unavoidable?   • How are the adults (parents, adult siblings, teachers) closest to the child coping? Are they safe and available to the child?   • Are the adults around the child able to connect with the child and make them feel regulated?   • Is the network feeling regulated witnessing the family's distress? Is it able to communicate effectively and calmly?

Table 14.3 Safety-based approaches and interventions

	What interventions can look like
Interventions to ensure the child is physically and emotionally safe	These are usually social work or joint work interventions to contract safety measures with the family. Consider: • Does mum/dad/older sibling/carer need to be out of the house for the young person's safety? • How will this work? What support will this individual be given? • Does the family need support meeting basic human needs? E.g., food, shelter and rest.
Enabling caregivers to access their own support	• Consider what they need to feel safe and provide a safe, containing and warm environment at home. This can include therapeutic support, social care and community interventions.
Providing psychoeducation and creating a shared formulation	• Understanding the child's behaviour in the context of trauma. • Supporting the network and caregivers to help the young person 'live out' their survival states in a safe way and develop strategies to help them regulate. • Helping the family and school consider what stimuli in the child's environment may be a trigger and considering whether these are removable and if not, what distress tolerance techniques the young person may need in these moments.
Co-regulating the network	• High risk survival states and coping strategies that can be difficult to manage will trigger the network into their own

(Continued)

Table 14.3 (Continued)

	What interventions can look like
	survival states which can lead to reactive decision-making. Therefore, providing consultation and reflective spaces to reflect on the feelings elicited by the child and family's behaviour helps to regulate the professionals so that they can access their own cortical systems. • These spaces can help the network come together to think how the system can respond consistently and calmly to co-regulate the young person and family in distress.
Routine and Rhythms	• Building structure and predictability into a child's daily life. • Incorporating supportive and soothing rhythmic activity into daily routine. • Clear boundaries and expectations within the home and school environment. • Building predictable and safe responses to the child's behaviours that are trauma sensitive.

The limbic/emotional brain: Regulation and social engagement interventions

Once it is established that the environment is 'safe enough', the goals of interventions can shift to focus on the three following areas: developing the child's capacity to understand and regulate their own emotions and bodily sensations; developing caregivers' capacities to continue to protect the child and help them regulate; and supporting the reparation of relationships and the development of positive attachment experiences for the young person. This is where the network can begin focusing on developing the part of the brain that has the power to mediate our survival responses: our emotion and attachment system. Perry and Szalavitz (2007) emphasise that relationships, not specific procedures, are the best support for recovery from trauma. Furthermore, the greater number of safe and healthy relationships a child has, the more likely they will be able to heal from traumatic experiences and thrive. In cases where a young person has witnessed IPV it may not always be possible for parents to engage fully in this work due to the impact of their own experiences of trauma and need for mental health support to be in a safe enough relationship for the child. Therefore, when we use the word 'caregiver' we do not mean only parents, but any adult with caring responsibilities and/or attachment to the child including foster carers, teachers, pastoral care workers, third sector workers, therapists and adult siblings. For older children, their peer group may also play a vital role (Tables 14.4 and 14.5).

Table 14.4 Questions for practitioners engaging in *Regulation and Social Engagement approaches*

Helpful questions for practitioners during this stage
• Is the child able to form safe relationships with any adults? Who are they and how many?
• Are the adults around the child able to connect with the child and make them feel regulated? Do they feel confident in this?
• How able are the adults to regulate their own responses to the child, particularly while they are in survival states?
• What opportunities are there for regulating the senses at home and school throughout the day?
• What opportunities are there for play at home and school with important attachment figures?
• What are the child's peer relationships like? How many healthy friendships do they have?
• Is the child showing signs of wanting to talk about what they have witnessed?
• Are there specific memories that are triggering a survival response and causing the young person distress?

Table 14.5 Regulation and social engagement approaches

	What interventions can look like
Parent work	• Supporting parents to seek out interventions for their own mental health and to prioritise their own self-care and to understand this as the bedrock for caring for their child.
	• Direct work to help parents mentalise their child's thoughts, feelings and behaviours and their own reactions to their child's experiences.
	• Supporting parents to accept and respond to distress empathically, to be curious about what might help and encourage opportunities for playfulness.
	• Examples of approaches that might be helpful here are: Dyadic Developmental Psychotherapy (DDP), Mentalization Based Treatment for families/children (MBT-F/C), Therapeutic Parenting, Non-violent resistance (NVR), Child-Parent psychotherapy and Video Interaction Guidance (VIG).
Exploration and strengthening of the child or young person's relationships	• Working with the child, family and network to explore and understand the quality of the child's relationships.

(Continued)

Table 14.5 (Continued)

	What interventions can look like
	• Thinking collaboratively with the child about options for increasing time with healthy attachment figures and reducing time with people who can be triggering or unhelpful. • Linking the child into pastoral support at school and exploring opportunities for experiences of mastery through schoolwork and extra-curricular activities such as cooking, sport, dance/music and art. • Potential approaches, depending on the family's resources and needs include: systemic family therapy, narrative approaches, genograms and eco-maps, family group conferences and parent-infant/ parent-child psychotherapy.
Trauma memory processing	• If a young person is seeking a space to process specific trauma memories, and the environment is safe enough to do so, it may be helpful to offer individual therapeutic work such as: • Eye Movement Desensitisation Reprocessing (EMDR), Trauma-Focused-CBT, Narrative exposure therapy, Sensorimotor Psychotherapy, drama, movement & art therapies and theraplay.
Regulation based approaches	• These approaches attend to the needs of the child during periods of distress and dysregulation. • The aims of these therapeutic approaches are broadly similar in that they seek to support children and young people to develop internalised 'islands of safety' and a broader awareness of internal experiences so they can best navigate the world without the disruptive impact of their unregulated survival states. • Approaches that fall within this domain include: MBT, CBT, DBT, ACT, EMDR, Compassion focused therapy, creative and expressive therapies, narrative therapy and ego-state type interventions such as Internal-Family systems therapy.
Sensory and body-based interventions	• It is important for young people managing distress and survival states to be moving and engaging in activities that up or down regulate their bodies.

(*Continued*)

Table 14.5 (Continued)

	What interventions can look like
	• If a young person is frequently dissociating and appearing frozen, it may be helpful to teach activities that increase energy and bring them back into their bodies.
	• If a young person is finding themselves often if fight or flight mode, it may be helpful to teach them down regulating techniques such as paced breathing techniques, mindfulness, relaxation & yoga, to calm bodily sensations.
	• Potential interventions and approaches to support somatic/body regulation: EMDR, Sensorimotor Psychotherapy, Sensory Attachment Intervention, Mindfulness based approaches, Neurofeedback, grounding techniques; activities or exercises that involve rhythmic movements e.g., dance, yoga, running, swimming; occupational therapy sensory assessment, sensory diet and sensory integration therapies.

The cortical/learning brain: Processing 'Beyond Trauma'

Many of the approaches discussed work to support the meaning and sense-making of traumatic experiences through the integration of cognitive, emotional and somatic/sensory domains. As well as the specific processing of traumatic memory this stage of intervention can support the child in developing their identity beyond trauma, strengthen existing supportive relationships, build cognitive and emotional resilience and orient the child and family towards the future. The primary goal of this stage is to support the child and family to move beyond trauma and derive lasting meaning from their experiences and treatment. Another important aspect of this work is building towards a safe and reparative ending of support and a transition to safe relationships (Tables 14.6 and 14.7).

Table 14.6 Questions for practitioners engaging in *Processing 'Beyond Trauma' approaches*

Helpful questions for practitioners during this stage

• *Is the child showing signs of wanting to talk to someone about traumatic experiences?*
• *Are they engaging in any meaning-making processes themselves?*
• *How does the families cultural, historical and social context shape the meaning-making process? What aspects can be integrated into this stage?*

Table 14.7 Processing 'Beyond Trauma' approaches

	What interventions can look like
Thinking about child's identity and life story	• Interventions to support the child making sense of who they are beyond the trauma- Narrative therapy, therapeutic life story work, the Tree of Life (Ncube, 2006), Compassion-Focussed Therapy, parts-work and ego-state interventions, creative and expressive therapies. • Building a resilient and balanced self-identity.
Strengthening relationships	• Systemic family therapy-based approaches • Continuing to build structure and routine into the child and family's lives. • Orientation towards future goals and outcomes. • Helping build skills in effective socialisation and communication with others.
Further trauma memory processing	• Eye Movement Desensitisation Reprogramming (EMDR), Trauma-Focused-CBT, Narrative exposure therapy, Sensorimotor Psychotherapy and drama and movement therapies and theraplay.
Relational and cognitive therapies	• MBT, DBT, CBT, ACT, CFT. • Building the capacity to evaluate situations, inhibit responses and build internal resources (positive self) • Helping the development of 'higher-level' thinking skills including problem-solving, planning and organisation.

Conclusion

The impact of IPV on children and adolescents is complex, multi-faceted and highly individualised, being shaped by the social, cultural, psychological and biological systems around and within these young people. Responses to the mental health needs of this group must therefore hold this in mind and be guided by the principles of trauma-informed care and assessment. This chapter has provided a brief, broad overview and guidance to aid professionals in developing holistic sequenced interventions and/or support plans based on collaborative assessments of young people and their families. Although brief, this overview and guidance highlights the complexity of IPV experiences for the child and the family as well as the skilfulness and sensitivity needed for workers and professionals in the field. We note that growth and change occur within safe and nurturing relationships, which are foundational to the success of any intervention and the effectiveness of the teams which support these children. We also consider the importance of staging interventions to meet the young people's developmental needs at each part of their life stage, as well as considering the barriers which professionals may encounter and how these may be managed. We hope to have provided the tools to support readers to map these children's experiences, alongside them and their families, to draw together a destination that both honours their hurt and provides new roots for growth.

References

Adamson, J. L., & Thompson, R. A. (1998). Coping with interparental verbal conflict by children exposed to spouse abuse and children from nonviolent homes. *Journal of Family Violence, 13*(3), 213–232. 10.1023/a:1022896804777

Bateman, A., & Fonagy, P. (2016). *Mentalization-based treatment for personality disorders: A practical guide.* Oxford University Press.

Blaustein, M. E., & Kinniburgh, K. M. (2018). *Treating traumatic stress in children and adolescents: How to foster resilience through attachment, self-regulation, and competency.* Guilford Publications.

Berger, R., & Quiros, L. (2016). Best practices for training trauma-informed practitioners: Supervisors' voice. *Traumatology, 22*(2), 145–154. 10.1037/trm0000076

Bevington, D., Fuggle, P., Cracknell, L., & Fonagy, P. (2017). *Adaptive mentalization-based integrative treatment: A guide for teams to develop systems of care.* Oxford University Press.

Barfield, S., Dobson, C., Gaskill, R., & Perry, B. D. (2012). Neurosequential model of therapeutics in a therapeutic preschool: Implications for work with children with complex neuropsychiatric problems. *International Journal of Play Therapy, 21*(1), 30–44. 10.1037/a0025955

Corrigan, F. M. (2014). Defense responses: Frozen, suppressed, truncated, obstructed, and malfunctioning. In U. F. Lanius, S. L. Paulsen, & F. M. Corrigan (Eds.), *Neurobiology and treatment of traumatic dissociation: Towards an embodied self* (p. 131–152). Springer Publishing Company.

Cook, A., Spinazzola, J., Ford, J., Lanktree, C., Blaustein, M., Cloitre, M., DeRosa, R., Hubbard, R., Kagan, R., Liautaud, J., Mallah, K., Olafson, E., & van der Kolk, B. (2005). Complex trauma in children and adolescents. *Psychiatric Annals, 35*(5), 390–398. 10.3928/00485713-20050501-05

Cusack, K. J., Frueh, B. C., & Brady, K. T. (2004). Trauma history screening in a Community Mental Health Center. *Psychiatric Services, 55*(2), 157–162. 10.1176/appi.ps.55.2.157

Daniels, M. A., & Robinson, S. L. (2019). The shame of it all: A review of shame in organizational life. *Journal of Management, 45*(6), 2448–2473. 10.1177/0149206318817604

Deblinger, E., & Runyon, M. K. (2005). Understanding and treating feelings of shame in children who have experienced maltreatment. *Child Maltreatment, 10*(4), 364–376. 10.1177/1077559505279306

El-Sheikh, M., Cummings, E. M., Kouros, C. D., Elmore-Staton, L., & Buckhalt, J. (2008). Marital psychological and physical aggression and children's mental and physical health: Direct, mediated, and moderated effects. *Journal of Consulting and Clinical Psychology, 76*(1), 138–148. 10.1037/0022-006x.76.1.138

Fonagy, P., & Allison, E. (2014). The role of mentalizing and epistemic trust in the therapeutic relationship. *Psychotherapy, 51*(3), 372–380. 10.1037/a0036505

Kitzmann, K. M., Gaylord, N. K., Holt, A. R., & Kenny, E. D. (2003). Child witnesses to domestic violence: A meta-analytic review. *Journal of Consulting and Clinical Psychology*, 71(2), 339–352. 10.1037/0022-006x.71.2.339

Knight, C., & Borders, L. D. (2018). Trauma-informed supervision: Core components and unique dynamics in varied practice contexts. *The Clinical Supervisor*, 37(1), 1–6. 10.1080/07325223.2018.1440680

Kurtz, A. (2019). *How to run reflective practice groups: A guide for healthcare professionals.* Routledge.

Layne, C. M., Ippen, C. G., Strand, V., Stuber, M., Abramovitz, R., Reyes, G., Jackson, L. A., Ross, L., Curtis, A., Lipscomb, L., & Pynoos, R. (2011). The core curriculum on childhood trauma: A tool for training a trauma-informed workforce. *Psychological Trauma: Theory, Research, Practice, and Policy*, 3(3), 243–252. 10.1037/a0025039

MacMillan, H. L., Wathen, C. N., Barlow, J., Fergusson, D. M., Leventhal, J. M., & Taussig, H. N. (2009). Interventions to prevent child maltreatment and associated impairment. *The Lancet*, 373(9659), 250–266. 10.1016/s0140-6736(08)61708-0

Minze, L. C., McDonald, R., Rosentraub, E. L., & Jouriles, E. N. (2010). Making sense of family conflict: Intimate partner violence and preschoolers' externalizing problems. *Journal of Family Psychology*, 24(1), 5–11. 10.1037/a0018071

Ncube, N. (2006). The tree of life project. *International Journal of Narrative Therapy and Community Work*, 2006(1), 3–16. https://search.informit.org/doi/10.3316/informit.197106237773394

Perry, B. D. (2006). Applying principles of neurodevelopment to clinical work with maltreated and traumatized children: The neurosequential model of therapeutics. In N. B. Webb (Ed.), *Working with traumatized youth in child welfare* (pp. 27–52). The Guilford Press.

Perry, B., & Szalavitz, M. (2007). Stairway to heaven: Treating children in the crosshairs of trauma. *Psychotherapy Networker*, 31(2), 56–64.

Porges, S. W. (2011). *The polyvagal theory: Neurophysiological foundations of emotions, attachment, communication, and self-regulation (Norton Series on Interpersonal Neurobiology).* WW Norton & Company.

Read, J., Harper, D., Tucker, I., & Kennedy, A. (2018). Do adult mental health services identify child abuse and neglect? A systematic review. *International Journal of Mental Health Nursing*, 27(1), 7–19. 10.1111/inm.12369

Rivett, M., Howarth, E., & Harold, G. (2006). "Watching from the Stairs": Towards an Evidence-based Practice in Work with Child Witnesses of Domestic Violence. *Clinical Child Psychology and Psychiatry*, 11(1), 103–125. 10.1177/1359104506059131

Saxe, G. N., Ellis, B. H., & Brown, A. D. (2016). *Trauma systems therapy for children and teens.* Guilford Publications.

Skuse, T., & Matthew, J. (2015). The trauma recovery model: Sequencing youth justice interventions for young people with complex needs. *Prison Service Journal*, 220, 16–25.

Sternberg, K. J., Lamb, M. E., Guterman, E., & Abbott, C. B. (2006). Effects of early and later family violence on children's behavior problems and depression: A longitudinal, multi-informant perspective. *Child Abuse & Neglect*, 30(3), 283–306. 10.1016/j.chiabu.2005.10.008

Sweeney, A., Clement, S., Filson, B., & Kennedy, A. (2016). Trauma-informed mental healthcare in the UK: What is it and how can we further its development? *Mental Health Review Journal*, 21(3), 174–192. 10.1108/mhrj-01-2015-0006

Snodgrass, C., & Selman, M. (2019). The psychologically-informed partnership approach: Innovation in working with vulnerable and marginalised children, young people and families. *Clinical Psychology Forum, 1*(321), 12–18. 10.53841/bpscpf.2019. 1.321.12

The National Child Traumatic Stress Network (2018). *Assessment of Complex Trauma by Mental Health Professionals.* Online publication: https://www.nctsn.org/ resources/assessment-complex-trauma-mental-health-professionals

Treisman, K. (2016). *Working with relational and developmental trauma in children and adolescents.* Taylor & Francis.

Treisman, K. (2017). *A therapeutic treasure box for working with children and adolescents with developmental trauma: Creative techniques and activities.* Jessica Kingsley Publishers.

Treisman, K. (2021). *A treasure box for creating trauma-informed organisations: a ready to use resource for trauma, adversity, and culturally informed, infused and responsive systems (1st ed.).* Jessica Kingsley Publishers.

van der Kolk, B. A., Roth, S., Pelcovitz, D., Sunday, S., & Spinazzola, J. (2005). Disorders of extreme stress: The empirical foundation of a complex adaptation to trauma. *Journal of Traumatic Stress, 18*(5), 389–399. 10.1002/jts.20047

Zarling, A. L., Taber-Thomas, S., Murray, A., Knuston, J. F., Lawrence, E., Valles, N.-L., DeGarmo, D. S., & Bank, L. (2013). Internalizing and externalizing symptoms in young children exposed to intimate partner violence: Examining intervening processes. *Journal of Family Psychology, 27*(6), 945–955. 10.1037/a0034804

15 Mind the blind spot

Accounts of fathering by domestically violent men

Susan Heward-Belle
Sydney University, Australia

Introduction

Matthia recently graduated from social work and has been working as a front-line worker in a statutory child protection service. After six months of employment, she notices that fathers who use domestic violence pose significant short and long-term dangers to most of the women and children she works with. However, Matthia notices that the primary focus of most of her work pivots on assessing women's capacity to protect their children from their partner's violence. She rarely engages with men to assess their fathering or to work towards changing their abusive patterns of behaviour. She starts to worry that she may be burdening mothers with unrealistic demands to separate from or take most of the responsibility for changing the abusive behaviours of their partners or ex-partners. Occasionally, Matthia hears more experienced workers remonstrate in frustration about women 'choosing to stay' in destructive relationships with abusive men. When she turns to the research, she discovers a lot of information about the adverse impact of domestic violence on children and young people but very little about fathers who perpetrate domestic violence to guide her practice.

Matthia's observations on practice are reflective of the complex experiences of many practitioners who work with families experiencing domestic violence. Her observations point to an entrenched and gendered pattern commonly observed in institutional responses to families, particularly within child welfare and family law settings (De Simone & Heward-Belle, 2020). Characteristically, this response involves minimal to no engagement with men/fathers and a simultaneous over-reliance on women/mothers. Edleson (1998) described this pattern, as the 'invisible father/over-responsible mother phenomenon', although I will use the term 'exonerated fathers/over-responsible mothers' to signify my belief that there is a more active process occurring within the

DOI: 10.4324/9781003124634-19

institutional responses to fathers who perpetrate domestic violence. This involves more than just passively failing to see them, it involves actively making choices which results in failing to hold many accountable for their behaviours. Examples of the ways in which professionals may participate in practices that exonerate fathers who use domestic violence are described in Table 15.1. This phenomenon frequently results in women's private lives and mothering being laid bare, increasingly through the use of procedural and overly technocratic risk assessment processes. Professionals often construct mothers as 'failing to protect' their children, leading oftentimes to the initiation of statutory action by child protection authorities and judicial officers. In the most extreme cases, this can involve children being removed from their immediate family and placed into out-of-home-care (Higgins & Kaspiew, 2011). Other examples of the ways in which professionals may participate in practices that result in the 'over-responsibilisation' of women mothering through domestic violence are described in Table 15.2.

This chapter seeks to redress sexist institutional practices inherent within the exonerated father/responsible mother paradigm by contributing to the growing body of knowledge exploring the attitudes and behaviours of men who use violence and coercive control. Research in this area will be reviewed and some findings from a research study conducted in Australia with men who were involved in a men's behaviour change programme regarding their accounts of exposing children to domestic violence will be presented. It will contribute to understandings of children's and young people's responses to experiencing domestic violence. It provides important insights into how fathers' behaviours and attitudes may contribute to childhood development and the ecology of the family. This is an area of enquiry that is often neglected or left as a professional 'blind spot'. This chapter will also contribute practice ideas about the professional assessment of domestically violent men's fathering.

Literature review

It is estimated that between 133 and 275 million children globally are exposed to domestic violence (UN Secretary General's Study on Violence Against Children, 2006). Twenty to twenty-five percent of children living in the United Kingdom and the United States, witness domestic violence during their childhood and adolescent years (Finkelhor et al., 2015; Radford, 2011). Although these numbers are shocking, they are considered conservative estimates given that there is limited reliable data available on the prevalence of domestic violence internationally (Ruiz-Pérez et al., 2007). In countries that have adequate reporting systems in place, domestic violence remains a crime that is significantly under-reported often due to the dynamics associated with domestic abuse that include silence, fear, stigma and helplessness (Ahmad & Jaleel, 2015). Even when domestic violence is reported, children and young people's experiences often go unseen and when their experiences are

Table 15.1 Institutional exonerating practices

Colludes with father's use of minimisations, denials, justification (accepts father's accounts that obfuscate responsibility – i.e., I was drunk, I was stressed, nothing happened, etc)	Subtly or overtly blames mother for her victimisation (i.e., frames her as provoking her partner's violence)	Does little to investigate or acknowledge the multiple ways that the father's use of violence and control might affect each child in the family	Renders the father invisible (i.e., asks very few questions about the father and his fathering experiences, practices and capacity)
Fails to collect information that can assist in assessing the level of dangerousness that the father poses to the mother and children	Avoids talking about the impact of the father's use of violence and control on the mother's sense of wellbeing; her ability to mother her children in the way she wants to	Problematises the mother's responses to violence rather than the father's use of violence and control that have contributed to the mother's responses	Demonstrates a narrow understanding of domestic violence (i.e., mainly asks/ documents physical violence – does not canvas the myriad of tactics of power and control used by the father)
Separates father's use of violent control from his fathering practices (i.e., 'bad partner but good parent')	Concentrates mainly on assessing mothers' parenting capacity	Demonstrates limited curiosity about how each child in the family is developing	Mutualises responsibility for domestic violence rather than clearly articulating that the father's use of violence and control is the issue of concern
Does something that potentially increases the level of dangerousness for the mother and/or the children	Offers up explanations for domestic violence that help the father avoid taking responsibility for his decisions and actions	Constructs mother's resistance and/or survival strategies as pathological (frames her as having a mental illness and/or a substance use problem)	Engages in behaviour that is disrespectful or overly judgmental and shaming

Table 15.2 Institutional survivor-blaming practices

Giving the mother an ultimatum or veiled threat	Subtly or overtly blames mother for her victimisation (i.e., Frames her as provoking violence)	Does little to investigate or acknowledge the multiple actions that the mother takes to provide care, love, support and protection to her children within the context of great adversity	Renders the father invisible (i.e., asks few questions about the father and his fathering practices, experiences or capacity).
Demonstrates little empathy or understanding of the difficult context in which the mother is parenting	Overburdens the mother with research findings about the adverse outcomes of childhood exposure to domestic violence	Makes the mother feel responsible for children's behaviour problems that arise in the context of chronic exposure to their father's violence and coercive control	Demonstrates a narrow understanding of domestic violence (i.e., Mainly asks questions/documents information about physical violence – does not establish the perpetrator's pattern of violence and coercive control
Separates the father's use of violence and coercive control from his fathering practices (i.e., Bad partner but good parent)	Concentrates mainly on assessing mothers' parenting capacity	Demonstrates limited curiosity about how each child in the family is developing	Mutualises responsibility for domestic violence (i.e., uses phrases like 'violent/dysfunctional/toxic/co-dependent/volatile relationship'
Engages in practices that decrease the safety and wellbeing of women and their children	Problematises the mother's responses to violence and coercive control (i.e., Frames her as 'resistant', 'uncooperative', 'difficult')	Constructs mother's resistance and/or survival strategies as pathological (frames her as having a mental illness and/or a substance use problem)	Expects the mother to pass on institutional messages to the perpetrator.

considered, they are often relegated to the status of 'secondary victims' of intimate partner violence (Kovacs & Tomison, 2003).

Over the past three decades, the evidence base examining children's and young people's experiences of living with domestic violence has increased. It is now well accepted that experiencing domestic violence is a risk factor that can adversely impact children's and young people's health and development across their lifespan (Campo, 2015; Holt, Buckley & Whelan, 2008); Studies from multiple countries including India, China, Columbia, Egypt, Mexico, the Philippines and South Africa, show a strong relationship between childhood exposure to violence against women and violence against children (Krug et al., 2002). Children who experience domestic violence are at higher risk of experiencing additional forms of child maltreatment including neglect, sexualised violence, physical, psychological and other forms of emotional abuse (Tomison, 2000). The perpetrator's pattern of violence and control extends to their treatment of children who are often abused or neglected in order to exert power and control over both women and children (Radford & Hester, 2006).

Not all exposed children experience significant, or similar responses and individual variations are noted within the population of exposed children and young people (Australian Institute of Health and Welfare, 2020). A complex interaction of risk, resilience and protective factors operating at multiple levels influences how children and young people develop and respond to developmental traumas including domestic violence and other forms of childhood adversity (Bronfenbrenner, 2006). A meta-analysis of 118 studies involving 101,592 participants found protective factors across multiple contexts including families, school and peers, were key features influencing resilience within individual children exposed to violence (Yule, Houston & Grych, 2019). The developmental timing of victimisation (Dierkhising, Ford, Branson, Grasso & Lee, 2019); the presence of polyvictimisation (Turner, Finkelhor & Ormrod, 2010); access to responsive interventions that reduce and prevent domestic violence through empowering survivors (Memiah, Ah Mu, Prevot, Cook, Mwangi, Mwangi, Owuor & Biadgilign, 2018); and the level of maternal warmth and responsiveness (Lapierre, 2010) have also been identified as significant factors that moderate the impact of childhood exposure to domestic violence.

Whilst advances have been made in relation to our understanding of the factors that influence children's and young people's responses to domestic violence, the influence of paternal behaviour remains a largely unexplored area in both research and professional practice. There are many valid reasons to increase scholarly attention and develop practice in this area including to redress gender inequity and the pervasive practice of blaming mothers for children's behaviour problems linked to domestic violence (Edleson, 1998); to develop more effective and targeted programmes to improve the fathering practices of men who use domestic violence and coercive control; to increase our understanding of the dynamics involved in situations where violence is transmitted inter-generationally; and to inform public policy and institutional responses particularly in the child protection and family law arenas (Holden & Barker, 2004).

Institutional responses

The increased understanding about the potentially deleterious impact of domestic violence on children and young people led to the construction of childhood exposure to domestic violence as a form of child maltreatment (Richards, 2011). In Anglophone, colonised countries, this construction led to legal and policy remedies pivoting on the provision of a statutory child protection response to allegations of childhood exposure (Fernandez, 2014).

Child protection agencies receive high levels of reports annually from professionals and the public expressing concerns for the wellbeing of children and young people due to exposure to domestic violence. An Australian study using organisational reporting data found that approximately 71 000 children across three states were reported to authorities over a four-year period due to allegations of exposure to domestic violence (Humphreys & Healey, 2017), comprising 16% of total reports. Other studies using different methodologies have found higher rates. For example, the prevalence of domestic violence within families reported to child protection authorities in Canada accounted for 50% of the child protection caseload when a qualitative in-depth survey of child protection case files was used. (Cross, Mathews, Tonmyr, Scott & Ouimet, 2012). An unpublished study in South Australia which examined child protection reports, found one in four children under the age of 10 were reported to child protection authorities and of these children, 90% have had multiple reports being made about severe abuse and neglect, which often included exposure to domestic violence, parental substance misuse and parental mental ill-health (ABC, 2018). Childhood exposure to domestic violence is also a common feature of many allegations made within the context of family law matters. In the Australian Family Law Court, 68% of matters contained allegations of childhood exposure to domestic violence (Moloney et al., 2007) and allegations of domestic violence were present in over 51% of litigated family law cases and over 70% of cases that were not judicially determined (AIFS, 2007).

The ethics and effectiveness of reporting children exposed to domestic violence to statutory authorities is contested and many critics have argued that this approach has not delivered appropriate, proportionate or timely responses to the needs of women survivors and their children (Hesse-Biber, 2007; Waugh & Bonner, 2002). Instead, this framing has frequently delivered a sexist response that disadvantages women, rendering them responsible for men's violence. Moreover, women are frequently labelled as negligent in the performance of their maternal duties due to their so-called 'failure to protect' their children by not living up to societal standards embodied in the construct of the 'good mother' (Heward-Belle, 2017). As Strega et al. (2009) point out the practice pattern most often observed within western, colonial child welfare settings involves holding the victim of violence responsible, whilst the perpetrator is missing from the analysis.

In child protection and family law, the limited evidence base pertaining to the fathering of men who perpetrate domestic violence has profound implications. In these areas, ascertaining the risk of harm to women and children requires a thorough assessment of the fathering of men who perpetrate domestic violence. Too often, however, it has been and continues to be the survivor/mother whose parenting is scrutinised while the risks posed by the perpetrator are not adequately assessed (Humphreys & Absler, 2011). In the current Australian law context, which increasingly emphasises shared parenting post-separation, knowledge about the fathering of men who use domestic violence is vital to the assessments that inform post separation parenting arrangements. However, it is often not the focus of these assessments (Elizabeth, Gavey & Tolmie, 2010; Laing, 2010; Morris, 2009). The invisible father/responsible mother phenomenon often leads to the 'secondary victimisation' of women and children (Laing, 2017).

What do we know about the fathering practices and experiences of men who perpetrate domestic violence?

Recently, there has been a surge of interest in fatherhood from a variety of disciplines (Lamb, 2000; Marsiglio & Cohan, 2000), which has occurred against a backdrop of major shifts in family life, gender relations, economic changes and increases in both women's participation in the paid labour force and men's involvement as primary carers. The construction of fathering has broadened in many societies and there has been an increased interest in understanding how fathers influence childhood development (Rosenberg, 2006). However, the mainstream fatherhood scholarship has largely neglected the cohort of fathers who use domestic violence. The existing small body of research has focused on fathers' perceptions of how domestic violence affects children, their fathering patterns and practices and their over-representation as perpetrators of childhood abuse and neglect (Thompson-Walsh et al., 2021).

Fathers who use domestic violence are not a homogenous group and as such their perceptions of the impact of their abusive behaviour on children differs across studies. Salisbury et al. (2009) and Sternberg et al. (2006) found that few men in their samples acknowledged the adverse impact of domestic violence on childhood development. However, other researchers found that most fathers understood that domestic violence harms children and young people (Baker et al., 2001; Fox et al., 2001; Rothman et al., 2007). Heward-Belle (2016) found that whilst many participants reported understanding the impact of domestic violence on children, due to their own childhood experiences; they minimised the impact of domestic violence on their own children. Of particular relevance for policy makers and violence prevention campaigners is the finding that many men in these studies were aware of the potentially deleterious impact of domestic violence on childhood development yet continued to use domestic violence. This finding should lead to a degree of scepticism about assertions that prevention efforts should rest entirely on campaigns to educate people about the impact of domestic violence on children.

Research examining men's perceptions of their fathering has contributed to an increased understanding of the child-rearing practices of men who use domestic violence. Qualitative research studies have found that this subset of fathers are more likely to engage in abusive and neglectful parenting practices across a range of abuse types (Harne, 2011; Salisbury et al., 2009; Heward-Belle, 2016). Other qualitative research has highlighted the complex feelings experienced by men who use domestic violence reporting that whilst they yearn for positive relationships with their children, they are constricted due to their violence-promoting beliefs and abusive behaviours (Perel & Peled, 2008). Other studies have found that some men who use violence and control experience significant levels of shame, guilt and remorse (Fox & Benson, 2004; Fox et al., 2001). The remainder of this chapter will spotlight some research findings from an Australian study with fathers who were participating in a men's behaviour change programme.

Accounts of fathers use of domestic violence

Seventeen men who had used domestic violence against the mother of at least one of their children were recruited from a men's behaviour change programme in a coastal community in New South Wales, Australia into a study that explored their lived experiences of fathering. Men ranged in age from 26 to 46 years, with a mean age of 35 years. Collectively, they were biological fathers to 45 children, two of whom had died in two separate families. Each man was a biological father to at least one child and four men also identified themselves as stepfathers to an additional six children. The 51 children and young people ranged in age from three months to 22 years. Most participants had minimal formal education with 47% indicating that their highest educational level of attainment was year 10 (age 16) or below. Six men were unemployed, and they recorded an annual income level lower than the average.

The majority of fathers reported high levels of substance misuse and some also reported experiencing mental ill-health alongside severe and frequent use of domestic violence. Ten of seventeen fathers described long-standing substance misuse problems that adversely affected their day-to-day functioning and that of their family members. For most of these men, polysubstance use was reported to be a daily occurrence and included the use of substances including, alcohol, marijuana, heroin, amphetamines, cocaine and/or ecstasy. Five of the men indicated that they had received a mental health diagnosis which included depression, Bi-Polar, Post Traumatic Stress Disorder (PTSD) and/or drug-induced psychosis. Nearly half of the men reported that they had a criminal record for domestic violence-related offences and eleven had been the subject of a protection order, of which, five men had been charged with breaching.

Most men reported that they used a myriad strategies to exert power and control over women and children including physical abuse, sexualised violence, emotional degradation, verbal abuse, coercive control, financial abuse and social isolation. Men described perpetrating frequent and severe physical violence against their partners and ex-partners which children were exposed to. The following statements were common accounts of domestic violence experienced by women and children:

Angus: I wanted beer and she stood in front of the fridge and said you're not having any more to drink I said if I want a beer get out of the road and she wouldn't so I've grabbed her by the throat and I've basically thrown her across the um kitchen, not thrown her, thrown her but like pushed her.

Interviewer: And what happened to her on that occasion?

Angus: Um like she just went walking backwards sort of thing, didn't hurt, get any physical damage apart from a bit of a red mark around her neck ... Nelson (child) seen it and um he was pretty upset with it.

Jack: I was holding Stan (baby) in my arms and she got in my face and I, I pushed her out of the way and she fell back onto our lounge and cracked her head open on the window sill which was right up against the back of the lounge and she had to go to hospital so the police were called.

Ken: I was physically punching her in the head and in the body ... (the children) were in their rooms hiding ... they could hear and then they ran off.

More than a third of men reported that they had physically assaulted pregnant women and unborn children. Many of these assaults were potentially life-threatening as the following accounts illustrate:

Keith: ... we had an argument on the way home I don't know why or what it was about but I pulled the hand brake on as we were driving along and the car spun around a few times you know and I'm thinking shit she's pregnant with me child.

Anthony: I pushed her up against a cupboard when she was pregnant and knocked it down on her.

Angus: ... I pushed her and um she like we were having an argument she said something to me ... and she went like she was pregnant with Todd she went out the back screen door.

Most men denied using physical force against children. Men who reported using physical force against children described the precipitating events and their related feelings after the events. One man described physically assaulting his young son for a minor infraction of his rules and claimed to feel remorse about his actions:

Dennis: and I remember just pulling my strap out and telling him to lay across the bed and I strapped him and um cause that's what that's what was done to me and I just remember I saw the marks on his backside and I went I'll never do that again you know I remember just hitting him four or five times and with the belt going and you know it was just like it was just out of frustration and for myself and for rage not because what he did was deserving of that, it was just something, shit something minor I told him not to touch something a toy or something and then he lost it.

Another man described how he felt provoked by his 11-year-old step-son and did not appear to recognise the paradoxical bind that he placed the child in. This child, like many others, was actively taught to disrespect and abuse his mother. By siding with his step-father and supporting his view of the mother as 'useless, lazy, stupid and incompetent,' he was intermittently rewarded and protected. At other times, however, this placed him at risk as his step-father punished him for failing to demonstrate respect for his mother.

Many men perceived that their partners, ex-partners and children suffered intensely. Impacts included: the death of an infant due to premature labour allegedly precipitated by a domestic assault, the repeated suicide attempts of an 11-year-old boy, numerous miscarriages, serious and potentially life-threatening illnesses and injuries sustained by women and children, the removal of numerous children from their families, as well as the ongoing emotional and psychological effects of living in a chronic state of fear and terror were described by the fathers in this study. All men expressed their opinion of the impact of domestic violence on children and young people generally, with most describing it as potentially devastating and long lasting. Fewer men, however, perceived that their own children had been deleteriously affected and most men minimised the impact on their partners and ex-partners. Most men described their partners as culpable and believed that their abusive behaviours were usually provoked. A diverse range of fathering behaviours were described which were correlated with men's constructions of their masculinity and their beliefs about their locus of control. Even though men's fathering was diverse, all men posed significant but different risks to women and children.

Since conducting this research, I have often been asked, 'how did you get men to talk to you about their domestic violence?' This is not surprising given that most health and welfare professionals receive limited tertiary education about engaging men generally and practically no training about engaging those perpetrating domestic violence (Hegarty et al., 2016). For many professionals, it may not be part of their remit to engage fathers generally and domestically violent fathers specifically. Child protection workers and judicial officers receive specific training and may use specific risk assessment models and procedures, which are well summarised by Messing, Campbell and Snider (2017). However, they often do not receive sufficient training around starting conversations about fathering with men who use domestic violence and consequently may default to depending upon survivors as informants who are expected to answer questions about men's fathering. The following questions yielded some success in starting a conversation with the men who participated in this study and may assist professionals (particularly early career professionals) whose work involves engaging men who use domestic violence. These questions do not replace agency risk assessment protocols but may help initiate conversations that will place men's violence towards women at the centre of assessment and intervention efforts, rather than at the periphery.

- I am interested in finding out about your relationship with your child(ren) can you tell me a bit about that?
- How would you describe the relationship with your child(ren)?
- How do you think your children might describe their relationship with you?
- What do you like about this relationship?
- Do you have any concerns about your relationship?
- How do you spend time with your child(ren)?
- How would you describe your child's relationship with their mum/siblings/ other family members/friends?
- What is fatherhood like for you?
- How did you react when you found out you were going to become a father? Is this something that you had planned or wanted?
- What are the key ingredients of being a good father? How do you see yourself measuring up to these ideas?
- What do you like about being a father?
- What are your strengths?
- What do you find challenging?
- Is there anything that you would do differently as a father compared to how you were fathered? Compared to how you have fathered in the past?
- Can you tell me how you think that domestic violence may have affected your relationship with your child(ren), with their mother, with other family members?
- Does domestic violence affect children? If so, how? What makes you think this?
- What kind of father do you want to be? What do you need to do to get there? What might happen if you don't change?

Conclusion

The invisibility of men in most health and welfare services can result in professionals holding few expectations of fathers but unrealistic expectations of mothers. Professionals may perpetuate gendered social norms which place a disproportionate level of responsibility on mothers to meet children's physical, social and emotional needs. In situations where fathers use violence, gendered social norms frequently contribute to professionals holding attitudes that paradoxically hold women accountable for 'failing to protect' their children from abusive fathers rather than the person responsible. Professionals who work in non-statutory settings infrequently see men and many lack the confidence or organisational support to engage at-risk fathers in conversations about potentially abusive behaviour (Humphreys & Heward-Belle, 2020). What is urgently needed is research, practice guidance and clear policies on how to promote professional engagement safely and ethically with men who have or are at risk of perpetrating domestic violence, in order to prevent and reduce violence against women and their children.

References

Ahmad, A. & Jaleel, A. (2015). Prevalence and correlates of violence against women in Nepal: Findings from Nepal Demographic Health Survey, 2011. *Advances in Applied Sociology (Irvine, CA)*, *5*(4), 119–128. 10.4236/aasoci.2015.54011

ABC. (2018). Australia facing an epidemic of child abuse and neglect. Retrieved from https://www.abc.net.au/news/2018-09-16.

Australian Institute of Family Studies. (2007). *Cooperation and coordination: An evaluation of the family court of Australia's Magellan case management model.*

Australian Institute of Health and Welfare. (2020). Australia's children. Retrieved from https://www.aihw.gov.au/reports/children-youth/australias-children

Baker, C. K., Perilla, J. L., & Norris, F. H. (2001). Parenting stress and parenting competence among Latino men who batter. *Journal of Interpersonal Violence*, *16*(11), 1139–1157. 10.1177/088626001016011003

Bronfenbrenner, U., & Morris, P. A. (2006). The bioecological model of human development. In Damon, W. (Series Ed.) & Lerner, R. M. (Vol. Ed.), *Handbook of child psychology: Theoretical model of human development* (pp. 793–828). New York, NY: John Wiley.

Campo, M. (2015). *Children's exposure to domestic and family violence: Key issues and responses (CFCA Paper No. 36)*. Melbourne: Child Family Community Australia information exchange, Australian Institute of Family Studies.

Cross, T. P., Mathews, B., Tonmyr, L., Scott, D., & Ouimet, C. (2012). Child welfare policy and practice on children's exposure to domestic violence. *Child Abuse & Neglect*, *36*(3), 210–216. 10.1016/j.chiabu.2011.11.004

De Simone, T., & Heward-Belle, S. (2020). Evidencing better child protection practice: Why representations of domestic violence matter. *Current Issues in Criminal Justice*, *32*(4), 403–419. 10.1080/10345329.2020.1840957

Dierkhising, C. B., Ford, J. D., Branson, C., Grasso, D. J., & Lee, R. (2019). Developmental timing of polyvictimization: Continuity, change, and association with adverse outcomes in adolescence. *Child Abuse & Neglect*, *87*, 40–50. 10.1016/j.chiabu.2018.07.022

Edleson, J. L. (1998). Responsible mothers and invisible men: Child protection in the case of adult domestic violence. *Journal of Interpersonal Violence*, *13*(2), 294–298. 10.1177/088626098013002010

Elizabeth, V., Gavey, N., & Tolmie, J. (2010). Between a rock and a hard place: Resident mothers and the moral dilemmas they face during custody disputes. *Feminist Legal Studies*, *18*(3), 253–274. 10.1007/s10691-010-9159-9

Fernandez, E. (2014). Child protection and vulnerable families: Trends and issues in the Australian context. *Social Sciences (Basel)*, *3*(4), 785–808. 10.3390/socsci3040785

Finkelhor, D., Turner, H. A., Shattuck, A., & Hamby, S. L. (2015). Prevalence of childhood exposure to violence, crime, and abuse: Results from the national survey of children's exposure to violence. *JAMA Pediatrics*, *169*(8), 746–754. 10.1001/jamapediatrics.2015.0676

Fox, G. L., & Benson, M. L. (2004). Violent men, bad dads? Fathering profiles of men involved in intimate partner violence. In R. D. Day & M. E. Lamb (Eds.), *Conceptualizing and measuring father involvement* (pp. 359–384). Lawrence Erlbaum Associates Publishers.

Fox, N. A., Henderson, H. A., Rubin, K. H., Calkins, S. D., & Schmidt, L. A. (2001). Continuity and discontinuity of behavioural inhibition and exuberance: Psychophysiological and behavioural influences across the first four years of life. *Child Development*, *72*(1), 1–21. 10.1111/1467-8624.00262

Harne, L. (2011). *Violent fathering and the risks to children: The need for change*. Bristol, UK: Bristol University Press.

Hegarty, K., Forsdike-Young, K., Tarzia, L., Schweitzer, R., & Vlais, R. (2016). Identifying and responding to men who use violence in their intimate relationships. *Australian Family Physician*, *45*(4), 176–181. https://search.informit.org/doi/10.3316/informit.019749393759289

Hesse-Biber, S. (2007). *Feminist research: Exploring the interconnections of epistemology, methodology, and method*. Handbook of Feminist Research: Theory and Praxis. pp. 1–26.

Heward-Belle, S. (2016). The diverse fathering practices of men who perpetrate domestic violence. *Australian Social Work*, *69*(3), 323–337. 10.1080/0312407X.2015.1057748

Heward-Belle, S. (2017). Exploiting the "good mother" as a tactic of coercive control: Domestically violent men's assaults on women as mothers. *Affilia*, *32*(3), 374–389. 10.1177/0886109917706935

Higgins, D. & Kaspiew, R. (2011). Child protection and family law … Joining the dots. *National Child Protection Clearing House*, *34*, 1–24. https://aifs.gov.au/cfca/publications/child-protection-and-family-law-joining-dots/export

Holden, G. W., & Barker, T. (2004). Fathers in violent homes. In M. E. Lamb (Ed.), *The role of the father in child development* (4th ed., pp. 417–445). Hoboken, NJ: John Wiley & Sons.

Holt, S., Buckley, H., & Whelan, S. (2008). The impact of exposure to domestic violence on children and young people: A review of the literature. *Child: Care, Health & Development*, *34*(6), 840–841. 10.1111/j.1365-2214.2008.00904_5.x

Humphreys, C., & Absler, D. (2011). History repeating: Child protection responses to domestic violence: History repeating child protection. *Child & Family Social Work*, *16*(4), 464–473. 10.1111/j.1365-2206.2011.00761.x

Humphreys, C., & Healey, L. (2017). *Pathways and research into collaborative inter-agency practice: Collaborative work across the child protection and specialist domestic and family violence interface: Final report (ANROWS Horizons 03/2017)*. Sydney, NSW: ANROWS.

Humphreys, C., Healey, L., & Heward-Belle, S. (2020). Fathers who use domestic violence: Organisational capacity building and practice development. *Child & Family Social Work, 25*(S1), 18–27. 10.1111/cfs.12708

Kovacs, K., & Tomison, A. (2003). An Analysis of current australian program initiatives for children exposed to domestic violence. *The Australian Journal of Social Issues, 38*(4), 513–540. 10.1002/j.1839-4655.2003.tb01158.x

Krug E. et al., eds. (2002). *World report on violence and health.* Geneva: World Health Organization.

Laing, L. (2010). *No way to live: Women's experiences of negotiating the family law system in the context of domestic violence.* University of Sydney and Benevolent Society.

Laing, L. (2017). Secondary victimization: Domestic violence survivors navigating the family law system. *Violence Against Women, 23*(11), 1314–1335. 10.1177/107780121 6659942

Lamb, M. E. (2000). The history of research on father involvement: An overview. *Marriage & Family Review, 29*(2-3), 23–42. 10.1300/J002v29n02_03

Lapierre, S. (2010). Striving to be "good" mothers: Abused women's experiences of mothering. *Child Abuse Review (Chichester, England: 1992), 19*(5), 342–357. 10.1002/car.1113

Marsiglio, W., & Cohan, M. (2000). Contextualizing father involvement and paternal influence: Sociological and qualitative themes. *Marriage & Family Review, 29*(2-3), 75–95. 10.1300/J002v29n02_06

Memiah, P., Ah Mu, T., Prevot, K., Cook, C. K., Mwangi, M. M., Mwangi, E. W., … Biadgilign, S. (2018). The prevalence of intimate partner violence, associated risk factors, and other moderating effects: Findings from the Kenya National Health demographic survey. *Journal of Interpersonal Violence,* 1–21. 10.1177/088626051 8804177

Messing, J. T., Campbell, J. C., & Snider, C. (2017). Validation and adaptation of the danger assessment-5: A brief intimate partner violence risk assessment. *Journal of Advanced Nursing, 73*(12), 3220–3230. 10.1111/jan.13459

Moloney, L., Smyth, B., Weston, R., Richardson, N., Qu, L., & Gray, M. (2007). *Allegations of family violence and child abuse in family law children's proceedings: A pre-reform exploratory study.* Melbourne, Vic: Australian Institute of Family Studies.

Morris, A. (2009). Gendered dynamics of abuse and violence in families: Considering the abusive household gender regime. *Child Abuse Review (Chichester, England: 1992), 18*(6), 414–427. 10.1002/car.1098

Perel, G., & Peled, E. (2008). The fathering of violent men: Constriction and yearning. *Violence Against Women, 14*(4), 457–482. 10.1177/1077801208314846

Radford, L., & Hester, M. (2006). *Mothering through domestic violence.* London: Jessica Kingsley.

Radford, L. et al. (2011). *Child abuse and neglect in the UK today.* NSPCC

Richards, K. (2011). Children's exposure to domestic violence in Australia. *Trends and Issues in Crime and Criminal Justice, 419,* 1–7. https://search.informit.org/doi/10.3316/informit.673124328907485

Rosenberg, J., Wilcox, W. B., & United States. (2006). *The importance of fathers in the healthy development of children.* Washington, D.C.: U.S. Dept. Health and Human Services, Administration for Children and Families, Administration on Children, Youth and Families, Children's Bureau, Office of Child Abuse and Neglect.

Rothman, E., Mandel, D., & Silverman, J. (2007). Abusers' perceptions of the effect of their intimate partner violence on children. *Violence Against Women, 13,* 1179–1191. 10.1177/1077801207308260

Ruiz-Pérez, I., Plazaola-Castaño, J., & Vives-Cases, C. (2007). Methodological issues in the study of violence against women. *Journal of Epidemiology and Community Health, 61*(Suppl 2), ii26–ii31. 10.1136/jech.2007.059907

Salisbury, E. J., Henning, K., & Holdford, R. (2009). Fathering by partner-abusive men: Attitudes on children's exposure to interparental conflict and risk factors for child abuse. *Child Maltreatment, 14*(3), 232–242. 10.1177/1077559509338407

Sternberg, K. J., Lamb, M. E., Guterman, E., & Abbott, C. B. (2006). Effects of early and later family violence on children's behavior problems and depression: A longitudinal, multi-informant perspective. *Child Abuse & Neglect, 30*(3), 283–306. 10.1016/j.chiabu.2005.10.008

Strega, S., Brown, L., Callahan, M., Dominelli, L., & Walmsley, C. (2009). Working with Me, Working at Me: Fathers' Narratives of Child Welfare. *Journal of Progressive Human Services, 20*(1), 72–91. 10.1080/10428230902871207

Thompson-Walsh, C., Scott, K. L., Lishak, V., & Dyson, A. (2021). How domestically violent fathers impact children's social-emotional development: Fathers' psychological functioning, parenting, and coparenting. *Child Abuse & Neglect, 112,* 104866–104866. 10.1016/j.chiabu.2020.104866

Tomison, A. M. (2000). Exploring family violence: Links between child maltreatment and domestic violence. *Issues in child abuse prevention, 13,* 1–23. https://search.informit.org/doi/10.3316/agispt.20004148

Turner, H. A., Finkelhor, D., & Ormrod, R. (2010). The effects of adolescent victimization on self-concept and depressive symptoms. *Child Maltreatment, 15*(1), 76–90. 10.1177/1077559509349444

UN: Secretary-General welcomes conclusion of study on violence against children. (2006). Report presents sobering picture, recommendation for prevention, response: 1. *M2 Presswire.*

Waugh, F., & Bonner, M. (2002). Domestic violence and child protection: Issues in safety planning. *Child Abuse Review (Chichester, England: 1992), 11*(5), 282–295. 10.1002/car.758

Yule, K., Houston, J., & Grych, J. (2019). Resilience in children exposed to violence: A meta-analysis of protective factors across ecological contexts. *Clinical Child and Family Psychology Review, 22*(3), 406–431. 10.1007/s10567-019-00293-1

16 Wellbeing development for young people who have experienced violence and abuse

Kaz Stuart[1] *and Lucy Maynard*[2]
[1] *YMCA George Williams College*
[2] *Brathay Trust*

Introduction to the chapter

Wellbeing is an increasingly critical agenda for professionals across multiple disciplines (health, social, education, criminal justice, community, etc.). There is growing evidence of *why* we need to work with young people to support their wellbeing, particularly those most in need of support. However, less is known about *how* professionals support wellbeing development. This is of particular significance as we are increasingly working within multiagency and interdisciplinary settings bringing multiple perspectives, practices and definitions of wellbeing. The interdisciplinary theoretical framework for wellbeing development is based on over ten years of participatory action research with professionals who work across multiple disciplines to support young people, families and community wellbeing. This chapter will present this theoretical framework through a case study of a young person who has experienced violence and abuse, as well as insights gained from the practice of applying the framework.

Problematising wellbeing

We hear the term "wellbeing" on a daily basis, across a range of contexts and through a variety of media. Policy makers, services and practitioners are increasingly concerned about wellbeing. But why is this? Has wellbeing been decreasing or are we simply more aware of it as a concept and a need to support it? What is clearer, is that in this "modern era" young people have very different and unprecedented levels of challenge to their wellbeing. With increased demands to process information and manage online lives, fulfil multiple goals, as well as climate change and a pandemic, to name but a few. A new modernity has seen both increased options and increased complexity in life trajectories (Nijs, 2015). The transition from youth to adulthood is increasingly non-linear and heterogeneous (Thomson et al., 2002). Margo (2008) states "children find it difficult to cope with the complex adult environment, which is increasing their levels of anxiety and rebelliousness" (p.27). Thus, of particular significance is the relationship between wellbeing

DOI: 10.4324/9781003124634-20

and mental health, especially for those who have experienced violence and abuse, whose experience is likely to have left them with poorer wellbeing.

The literature is dominated with debate on the types of wellbeing and its subsequent measurement (for example, hedonic and eudemonic or subjective and objective, Maynard & Stuart, 2018, p.3). Stark data from this measurement and particularly in relation to mental health, are fuelling the need for wellbeing policy, for example, the Department of Health England's (2013) paper on wellbeing and why it matters to health policy, as well as "Measures of Wellbeing" (ONS, 2020).

Wellbeing received heightened attention in the UK with the Every Child Matters (DfES, 2004) and Youth Matters (DfES, 2005) agendas. These strengthened the requirement for agencies to work together to ensure children and young people all attained a range of holistic outcomes that could broadly be said to encapsulate wellbeing. Since that time, however, wellbeing has again been positioned within health in the UK rather than all services for children and young people, as in the Improving Young people's Health and Wellbeing Framework (Public Health England, 2015). Fisher (2019) discusses the need for improved theory on public wellbeing to inform policy. They state that current theories on wellbeing are not well placed to inform this policy need, as they fail to take account of and explain evidence on social determinants of mental health.

Our argument aligns with Fisher's in considering the contingent nature of wellbeing within contemporary social environments and extending understanding of its social determinants. The social determinants perspective on wellbeing (Marmot, 2010; 2020) would encourage a focus on the issues that cause poor wellbeing, rather than the symptoms of poor wellbeing (Stuart, 2020).

But what does this mean to us in practice? How do we translate policy and theory into practice, and moreover, how do we influence this policy from practice? The theoretical framework for wellbeing development (Maynard & Stuart, 2018) was developed in practice with young people and thus goes some way to contribute to this debate.

Defining wellbeing

Amid this multi-sector setting, wellbeing has multiple broad and contested definitions across disciplines (La Placa, McNaught & Knight, 2013). We feel it is therefore important to state a founding definition in introducing this research and clearly state our starting position. We subscribe to the notion that wellbeing is about how one feels about one's self and situation and therefore how we can act, or function, in the world based on this feeling. Aked et al. (2008) summarise this with their stance that,

> ... feelings of happiness, contentment, enjoyment, curiosity, and engagement, to be characteristic of someone who has a positive experience of their life. Equally important for wellbeing is our functioning in the world (pp. 1–2).

Therefore, as a foundational reference point, in the multi-dimensional context, we define wellbeing to be *feeling good and functioning well*. This not only considers how we act in the world but it also considers how the world acts upon us and the conditions in which we find ourselves having to act.

Wellbeing and social justice

The wellbeing development theoretical framework offers a map of critical aspects to be considered in the process of young people's wellbeing development. Fundamentally, the framework proposes that the degree of wellbeing young people experience, sits in direct relation with the social justice of their context. The more equity and equality they experience (social justice); the greater their wellbeing (Wilkinson & Pickett, 2010). In turn, the more wellbeing they experience the more equity and equality supporting social justice they will experience and are likely to offer themselves and others. These two terms are therefore inter-related and inter-dependent, just as feeling and functioning are. This is represented by the outer circle of the wellbeing development theoretical framework (Figure 16.1).

Equity and equality are mediated through structures – the laws, customs, norms and expectations of the young people's surrounding systems and networks: families, communities, organisations or societies (La Placa, McNaught & Knight, 2013). These all act upon them to either enable or

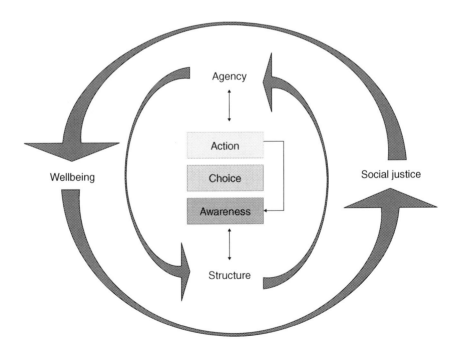

Figure 16.1 Wellbeing development theoretical framework.

constrain their wellbeing. These structures act in relationship with their personal agency (Archer, 1995), that is the ability to make choices that contribute to influencing structures and thus enabling social justice and wellbeing. Structure and agency therefore sit in relation to one another as the second circle in the model, working directly within, and thus contributing to, social justice and wellbeing (Figure 16.1). Young people who have experienced violence and abuse are likely to lack agency because of these very experiences that represent their surrounding structures. Thus, they may lack control and available choices to influence and enable social justice and wellbeing.

Agency is developed through empowerment (Parpart et al., 2003; Carr, 2003; Thompson, 2007). Our research simplified this complex interpersonal process into three key stages: (1) becoming aware of self and situation, (2) gaining control and making informed choices to bring about a desired future and (3) taking actions in line with those choices to enable one's own agency: Awareness-Choice-Action (ACA). These are shown as the central area of the wellbeing development theoretical framework in Figure 16.1.

One of our foundational assumptions, was proposed by Ledwith (2011) who stated, "when people have control over what is happening in their lives, their health and wellbeing improves" (p.36). Thus, what does a lack of control look like and what are the experiences of young people who don't have control. Furthermore, what are their experiences of gaining control and what does this teach us as practitioners, services and policymakers in our role in supporting this? This theoretical framework positions the empowerment process, supporting awareness, choice and action, as the key domain of wellbeing development practice. The central assertion is that empowerment is an intrinsic process, not something that can be done to people (Hand, 1995; Maynard & Stuart, 2018). Thus, we cannot empower others, increase their agency or do wellbeing to them, making them better. Our professional practice is to enable the conditions in which people can become empowered, develop more agency and foster their own wellbeing.

Wellbeing and empowerment

Broadly, empowerment can be seen as people gaining greater control of their lives and circumstances (Thompson, 2007). Of most significance is exploring what "power" means in empowerment. Gutierrez (1990) described empowerment as *"a process of increasing personal, interpersonal, or political power so that individuals, families, or communities can take action to improve their circumstances"* (p.149).

Young people who have experienced violence and abuse may have been disempowered by their experience and specific perpetrators, as well as the structures and conditions that surround them. This may manifest in destructive attempts to gain control which can be misinterpreted by the professionals supporting them (Leveneson, 2017; Jansen, 2010). This presents many challenges for professionals working with these young people, that they need to be aware of, and manage, their own power. This is important because failure to do this effectively may reinforce to the young person the sense that adults are powerful and young people are powerless. In turn, this may lead to discrimination against the young person on the basis of their actions which will likely marginalise them further.

The challenge for practitioners is therefore to create an environment for young people to develop power. The process of empowerment that follows provides a road map for the creation of those conditions. We will exemplify this through a young person's case study.

The reactive self

Many young people find themselves "reacting" to the world and constrained by the structures and injustices in which they find themselves and often feel out of control of their lives. For example, Adam grew up amid chaotic circumstances, including neglect, abuse, alcoholism, drugs and criminal activity. His own words provide the most powerful account of the constraining structures surrounding him:

> *Me upbringing; I had a bad-un. I think it was just what I was used to, so as I got older I didn't know different. I knew now't else and then when you start, like I knew I was in the wrong at 13 and stuff, but that was the lifestyle I was in.*
>
> *Like from a young age, I used to tick school at like five! And my Dad wasn't a very good role model, because you always wanna be like your Dad. But my Dad was in and out of jail, till I was about 11. So from a young age I was taking all that in. Like I'd be in a room with like me Mam, me Dad and all their friends and they were drinking and taking drugs, so that was what I was used to.*
>
> *I was 12 [when I first got in trouble with the police] I set a bin on fire in the middle of the street. But I can remember as young as six being took home by the police, when I lived with my Mam and Dad, so ... But [Grandad] went awol; give us a couple of slaps. He was strict but I didn't listen to him.*

Campbell and Macphail (2002) suggested that most empowerment work starts with the assumption that there is powerlessness or lack of control over destiny. We therefore can assume that empowerment comes from a disempowered place. This is defined in the model of empowerment (Figure 16.2) as a reactive place. Young people may be reacting to the world in which they find themselves because they not only lack control but they may also not know what other options there are. They are going with the flow and are stuck in the status quo. For many young people who have experienced violence and abuse this may be a world of chaotic family situations (Holt, Buckley & Whelan, 2008; Almgren, 2005), a feeling of a lack of love and security (Holt, Buckley & Whelan, 2008), disengagement from education

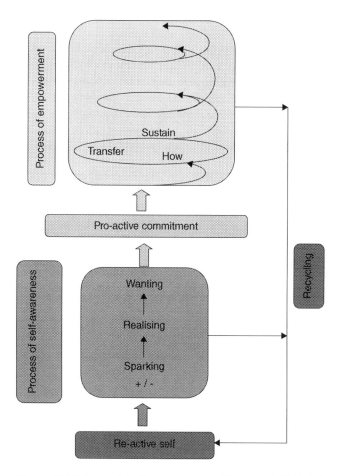

Figure 16.2 The model of empowerment (Maynard, 2011; Maynard & Stuart, 2018).

(Dube & McGiboney, 2018; Graveson et al., 2021), external pressure from peers and society (Albert, Chein & Stenberg, 2013) and disconnection from what we and they might come to know as positive trajectories.

Many young people who have experienced violence and abuse do not describe or recognise themselves as disempowered or oppressed (Fellin et al., 2018). They may, however, demonstrate powerlessness to us even though they do not see it in themselves. There may be little reference to powerlessness whilst powerless and critically unaware. This may only become apparent to them once they have recognised that there are other ways of being and thus people may only recognise their disempowerment once empowered. Freire (1973) defined this as where people are naïve rather than critically conscious. At this stage, people lack insight into the way in which their social conditions undermine their wellbeing and so do not see their own actions as capable of changing these conditions (Campbell & MacPhail, 2002).

Freire argued that people need to become aware of their own oppression before they can do anything about changing it. However, we argue that young people cannot be told this and we must be particularly careful with this in the context of violence and abuse, as young people may often still be protecting perpetrators at this disempowered stage. Being told is more likely to lead to pushing back against the teller. Many of us are guilty of saying "stop hanging around with them; they're no good for you", but this must be realised, not told. Thus, our role as professionals is to create time and space to discover they have control and power, there are other options and they are capable (they have agency). This inadvertently can reveal powerlessness to young people. This can be traumatic, and we may worry about "opening a can of worms" but this is the process of becoming critically conscious.

With time and space comes the opportunity for the discovery of self. An increased self-awareness is underpinned by the concept of raising critical consciousness. This can be seen by understanding an individual's journey through gaining awareness of their power (or lack of); learning to question, rather than simply accept the status quo; which leads to insight into other opportunities and ways of being and their potential to change their circumstance (Robins, Chatterjee & Canda, 1998). Increased self-awareness, and thus critical consciousness, is depicted in the empowerment model as three levels: Sparking, Realising and Wanting. Each of these is considered in the following.

Sparking

Coleman (2007) identified the need to provide positive experiences to "interrupt" the chain reaction of negative events. This in turn is a catalyst, sparking a different chain of events. Similarly, Henderson et al. (2007) worked with the concept of "critical moments" and Giddens's (1991) discussed "fateful moments". Giddens (ibid.) defined these moments as *"times when events come together in such a way that an individual stands at a crossroads in their existence or where a person learns of information with fateful consequences"* (p.143). Hart (1996) suggested that new experiences or special challenges often served to spark the empowerment process. Whereas Gutierrez (1994) proposed that stressful life events could also catalyse the empowerment process. Both perspectives are represented by the positive and negative sparking in Figure 16.2. Young people have described sparking that came about from negative events, such as an assault or abuse. We also see sparking from positive events, such as being listened to for seemingly the first time. Therefore, as practitioners, much of our early work is focused on sparking. We can create these sparks with our approach to practice – our critical pedagogy. Our equity, our listening and not telling and our questioning, provide a different perspective to the disempowered or oppressed.

Adam participated in a programme to support 18–25-year-old ex-offenders, or those at risk of offending, towards full-time employment. The programme took a holistic approach to supporting participants personal, social and employability skills. Adam described the sparking phase as "lightbulb" moments:

> *You're just going with the flow [reactive]. You have a light bulb moment; what am I doing, I need to change, I'm going nowhere. I thought I'd had enough and was being good for quite a while and then the [programme] came along and I done it and got stuck in and then after that I got locked up! I was doing the programme and then this time last year, [laugh] it was [festival], I had a bit too much to drink and I got locked up, for fighting, but luckily, I didn't get prosecuted or 'owt. So I thought right, I'm gonna have to change. I'm gonna have to use everything I've learnt from the programme and put it into action here and just go for it. I thought I don't want any more of this. And that turned into another one [light bulb moments] and I thought that's it, final straw.*

Realising

Asking young people to reflect on critical questions at this heightened time can pave a path for them to begin to make connections and realisations. Becker (2008) sees this point as crisis, as it is asking them to question what they have come to know as the truth previously. He states that *"In the crisis the individuals are confronted with themselves. They learn something about themselves … Thus the crisis turns into a kind of self-enlightenment"* (ibid; p.11).

Gibson (1995) similarly referred to a phase of "discovering reality". This may be realising a heightened sense of one's self and/or situation, which leads to an awareness. As Adam states:

> *So it's options, but people will only do it if they want to do it. You can advise them, so they've got everything for when they decide to go for it. I'd had a realisation and I wanted to change and I wanted to make the most of the programme. They [youth workers] know what they're doing, so I might as well use what they know to help me.*

Wanting

Summerson Carr (2003) suggests that opening a range of possibilities about who one can be and how one can act, inspires mobilisation for change. This is characterised in the model by realising what you want. This is an intrinsic motivation, in that it comes from within the participant, from the realisations they make, rather than something they are told to do or have imposed upon them and which they may have previously pushed away or fought. Parpart, Rai and Standt (2003) referred to this phase as strengthening the *"power within"*.

Arneson (1999) made an important critique to using the term "wanting", arguing that something can intrinsically enhance an individual's wellbeing even though they might not want it. However, "wanting" is not simply desire fulfilment, but a raised critical consciousness that leads to knowledge and aspirations that contribute to enhancing one's own wellbeing. Adam explained this from his perspective:

> *The people on the course, I think there was only me that really wanted to change on the course. But the other guys, they were probably in that stage in their life where they didn't want to change. So if they wanted to change the help was there. Just take the help, but they obviously didn't want it and it wasn't the right time for them.*

Proactive commitment

An intrinsic motivation for change can initiate proactive commitments, illuminating a distinct shift from the previous reactive state. This is a commitment to action and marks the mobilisation for change (Friedmann, 1992). This is a significant point, as it distinguishes action from reflection; active from passive; from realising and wanting something, to doing something about it. Freire (1973), amongst other authors (e.g., Friedmann, 1992), identified a similar "turning point". Adam explains,

> *I think I committed to changing, all together. But growing up as well, that was a big change. I know now I am in control, but there is always this little thing in the back of my head saying I could always go back and do something silly and make a stupid mistake. So that's why I wanted to get away as well. I was just a teenage boy who thought life will sort itself out. But, you have to sort it out yourself. You have to go out and get what you want. So I learnt that. The hard way, but in a good way.*

Learning how

Within this proactive process, people seek answers to their own questions. They develop belief in their ability (self-efficacy) to be different and seek out new skills. At this point, as facilitators of this process, we also become a resource for young people to draw information from, through suggestion or signposting. However, this is only once this point has been reached intrinsically. If we input before this, we run the risk of being interpreted as "telling".

At this stage, we can introduce more tools and strategies for young people to utilise in their forward momentum. For example, if people acknowledge anger as a barrier for them, we can introduce activities directly related to anger management. One of the things that supported Adam was the way he was treated. The staff on the programme helped him realise choices, rather than telling him what to do, and they treated him as an equal:

> *I think that when you're getting cornered and you're getting attacked and attacked [told what to do] you put a defensive shield up. And I think if ya just talk, like we are now, and given advice and shown; then it's different. So I think it's the way people behave with ya that will influence what you do.*

Transferring learning

As young people start to think about how they can implement the changes they have started to make, we need to consider how we facilitate the transfer of learning from one context to another. They may make realisations and commit to changes on a programme with us, but what is crucial is how this is able to be transferred and implemented in different aspects of their lives. Research has shown that benefits gained from projects supporting young people have been transferred to the daily lives of participants (Holman & McAvoy, 2005). Luckner and Nadler (1997) state the importance of the generalisation of learning and application of what young people learn. As facilitators of the empowerment process, we need to make sure we help people transfer learning beyond their time with us. We need to make this explicit and moreover allow time to explore how young people will feel being critically conscious in an environment that may not change. Adam explains,

> *Like I was on my last week of probation and I thought probation was keeping me on track and I thought I'm just going to go back to my old ways and I thought NO! No, come on, I can do this. It means I've got no more tags and I can go out and do it for myself. And as I walked through the door she [probation officer] said 'I've got some good news for you. I've got a job application for ya'. And I thought you're winding me up! [laugh] After all that hard work and keeping myself on track and today could be the day. It's like I know I can do it and I just need to get the chance.* (Adam)

Sustaining

Ryan and Deci (2000) stated that comparisons between people whose motivation was authentic (literally, self-authored or endorsed) had more interest, excitement and confidence than those who were externally controlled for an action (because they have been told to by another, law or policy). This manifests in enhanced performance, persistence and creativity, as well as heightened vitality, self-esteem and general wellbeing. Persistence is crucial for young people to be resilient to external disabling structures and have agency. It follows that, an individual who develops an ability to optimally function, in their worlds, is likely to show more sustained empowerment;

upwardly spiralling and growing, proactive, problem solving and flourishing for longer periods of time. Adam explains,

> *It's the positive attitude, the job, a good lifestyle, a healthy lifestyle. I have a couple of drinks now and again, but I'm entitled. Back then it was every day like carrying on, now maybe once a week a drink. But when I go home, I've prepared for it so, it's alight. So I'm sustaining a lifestyle that I've wanted though for a while.*

Recycling

Ryan and Deci (2000) suggested that despite humans being liberally endowed with intrinsic motivational tendencies, evidence suggests that the maintenance and enhancement of this propensity requires supportive conditions and networks (structures), as it can be disrupted by various non-supportive ones. Non-supportive conditions are social environments that are antagonistic towards positive developmental tendencies.

The Transtheoretical Model of Behaviour Change (Prochaska and DiClemente, 1984) offers some theoretical underpinning to understanding this unsustainability. The authors suggest that most people would "relapse" to previous stages before successful behaviour change was achieved. Sutton (1996) states that it is likely that individuals will relapse and typically cycle through the stages several times before achieving long-term maintenance or change.

We suggest that if this is likely, we should plan for it and actually see it as an experiential process and therefore frame it as positive. Thus, we refer to this as "recycling", rather than relapse. Practitioners can make this explicit through activities that can raise awareness of the pressures of social networks, for example. We also need to provide ongoing opportunities to spark the recycling through the empowerment process again, in realising themselves to have recycled to a reactive place.

Young people can gain greatly by learning from their disempowerment having previously been critically conscious as they can tune in to more specific details and strengthen their commitment to action. This can also be experienced negatively, particularly the frustration that can be felt by a disempowered-empowered person. We may see this within repeated abusive or violent relationships.

As a result of the programme and Adam's openness to change, he became more self-aware, developed support networks, developed healthier habits, gained a job and learned how to look after himself. These are significant outcomes that have enhanced Adam's wellbeing and equality of opportunity. However, Adam experienced ongoing challenges and at times recycled – drinking and fighting. However, these appear to be shorter-lived experiences and he increasingly engaged in work and training.

> *I need to give myself a few kicks up the butt. I'm not as scared to ask for help. I know there's people out there willing to help. Why push them away when they want to help.*

Summary

Empowerment is an intrinsic process; it comes from within – be this individually, in families or in communities. As such, it cannot be given to someone and therefore we cannot empower others. As soon as we suggest this, we are stating our power over them and that power is ours to gift. Our work doesn't empower people; we provide catalytic conditions for young people to become empowered. Ledwith (2011) cautioned against policy that is strong on the rhetoric of empowerment and weak on equality. The process of empowerment demands a high level of critical pedagogy to avoid working on a superficial level or reinforcement of existing dominant structures and benignly reinforcing oppression. We must be careful in how we talk about practice that is empowering. Whilst we may "teach" a child to read in a step-by-step logical way, developing skills progressively, there is no core set of skills that comprise empowerment. It is a complex state, a feeling or sense. The challenge for practitioners is therefore to create an environment for disempowered young people to develop power. The model of empowerment provides a road map for the creation of those conditions. This is our practice and it sits at the heart of wellbeing development; supporting agency to influence structures and thus enabling social justice and wellbeing.

References

Aked, J., Marks, N., Cordon, C., & Thompson, S. (2008). *Five ways to wellbeing: The evidence*. London: nef.

Albert, D., Chein, J., & Steinberg, L. (2013). Peer influences on adolescent decision making. *Current Directions in Psychological Science, 22*(2), 114–120. 10.1177/0963 721412471347

Almgren, G. (2005). The ecological context of interpersonal violence. *Journal of Interpersonal Violence, 20*(2), 218–224. 10.1177/0886260504267741

Archer, M. (1995). *Realist social theory: The morphogenetic approach*. Cambridge: Cambridge University Press.

Arneson, R. J. (1999). Human flourishing versus desire satisfaction. *Social Philosophy and Policy, 16*(1), 113–142. 10.1017/s0265052500002272

Becker, P. (2008, November). Outdoor practices and outdoor equipment – Fields and spaces to form, to test and to present different forms of (bourgeois) subjectivity. Paper presented at the *International mountain and outdoor conference*, Hruba Skala.

Campbell, C., & MacPhail, C. (2002). Peer education, gender and the development of critical consciousness: Participatory HIV prevention by South African youth. *Social Science & Medicine, 55*(2), 331–345. 10.1016/s0277-9536(01)00289-1

Carr, E. S. (2003). Rethinking empowerment theory using a feminist lens: The importance of process. *Affilia, 18*(1), 8–20. 10.1177/0886109902239092

Coleman, J. (2007). Emotional health and well being. In J. Coleman, L. Hendry & M. Kelop (Eds.), *Adolescence and health* (pp.41–60). London: John Wiley.

Department for Education and Skills (2004). *Every child matters: Change for children*. London: DfES.

Department for Education and Skills (2005). *Youth matters*. Cm 6629. London: HMSO.

Department of Health. (2013). *Wellbeing why it matters to health policy health is the top thing people say matters to their wellbeing* (p. 6). Department of Health. https://assets.publishing.service.gov.uk/government/uploads/system/uploads/attachment_data/file/277566/Narrative__January_2014_.pdf

Dube, S. R., & McGiboney, G. W. (2018). Education and learning in the context of childhood abuse, neglect and related stressor: The nexus of health and education. *Child Abuse & Neglect, 75*, 1–5. 10.1016/j.chiabu.2017.09.029

Fellin, L. C., Callaghan, J. E., Alexander, J. H., Harrison-Breed, C., Mavrou, S., & Papathanasiou, M. (2018). Empowering young people who experienced domestic violence and abuse: The development of a group therapy intervention. *Clinical Child Psychology and Psychiatry, 24*(1), 170–189. 10.1177/1359104518794783

Fisher, M. (2019). A theory of public wellbeing. *BMC Public Health, 19*(1). 10.1186/s12889-019-7626-z

Freire, P. (1973). *Education for a critical consciousness.* New York: Seabury Press.

Friedmann, J. (1992). *Empowerment: Politics of alternative development.* Malden, MA: Blackwell Publishers.

Gibson, C. H. (1995). The process of empowerment in mothers of chronically ill children. *Journal of Advanced Nursing, 21*(6), 1201–1210. 10.1046/j.1365-2648.1995.21061201.x

Giddens, A. (1991). *Modernity and self identity: Self and society in the late modern age.* Cambridge: Polity.

Graveson, D., Stuart, K., Bunting, M., Mikkelson, S., Frostholm, P. (eds). (2021). *Combatting marginalisation by co-creating education. Methods, theories, and practices from the perspectives of young people.* London: Emerald.

Gutierrez, L. (1994). Beyond coping: An empowerment perspective on stressful life events. *Journal of Sociology and Social Welfare, 21*, 201–219. https://heinonline.org/HOL/LandingPage?handle=hein.journals/jrlsasw21&div=43&id=&page=

Gutiérrez, L. M. (1990). Working with women of color: An empowerment perspective. *Social Work.* 10.1093/sw/35.2.149

Hand, M. (1995). Empowerment: You can't give it, people have to want it. *Management Development Review, 8*(3), 36–40. 10.1108/09622519510092595

Hart, J. (1996). *New voices in the nation.* New York: Cornell University Press.

Henderson, S., Holland, J., McGrellis, S., Sharpe, S., & Thomson, R. (2007). *Inventing adulthoods. A biographical approach to youth transitions.* London: Sage Publications.

Holman, T., & McAvoy, L. H. (2005). Transferring benefits of participation in an integrated wilderness adventure program to daily life. *Journal of Experiential Education, 27*(3), 322–325. 10.1177/105382590502700316

Holt, S., Buckley, H., & Whelan, S. (2008). The impact of exposure to domestic violence on children and young people: A review of the literature. *Child Abuse & Neglect, 32*(8), 797–810. 10.1016/j.chiabu.2008.02.004

Jansen, A. (2010). Victim or troublemaker? Young people in residential care. *Journal of Youth Studies, 13*(4), 423–437. 10.1080/13676261003801770

La Placa, V., McNaught, A., & Knight, A. (2013). Discourse on wellbeing in research and practice. *International Journal of Wellbeing, 3*(1), 116–125. 10.5502/ijw.v3i1.7

Ledwith, M. (2011). *Community development: A critical approach* (Second Edition). Bristol: Policy Press.

Levenson, J. (2017). Trauma-informed social work practice. *Social Work*, *62*(2), 105–113. 10.1093/sw/swx001

Luckner, J., & Nadler, R. (Eds.). (1997). *Processing the experience: Strategies to enhance and generalise learning*. London: Kendall Hunt.

Margo, J. (2008). *Make me a criminal. Preventing youth crime*. London: IPPR.

Marmot, M. (2010). Fair society, healthy lives: The Marmot Review. http://www.marmotreview.org/ Accessed: 19/6/2012.

Marmot, M. (2020). Health equity in England: The Marmot review 10 years on. *BMJ*, *368*(1), m693. 10.1136/bmj.m693

Maynard, L. (2011). "Suddenly I See" Outdoor Youth Development's Impact on Women's Wellbeing: A Model of Empowerment. PhD Thesis. Lancaster: Lancaster University.

Maynard, L., & Stuart, K. (2018). *Promoting young people's wellbeing through empowerment and agency: A critical framework for practice*. 179 pages. London: Routledge.

Nijs, D. E. L. W. (2015). Introduction: Coping with growing complexity in society. *World Futures*, *71*(1-2), 1–7. 10.1080/02604027.2015.1087223

Office for National Statistics (2020). Well-being. Accessed 20/3/20 at https://www.ons.gov.uk/peoplepopulationandcommunity/wellbeing#:~:text=Average%20ratings%20of%20life%20satisfaction,10%20in%20the%20second%20quarter.

Parpart, J. L., Rai, S. M., & Standt, K. (2003). *Rethinking empowerment: Gender and development in a global/local world*. New York: Routledge.

Public Health England (2015). Improving Young People's Health and Wellbeing: A Framework for Public Health. Accessed 6 June 2021 at: https://www.gov.uk/government/publications/improving-young-peoples-health-and-wellbeing-a-framework-for-public-health

Prochaska, J. O., & DiClemente, C. C. (1984). *The transtheoretical approach: Crossing the traditional boundaries of therapy*. Malabar, FL: Krieger Publishing Co.

Robins, S. P., Chatterjee, P., & Canda, E. R. (1998). *Contemporary human behaviour theory: A critical perspective for social work*. Boston, MA: Allyn and Bacon.

Ryan, R. M., & Deci, E. L. (2000). Self-determination theory and the facilitation of intrinsic motivation, social development, and well-being. *American Psychologist*, *55*(1), 68–78. https://psycnet.apa.org/doi/10.1037/0003-066X.55.1.68

Stuart, Kaz (2020). Tinker, tailor, soldier, sailor: Social determinants of wellbeing. In: *University of Cumbria Professorial Inaugural Lectures*, 27th January 2020, University of Cumbria, Fusehill Street, Carlisle, CA1 2HH. (Unpublished).

Sutton, S. (1996). Can 'stages of change' provide guidance in the treatment of addictions? A critical examination of Prochaska and DiClemente's model. In G. Edwards & C. Dare (Eds.), *Psychotherapy, psychological treatments, and the addictions* (pp. 189–206). Cambridge: Cambridge University Press.

Thompson, N. (2007). *Power and empowerment*. Lyme Regis: Russell House Publishing.

Thomson, R., Bell, R., Holland, J., Henderson, S., McGrellis, S., & Sharpe, S. (2002). Critical moments: Choice, chance and opportunity in young people's narratives of transition. *Sociology*, *36*(2), 335–354. 10.1177/0038038502036002006

Wilkinson, R., & Pickett, K. (2010). *The spirit level: Why equality is better for everyone*. London: Penguin.

Concluding thoughts

Future research directions and recommendations for practice

Julie C. Taylor and Elizabeth A. Bates

In this edited volume, experts from the UK, Canada, US, Australia and Europe have shared insights from their research and/or professional experiences. Each chapter has explored an area of children's experiences of living in homes with domestic violence and abuse (DVA) and made associated recommendations for ways to improve how we listen to and support these young people.

In the introduction, we identified five overarching themes: 1. the importance of accessing the child victim/survivor voices as opposed to relying on the voices and assumptions of others; 2. The methodological challenges of working with child/adult victim populations; 3. The gendered assumptions around children's experiences of domestic abuse; 4. The adult sequelae of child victimisation, strengths and challenges; and 5. What the evidence tells us about ways of working in practice with children and young people affected by child victimisation. In the conclusion and recommendations that follow we reflect upon these themes.

Part I

Professor Jane Callaghan opened the volume with her discussion of agency, resilience and resistance in child victims of domestic violence and abuse. Callaghan's discussion reminds the reader of both the harmful impacts of abuse on children and the lack of agency they are afforded within research literature and practice settings. Callaghan utilises published data to highlight the important ways children demonstrate resilience and readdress power imbalances through resistance strategies. Whilst these strategies may not always seem adaptive to an observer, they serve an important function for embracing agency in the situation. This discussion points to the need for us to explore and understand the complex ways in which children cope with violence and abuse.

In Chapter 2, following an extensive review of the available literature Professor Nicola Graham-Kevan, challenged some of the gendered assumptions relating to children who have experienced intimate partner violence (IPV) within their homes. In response to Graham-Kevan's primary questions, the literature suggested that exposure to IPV (EIPV) can come via father's, mother's or both parents' perpetration. Additionally, there is no support for gender differences in adult outcomes of EIPV in terms of the likelihood that any exposed child would become an adult victim or perpetrator of IPV themselves. Indeed, boys and girls appear similarly exposed and similarly harmed by EIPV. These conclusions challenge several of the gendered assumptions associated with IPV and whilst superficially may infer homogeneity, a deeper look at Graham-Kevan's discussion suggests that while there are no demonstrable gender differences, there are a host of ways in which children can respond to EIPV. Therefore, this review adds further support to the calls for an individualised approach to supporting victim-survivors of EIPV, one that is not based on unsubstantiated gendered narratives.

In Chapter 3, Dr Julie Taylor and colleagues report on their work with adults who were victims of domestic abuse as children. The findings from this retrospective study found that most participants, whether they identified as male, female or non-binary reported ongoing negative sequelae. In addition, our participants indicated that several things might have made a positive difference to them. The most consistently reported being their school experience. Those participants who reported feeling safe and supported at school were most likely to continue their education and succeed in careers. Unsurprising to those who work in trauma-related fields, but possibly not something widely considered elsewhere, some teachers may inadvertently engage in "triggering" behaviours whilst in the classroom, (e.g., shouting, singling children out) and what may be experienced as unhelpful control (e.g., deciding where the children can sit and changing their seating plans from session to session or within sessions). Taylor et al. concluded that there is a need for more UK-based research relating to the effects of the school ethos and environment on children who have experienced DVA.

In Chapter 4, Professors Stephanie Holt and Carolina Øverlien reflected on the rationale and challenges underlying the practice of engaging children in research. They presented an overview of research conducted across Europe both with and about children and young people who experience living with DVA and noted differences between the North American and European approach to DVA research. Following their review, they concluded that participating in research should not only be seen as a right but also that participation can be experienced as empowering for children, as their lived experience can contribute to research and ultimately, to improved practice and policy. Their final sentence captures the perspective of several authors within the text, stating that they concur with Houghton's (2018) call for people to 'listen louder' to children and young people and see them as 'experts in their own lives'.

Following the discussion of the European perspective, Dr Nassra Khan introduced a South Asian perspective, drawing upon her research with members of a rural community in Pakistan. Khan's observations remind us of the importance of culture and social structures when drawing conclusions about children's experiences. Khan concluded that the villagers did not recognise exposure to DVA at home as having a negative impact on children; nor did they consider these children as victims. She argued that this type of 'cultural conditioning' ran the risk of masking any psychological repercussions of early exposure to DVA. Khan concluded that further research was needed to explore the issues raised here further, with cultural awareness and sensitivity underpinning all aspects of the research process, including design, implementation, analysis and interpretation.

In Part I of the book, two of the main themes discussed were the critical nature of the victim/survivor voice, whether as children or from a retrospective perspective; this crucially included the importance of learning from the experts by experience and using their lived experiences to inform both prevention and intervention strategies. The second primary theme relates to the application of gendered narratives to our interpretation of research in this area. Professor Nicola Graham-Kevan's review suggests that gendered assumptions are not clearly supported by the available evidence, arguing that both men and women can be perpetrators and victims and that children whether male/female or non-binary can be similarly affected by EIPV. This evidence-based conclusion is particularly pertinent to the design of policy, therapeutic interventions and prevention campaigns.

Part II

In Part II of the book, our attention was drawn to discussions relating to the impact of DVA on child victims. In the first chapter of this section, Dr Bethan Carter explored the challenges associated with research in the field. Dr Carter concluded that methodological flaws plague the research relating to the effect of DVA on child and adolescent outcomes including internalising symptoms. She concluded that more research is needed to assess the causal effect of DVA on internalising symptoms and other emotional and behavioural problems in order to better understand how best to support children and adolescents who have been exposed to DVA. In the next chapter Professor Kathryn Maurer discussed the self-regulation capacities of young people exposed to violence. Professor Maurer concluded that family violence is one of several forms of violence that children and young people may be exposed to within their social ecologies and that intervention and treatment models need to acknowledge the complex environments in which children are raised. Professor Maurer explained that to help mitigate the effects of family violence the whole ecology needs to be understood. Maurer concluded by advocating a value and justice-based response to adversity exposure. Arguing that such an approach could be supported by a commitment to participant-researcher collaborations to help challenge the narrative that supports the pathologisation of adolescent behaviour. Consistent with theme two of the text both Carter and Maurer concluded that research in this field is complex indicating that one size fits all approaches are unlikely to be successful because each child's environment is different and experienced uniquely. Both indicated that more research is necessary with Maurer pointing to the need for expert (participant) informed research collaborations. This need to listen to the expert voice of the child/young person has been a recurrent theme throughout the volume.

In the third chapter of this section, Dr Sabreen Selvik and Dr Carolina Øverlien progress the discussion from the outcome data itself to how to learn from the data and offer opportunities that can mitigate the effects. Several of the prominent outcomes relate to school and the educational experience more broadly, with child victims of DVA often having additional barriers to educational engagement compared with their non-victim counterparts. Selvik and Øverlien explain that school is an opportunity for both safe disclosure and intervention for children experiencing DVA. They situate their discussion within a Human Rights Agenda, referring in particular to the United Nations Convention on the Rights of the Child (UNCRC, 1989). They conclude that school offers an opportunity for disclosure, intervention and wider education but that investment and infrastructure is required to enable this. They are very explicit in their recommendation that the responsibility for this should not fall upon the shoulders of existing school personnel. Indeed, they call for intervention at government level to prioritise DVA, allocate resources to schools and strengthen laws and policies concerning schools' abilities to safeguard and support their students. In the next chapter, Dr Bates and colleagues further explore the barriers to help-seeking by victim/survivors. Drawing on retrospective accounts from adults, Dr Bates and colleagues concluded that whilst a range of barriers to disclosure and help-seeking were identified the influence of the attitudes and responses of adults was a powerful determinant, coupled with a lack of awareness about available or appropriate support. This conclusion led to a series of recommendations including the reiteration of some from previous research (e.g., Callaghan et al., 2017). For example, the call for professionals and practitioners to value the accounts of children and young people and afford them the same credibility afforded adult victims. Several of the recommendations came from participants themselves in terms of how we can improve service availability and responses, with the need for trusted and reliable people to confide in being a priority. This call echoes that of Selvik and Øverlien in the preceding chapter.

In the final chapter of this section, Angie Boyle progresses the discussion from victimisation to survival. Boyle's work with child victims now in adulthood shifted the focus to survival strategies. Boyle concluded that her participants capacity for agency and the role that they play in DVA contexts had the potential to positively contribute to discussions about being able to regain power, autonomy and self-belief. Moreover, her tentative recovery framework offers hope to counteract some of the negative discourse about children and young people's outcomes. The consistent messages in this part of the book have been that research needs to acknowledge the heterogeneous experiences of participants and work collaboratively with the experts by experience. In addition, safe opportunities for disclosure and intervention need to be made available and visible to all children and young people.

Part III

In Part III of the book, the emphasis shifts to working with victims of DVA and includes insights from several researcher-practitioners across a range of services. Themes 1, 3, and 5 are prominent across this section: 1. the importance of accessing the child victim/survivor voices as opposed to relying on the voices and assumptions of others. 3. The gendered assumptions around children's experiences of domestic abuse. 5. What the evidence tells us about ways of working in practice with children and young people affected by child victimisation. In the first chapter of this part of the book, Dr Tanya Frances and Dr Grace Carter discussed the negotiation of power, ethics and agency with participants when developing interventions. They make the important point that those who have experienced violence and abuse have experienced both subordination and disempowerment at the hands of adults. Consequently, to develop interventions without their full and meaningful involvement may perpetuate these experiences. One of the main insights from this chapter is that the children and young people wanted to be fully informed, included and consulted. Moreover, they knew when this was not the case and how it made them feel. This is a particularly powerful message to all those working in the field whether as researchers, intervention designers or therapists. This message is also evident from the work of Drs Larner and McGlashan whose analysis of how children talk about their experiences offers support to practitioners. Their work reveals that even the language used by children to articulate their experiences is different to that of their adult counterparts. One of the challenges they identified was that children may be trying to tell adults about DVA but in words that are not recognised as such by adults. This suggests that adults need to listen and adjust their frame of reference if they wish to capture and appropriately interpret the messages being conveyed to them. Moreover, Larner and McGlashan propose that a space for children to disclose and report their experiences in their own way is essential.

In the next chapter, Dr Di Basilio discussed the impact of IPV on children's internal working models. Di Basilio proposed that one of the problems with current interventions is that they do not engage with the individual's emotional core and therefore do not address the underlying emotional experiences associated with being a child victim of DVA. Consequently, Di Basilio concluded that children and young people may benefit from attachment-restructuring and emotional regulation-focused interventions, recommending a combination of training of DVA professionals on affect-regulation interventions and developing children's school-led programmes. This discussion was followed by Dr Papamichail and colleagues who focused explicitly on the mental health needs of children who have experienced DVA.

They offered confirmation from a practitioner perspective of the heterogenous nature of victimisation and the importance of the context in which the child is situated. In addition to discussions of current evidence and practice, Dr Papamichail et al. offered guidance to other professionals relating to the development of holistic sequenced interventions based on the collaborative assessment of young people and their families.

In the penultimate chapter of this volume, Professor Heward-Belle revisited the gendered assumptions that may be detrimental to child victims of DVA. Heward-Belle reminds us of the expectations placed on mothers when their children have been victims of DVA. These expectations reflecting the pervasive assumption that women are responsible for the protection of their children in DVA situations. Assumptions that help to conceal adult male victimisation as well as reinforcing the belief that only males perpetrate DVA. Moreover, this also fails to recognise that fathers have an important role to play in recovery and prevention. Heward-Belle recommends as a matter of urgency the development of research, practice guidance and clear policies on how to promote professional engagement safely and ethically with men who have or are at risk of perpetrating domestic violence. In the final chapter of the book, Professor Kaz Stuart and Dr Lucy Maynard propose a framework to enable the empowerment of children and young people who have been victims of DVA. Their framework is focused on providing a catalyst for children to regain power. They argued that one of the main challenges for practitioners was their ability to create an environment for disempowered young people to develop power. They offered a model of empowerment to support practitioners in the creation of those conditions.

In Part III, there were several recurrent themes: the importance of listening to children and learning how they communicate their experiences; involving children in the development of interventions; recognising the individualised needs of children who have been victims of DVA and finally the need to revisit gendered assumptions that may be influencing professionals' ways of working and inadvertently hindering successful intervention and prevention.

This volume is one of the first to bring together a comprehensive body of contemporary research and practice related to working with child victims of domestic violence and abuse. The authors' contributions can be synthesised into several recommendations for both future research and practice, these have been organised to reflect the themes identified in the introduction of the volume and throughout this concluding chapter.

1 **Recommendation Theme 1: Accessing the child victim/survivor voices.** The recommendations throughout this volume have been to centralise the voice of the child at all levels of engagement, from learning the language they use to communicate their experiences, to prioritising their role in the design and execution of research, intervention and prevention strategies. It appears clear that a failure to do this effectively has the potential to further disempower and disillusion the children and young people we are seeking to support.

2 **Recommendation Theme 2: The methodological challenges of working with child/adult victim populations.** There are inevitably challenges associated with populations who have experienced trauma however we have seen in this volume that there are ethical and creative solutions available. The main barriers to which are the scientific value placed on non-traditional approaches to research and the associated impact on resource allocation. The recommendation is that authentic participant-informed research and practice is elevated to the status it deserves. The evidence and practice discussed in this volume indicates that this research genre has the potential to be impactful and support meaningful change.

3 **Recommendation Theme 3: The gendered assumptions around children's experiences of domestic abuse.** The problem with gendered assumptions, as with all assumptions, is that they have the potential to influence judgement, decision making and action. In two chapters of this volume, Chapters 2 and 15, the impact of these assumptions was shown to be counter-productive i.e., rather than offer clarity and improve research and practice they hindered it. In several other chapters of this book, the complex and idiosyncratic nature of victimisation was highlighted. Synthesising these positions leads to the recommendation that when working with victims it is their experience and needs that are centralised. To support this, it is further recommended that researchers and practitioners can access training to help them work from the participant's/client's perspective.

4 **Recommendation Theme 4: The adult sequelae of child victimisation, strengths and challenges.** It is clear from several contributors that the emphasis in the research has traditionally been about the negative outcomes for children and young people. The problem with this emphasis is that it fails to acknowledge the resilience and strengths of many victim/survivors. It is therefore recommended that strengths and resilience are afforded equal attention in the research so that they can inform intervention and prevention and also, as Boyle suggests, offer hope.

5 **Recommendation Theme 5: What the evidence tells us about ways of working in practice with children and young people affected by child victimisation.** There is the potential here to make a host of recommendations based on the many and varied insights within the chapters of this volume. However, perhaps the urgent recommendations are related to providing spaces for children to articulate their experiences, these may be virtual and real spaces, allocating resources to schools as one of the consistent institutions within the child/young person's ecosystem to enable schools to provide safe disclosure and intervention spaces. Finally, train adults to listen to and hear the child's voice so they can interpret the message without imposing their own frame of reference.

Index

Note: **Bold** page numbers refer to tables, *italic* indicate figures, and page numbers followed by 'n' refer to notes.

Printed in the United States
by Baker & Taylor Publisher Services